THINKING
ON
MY FEET

Kate Humble

THINKING
ON
MY FEET

The small joy *of putting*
one foot in *front of another*

aster

An Hachette UK Company
www.hachette.co.uk

First published in Great Britain in 2018 by Aster, an imprint of
Octopus Publishing Group Ltd
Carmelite House, 50 Victoria Embankment, London EC4Y 0DZ
www.octopusbooks.co.uk
www.octopusbooksusa.com

First published in paperback 2019

Distributed in the US by
Hachette Book Group
1290 Avenue of the Americas, 4th and 5th Floors, New York, NY 10104

Distributed in Canada by
Canadian Manda Group
664 Annette St, Toronto, Ontario, Canada M6S 2C8

ISBN 978-1-78325-315-9 (Paperback)

A CIP catalogue record for this book is available from the British Library.

Printed and bound by CPI Group (UK) Ltd, Croydon, CR0 4YY

10 9 8 7 6 5 4 3 2 1

Publishing Director: Stephanie Jackson
Creative Director: Jonathan Christie
Senior Editor: Alex Stetter
Production Manager: Caroline Alberti

Contents

———

FOR MY MUM & THE BEAR

PREAMBLE

I walked out of the door of the hotel and into Africa.

Over the previous three days I had travelled more than five thousand miles, most of them in one hit on a plane from London to Nairobi. It was a daytime flight and we arrived in the evening. There was a long queue at immigration and quite a lot of faffing about waiting for customs officers to decipher paperwork and find a pen. I was there with a small team to make a documentary. There were five of us and forty pieces of luggage, much of it as heavy and unwieldy as the trolleys at Nairobi airport. We manhandled everything outside, squeezed it into every available inch of space in a minibus and drove to our hotel. By the time we had unloaded everything it was almost midnight and we were dead on our feet.

The next morning we were up at dawn and off. Ahead lay a two-day drive to our final destination, a small border town in the west of Kenya, not far from Lake Victoria. When we arrived, after a flurry of unloading and carrying bag after bag up the stairs, there was about half an hour of daylight left. 'I'm just going for a quick walk,' I said.

For me walking feels as vital as breathing. The first thing I do, every morning I can, is to go for a walk – for an hour, or longer if I can get away with it – usually alone apart from my dogs. I find the simple action of putting one foot in front of the other, and the rhythm of that action, incredibly therapeutic. It wakes me up, unscrambles my sleep-fogged head. But it also gives me a sense of immersion, of being rooted somewhere, makes me feel part of where I am, a sensory and physical connection to the bit of the world I find myself in.

After my three-day journey I was in another country, on another continent, in a different time zone. But despite having travelled so far I didn't feel I'd really *travelled*. I had hardly spent any time on my feet, barely taken a step. The travelling had been done for me. I felt, as I emerged from the hotel into the softening evening sunshine, discombobulated, stiff-limbed, tired and disconnected, as if somehow I had been blown in, Dorothy-like. Which, I suppose, in some ways I had. But as soon as I took my first few steps, I could feel my fatigue lift, my legs come back to life, my brain too, as my senses were flooded with the sights, sounds and smells of my new surroundings. I'd awoken at last from catatonia and was alive once more.

We stayed in Isebania, as the town is called, for just over a fortnight and I would get up every morning, sometimes before the sun, and walk for half an hour or so. Isebania is a typical border town: a strip of tarmac barely half a mile long which runs uphill to the big grey gates that mark the point where Kenya becomes Tanzania. Alongside the road is a jumble of buildings, shacks and makeshift stalls. You can buy a suitcase, a sim card, all manner of vegetables, have your tyres changed, your car washed, fill up with petrol, eat *chipsi mayai* (a chip omelette – the local speciality) or take home freshly cooked *chapatis* or golden puffs of fried dough called *mandazi*. People will change your money, fix your shoes, try to sell you a new coat or just – as I discovered – wish you good morning.

I was an anomaly. This is not a tourist town and I was the lone *mzungu* – the Swahili word used for anyone who is white, although the literal translation is 'someone who wanders without purpose or someone who is constantly on the move'. So the term seemed entirely appropriate for me as I wandered with little more intent other than to feel a part of the world going on outside the hotel. At home, although I vary the walks I do every day, there are many routes I've done time and time again at different times of day and at different times of year. There is nothing boring about this because one of the great joys of seeing a place on foot is that it allows you to notice things, little things, that would otherwise be missed. The more familiar a route becomes, the more, I find, it is easy to notice things that have either been overlooked previously or have changed.

It took me a day or two to settle into a route around Isebania. That first afternoon I wandered down the hill – past the police station and a couple of cows grazing on a verge – to a little knot of stalls, where women with bright wraps of cotton around their waists and heads were selling avocados, hands of the small, sweet local bananas, or cooking cobs of corn on little charcoal braziers. Set back from the road was a row of more formal shops selling bright plastic buckets and bowls, lurid fizzy drinks, packets of chewing tobacco, cooking oil and flour. Beyond these shops there was a pot-holed road, a few houses with goats tied to trees outside, dogs lolling, chickens scratching about. I'd reached the end of town. I turned and walked back the other way. The sun was setting, and darkness falls fast in Africa. I missed the hotel, which is set back a little from the road, and turned back when I realized I was in unfamiliar territory and the town's few lights started to come on.

The next morning I left the hotel at 6.30am and walked the other way, up the hill towards the border. I came across three young men cutting and frying *mandazi*, a queue already forming by their stall. A woman was sweeping the hard-packed earth in front of her shop with a bundle of twigs. A scrawny mutt scavenged in the roadside rubbish. A small market was set up on the corner of a side road, the women sitting among their piles of greens and tomatoes, some of them shredding kale with machetes at astonishing speed, packing it tightly into plastic bags and selling them for a shilling apiece. The barber's stall was just opening as I walked past, the *boda boda* boys (the motorcycle taxi drivers) had gathered in an audacious pack near the top of the hill, all vying for the first business of the day, hoping it might be the *mzungu* who they would try to charge double. 'I'm not going anywhere!' I laughed as they competed for my attention. 'I'm just walking.' 'Maybe tomorrow?' 'Maybe,' I laughed.

I knew I was smiling inside and out. I loved being there, loved the feeling of being part of the morning scene. At the border gates I turned off the main road and followed a dirt track which ran into the main residential area of the town. Here my fellow walkers were schoolchildren, dwarfed by outsize school bags, or people heading to work in neatly ironed shirts and smart shoes. Through chinks in the walls and fences of the little compounds I could see washing pegged out, goats being chivvied, water being carried. I tried not to look taken aback when I passed a woman with a large white bucket on her head from which poked the horns and the muzzle of what had recently been a cow. I discovered the rest of the animal in various big chunks awaiting further dismemberment outside the little butcher's stall, just beyond the police station.

And so my morning routine was set; I often saw the same people, like the woman selling goats' milk on the corner, who after a week of saying good morning to each other, invited me to her house. The *boda boda* boys joked 'Just walking today!' as I approached. The vast, smiling woman, who sat outside her house with a tray of *mandazi* glistening with oil, never failed to try to persuade me to buy one. But every morning was different too. If it had rained in the night – we were there during the short rains, when every day or two the clouds would burst in spectacular fashion, accompanied by sheets of lightning, explosions of thunder and rain or hail falling in Niagara-style torrents – the air would be fresh, the light clear and clean. If it hadn't rained, the sky would often be heavy with cloud, the heat sticky and oppressive, the lady from whom I often bought supplies for lunch fanning herself with her notebook, face glistening with sweat.

There was the time when a man emerged from the door of his house carrying a dead cat by the tail as if it were a handbag. Another time, after a particularly violent rainstorm in the night, the tree outside the police station had shed its spectacular, blousy orange flowers and they lay in colourful drifts on the ground beneath. The carpenter started work on a new piece of furniture. Someone walked towards me with a huge bundle of white rope on their head which made them look as if they were wearing an outrageous Seventies disco wig. On Sundays the rap music that blared from some of the shops and stalls during the week became hymns, and from every church and chapel came the sound of lusty singing. And then there was the morning that followed the night we drove back into town and there was a riot going on. The road was blocked, there were gun shots, knots of people shouting and throwing rocks, stalls being overturned. We had heard someone had been murdered, but it was only on my walk the next morning that I found out what had appened.

I walked down the hill to the junction where the riot had taken place.

A crowd was gathered, quiet but not silent, and tense, a simmering undercurrent which felt very close to the surface, ready to break out at any minute. Everyone was looking in the same direction, at a patch of sandy earth behind the stall selling corn. There was a dark stain, as if a puddle had recently dried up, but the stain was the red brown of spilt blood. I walked through the crowd, trying to gauge the atmosphere. There was anger, yes, sadness too, but the thing that struck me most of all was what was missing. There was no sense of horror. No sense of incomprehension at the enormity of what had happened. There was, I started to realize later as I walked away, back up the hill, almost an acceptance that this was just sometimes the way of things. It was the reaction of people who are more used to facing death than we are.

I went to see a shopkeeper I had met on the first morning, because he spoke enough English to make up for my less-than-rudimentary Swahili. 'It was the school teacher,' he told me, 'I was at church with him on Sunday. He was a good man. So well respected here.' 'What happened?' I ventured to ask. 'It was robbers. They attacked him when he came out of the shop. It was a knife. But they were on foot; they just ran away and the police were too slow. They didn't stop them and they could have. Now those robbers have got away with it. That is why there were riots last night. People were angry with the police. They still are. I think there will be more riots today.' 'I'm sorry,' I mumbled, 'sorry for your loss.' We shook hands and I left. The crowd outside was more restless, more vocal. Some of the men had broken away, were rolling tyres across the road, faces set, eyes blank with intent. I walked away, back up the hill, the image of the blood-soaked sand and a feeling of helplessness following along beside me.

I should probably explain at this point what I was doing in this unremarkable border town with a documentary crew. Isebania is within the territory that traditionally belongs to a tribe called the Kuria. The Kuria number about half a million people and their lands span the Kenya/Tanzania border. They predominantly survive by subsistence farming; poverty is rife, education – certainly beyond primary age – rare. They are infamous for their cattle-rustling habit, which makes them particularly hated by the Maasai, but it is another of their traditional practices that has thrown them in the spotlight: female genital mutilation (FGM).

FGM was made illegal by the Kenyan government in 2011, but for many of the Kuria the law of the land is meaningless. They are governed by their own gods, their own beliefs, a powerful council of elders, long-held tradition, fear, pride and, increasingly, defiance. But they are also in a time of transition. Change, however much some might resist it, is coming, and not just from outside pressure. There are people within the tribe who want to see change too, want the practice of circumcising girls to become a thing of the past. We were there to try to capture, as faithfully and honestly as we could, the complexities of this period of huge social upheaval, that in some cases divides families, pitches communities against the police and drives the practice underground, with the potential for truly dire consequences.

Over my time there, thanks to two local men who were my translators and guides and the patience and generosity of the people I met, I managed to get an insight into not just how they live, but what matters to them, the fundamental things that give them their identity, that make them Kuria. Rarely have I felt so challenged, both emotionally and intellectually. I would form what I imagined to be a well-thought-through, rock-solid opinion one minute, to have it turned on its head the next. And the more time I spent in the villages getting to know people – hanging out, doing jobs with them, dancing in church, sleeping on the floor of their huts, cooking and eating with them – the more and more I cared; the more and more it mattered that what we filmed was a true reflection of Kuria life.

At the end of every day – and they were often very long days – I would feel both elated and wrung out, relishing being so challenged and utterly exhausted by it too. If you've ever seen the film *Broadcast News*, which was made in 1987, you might recall that Holly Hunter plays a news producer who gets so wrapped up in her stories she reaches a point where she simply has to sit somewhere on her own for a moment and cry, with total abandon, before stopping abruptly and carrying on. It is something I confess I do too, and on this trip I did it a lot, but I would have had to do it a whole lot more if it wasn't for my walks. Because as well as noticing men with dead cats or joking with the *boda boda* boys or seeing the sun come up, it was time when I could simply think.

Now don't get the impression that I was walking along with a knitted brow, muttering to myself, wrestling with the complexities I was dealing with every day. That's not the case at all. What I have discovered about walking is that thoughts come, quite naturally. I never go for a walk – and didn't in Isebania – with the intention of solving a problem. It doesn't seem to work like that, at least not for me. But thoughts, ideas, solutions seem to come more easily when I'm thinking more about walking than about thinking. And my thoughts are often random, unconnected.

The philosopher Friedrich Nietzsche wrote, 'All truly great thoughts are conceived while walking.' Well, I'm not sure my thoughts on what to cook with the measly pickings in my fridge so I don't have to go to the supermarket count as great. But as well as coming up with a plan for dinner, I might also come up with the opening line of a paragraph I've been battling with, an idea for a documentary or the right colour to paint the bathroom. In Isebania my walks helped me find clarity when my emotions and my responses to them had felt irrecoverably tangled. But they also gave me a rest, my thoughts wandering as aimlessly as my feet.

It was on one of these mornings that it occurred to me that I had never kept a diary or a journal. And as I walked on along the now-familiar roads, I rolled this kernel of an idea around my head. I liked the thought of charting a year through walks: the seasonal changes, the weather, encounters and unexpected happenings. And I liked the idea of exploring the more personal aspect of walking: the reasons I might feel compelled to walk and the effect that walking might have on me. 'And what about other people?' I thought, 'Why do they walk? What does the simple act of putting one foot in front of the other do for all of us mentally, physically, spiritually?'

And so what follows is a journal, of sorts. It is a collection of observations and experiences, of feelings and responses. There are the stories of the people I met who were generous enough to share their reasons for walking – and they range from seeking inspiration to seeking a reason to carry on living. There are pieces of poetry and prose by writers who evoke the emotive power of going for a walk more eloquently than I ever could. And there's a bit of science too, because anecdotal evidence is one thing, but I wanted to try to understand why we humans have been extolling the virtues of walking for many hundreds of years.

Roman philosopher Seneca wrote this in the 1st century AD:

We ought to take outdoor walks, to refresh and raise the spirits by deep breathing in the open air.

And then there's the sad truth that even though there is so much evidence that walking is good for us, we are doing less and less of it. A UK All-Party Commission on Physical Activity found that today's children are 'the least active generation in history', and the World Health Organization cites lack of physical activity as being the fourth leading risk factor for global mortality.

We are recommended to walk 10,000 steps a day. Hardly any of us get close to that. But to stay healthy, both physically and mentally, we need to walk more. The problem is 'need' makes it a chore, another thing on the never-ending to-do list of life. And something as simple and as pleasurable as walking should never be a chore.

So I hope that by sharing my ramblings – in both senses of the word – and those of others, you may be inspired to stick on a pair of comfortable shoes and discover what novelist Elizabeth von Arnim describes so beautifully:

Walking is the perfect way of moving if you want to see into the life of things. It is the one way of freedom. If you go to a place on anything but your own two feet, you are taken there too fast, and miss a thousand delicate joys that were waiting for you by the wayside.

A
NEW
YEAR

January

1ST JANUARY
NEW YEAR'S RESOLUTION NUMBER 3:
GET FIT

*

It is New Year's Day, seven in the morning and I'm running. Well, shuffling at best. It is hot, probably about 28°C, the stiff breeze coming in off the sea unhelpfully sticky. I am jetlagged, with the remnants of a cold and aware that I am telling myself these things as a means of excusing, or perhaps justifying, the fact that if I gave up and just walked I would almost certainly cover the ground faster. Bloody New Year's resolutions.

I'm on an island called Bequia, pronounced '*beck-way*', which until a few weeks ago I hadn't heard of. It is one of the islands that trail behind St Vincent like, my husband Ludo observed, the tail of a sperm, although the tourist board puts it rather more poetically and likens the Grenadines to the tail of a kite. Bequia is the biggest Grenadine, at seven square miles, and is, as I am now discovering, basically one big hill that pokes up through the sea like the back of an iguana, with the Atlantic Ocean on one side and the Caribbean Sea on the other.

We arrived yesterday afternoon, delayed twenty-four hours by fog at Gatwick and a missed connection, just in time to have a ruinously expensive New Year's dinner and to take one of the pick-up trucks that are the island's taxis over to the harbour for the midnight fireworks. The island's population – which numbers less than five thousand – didn't turn up en masse for the firework display. I was expecting the harbour to be a thrumming throng of inebriated humanity, but there were probably no more than about a hundred or so people – mostly families – milling rather aimlessly about as if unsure what or where anything was going to happen. And the atmosphere was curiously muted, as if giving away any sense of excitement went against the national identity of laid-backness.

We joined the directionless milling. There was no obvious place to stand, nor could we work out exactly where the fireworks were going to be set off. 'Isn't it midnight now?' I asked Ludo. 'It is by my watch,' he replied and on cue a firework, set off from a distant hill, blazed a trail through the sky and burst into a shower of golden stars. A couple of the yachts in the harbour set off flares, but it was a good five minutes later that the first rocket screamed up from behind the rusting hulk of an abandoned cargo ship and the little knot of people standing alongside us on a wooden pontoon, all, as one, went 'Ooooooh!'

Given the low-key atmosphere and the small number of people watching, we were expecting, at best, a couple of Roman candles, a Catherine wheel and a rocket or two – perhaps one of those that explodes into stars which then explode again with loud bangs as a finale, and we would all be in bed by 12.30. But how wrong, and cynical, we were. What followed was twenty minutes – and what must have amounted to tens of thousands of pounds worth – of fabulous colour, noise and wonder, as the sky was alternately lit by blues and golds, silvers, reds and greens, as fireworks screamed, popped, boomed and banged, and the ooooohs were joined by aaaaahs and even the occasional smattering of applause. There were cheers from the yachts, Happy New Years exchanged on the pontoon and then everyone melted quietly away.

But it is clear the next morning that not everyone went home, like us, and gratefully tumbled into bed by 1am. The few cars and minibuses that pass me as I continue my tortuous progress along the road that leads to the airport are packed full of people still very much in party mode. Music blares out at a volume so extreme it makes me wince in a way I remember my mum doing when I was a teenager and we would constantly do battle with the volume knob of the radio in the car when she picked me up from the school bus. 'God,' I mutter, 'not only can I barely move, I've become completely, stereotypically middle aged over sodding night.'

A minibus overtakes me and stops to disgorge a man of senior years, so staggeringly plastered he weaves and stumbles to a roadside bench and sinks down, his hat askew. I'm dimly aware that I am passing houses, that they are all rather pretty and candy coloured, with verandas. There are great thickets of verdant vegetation, and garish flowers hang over fences and walls. There are lots of dogs about and every single garden seems to have a goat in it.

I round a corner and the road, which I had already thought was heading uphill, starts to climb with cruel purpose. I stop noticing anything at all beyond the pain in my legs and my bum and my inability to breathe in and out quick enough. 'Must get to the top. Must get to the top,' I mutter, like a mad person, but it becomes patently obvious that my body is going to give up long before the road flattens out. I stumble to a walk, holding my sides, feeling my face burning puce with exertion.

I stagger on to the crest of the hill outside the defunct whaling museum and stand, chest heaving, looking out at the sea and the other islands that lie scattered along the horizon, one of them Mustique. Below me is the green corrugated roof of a building with 'Church of Christ Bequia' written across it in large, proud white letters. I'm not a person with any sort of religious leanings, but at this precise moment I wonder if a quick prayer might help me press on for another mile or so.

I look at my watch, one of those devices that counts your steps and buzzes encouragingly when you've reached your daily target. I think I must have run at least two and a half miles, but I find I haven't quite reached one. Thoroughly disheartened and spurred on only by the fact that the next stretch is downhill, I push on. Another minibus passes me, 'LOVE IS D ANSWER' emblazoned across the back in gold and red lettering. 'No it's not,' I shout crossly at its receding form, 'love is not going to make me run like some lithe, young athletic whippersnapper, all bounce, swinging pony tail and perfectly tanned legs.'

The road swings round the corner and past the Church of the Seventh Day Adventist and I see my first non-drunk people of the morning, a father in a pink bow tie carrying his daughter in a frothy dress of net and frills in a matching pink. 'Good morning,' I gasp and receive a slightly concerned look in return.

I pass the harbour. There are no yachts here on the more rugged, less protected Atlantic side. These are the local boats – identical, fibreglass, with outboard motors – painted bright colours and called things like 'Not Guilty'. There's a man sweeping the steps outside his shack, a dog lolling in the gutter, a purple car propped up on breezeblocks. I'm heading for the airport, as it is the only place I know how to get to without getting hopelessly lost, and finally, wonderfully, I see the runway, a rectangle of manmade land stuck to the side of the hill, surrounded on three sides by the sea.

As runways go, this one is a tiddler, but it still seems to take me an inordinately long time to reach the airport building at its end. As I press on I am reminded of walking the length of the runway on Easter Island, 15 – maybe even 20 – years ago. Ludo and I had flown there from Chile and landed bubbling with excitement at the thought of being on one of the most remote inhabited islands in the world, and one so steeped in legend and mystery. We were therefore a little disappointed when, on being picked up by the owner of the B&B we were staying in for our first night, he switched on the engine of his rather dilapidated jeep and the music playing on the radio wasn't a local composition played on unfamiliar instruments fashioned out of shell and coral, but Fleetwood Mac.

We had decided that the best way to see and properly experience Easter Island, immerse ourselves in the landscape and the culture, was to walk around it, which I reckoned would take about four days. The next morning, rucksacks packed with tent, sleeping bag, water bottles and provisions, we headed out of Hanga Roa, the main town, and followed the island's runway to reach the opposite coast before heading east.

Easter Island may be small and remote, without many people and with little need for a runway that can take large aircraft, but its airport was chosen as an abort site for the US space shuttle and the runway was lengthened in 1987 to be able to do the job. It is now over three miles long (Heathrow's runways are under two and a half) and to walk the length of it, with little else to look at is, without a shadow of a doubt, the most boring, unstimulating walk either of us have ever done. And, just in case you want to know, the rest of the day's walk turned out to be headlong into a driving prevailing wind, along the treeless, totally exposed coastline, which left us so dehydrated we resembled husks by the evening and had to be rescued by an eccentric Frenchman, living on his own in a shack surrounded by great dark hunks of volcanic rock. We camped in his garden and he cooked for us while we drank jug after jug of water from his well.

The runway on Bequia is about three-quarters of a mile in length and has goats grazing alongside it, which helps distract me enough to get me finally stumbling into the concrete airport building. Security is provided by a man and woman sitting on plastic chairs in stiff uniforms gossiping in the shade, and they are kind enough to ignore me as I head straight to the ladies' loo and stick my head under the tap.

Every person I know who runs, even the fittest and most dedicated of them, say that the first mile or so of a run is always horrible, that you always feel sluggish and out of sorts, that it takes that time to find a rhythm, settle into it and, finally, hopefully, start to enjoy it – instead of, as I've been doing all morning, questioning the benefit of doing all this furious exercise if it never seems to get any easier. It was a little over two miles to the airport. Perhaps, I wonder as I leave the airport building, dripping water off my chin, I've broken through the pain barrier and I'll do the return journey in a fraction of the time, scampering up the hills like a spring lamb.

It's not to be. I end up walking most of the way back up to the whaling museum. There are a few more people about. A woman walks past with a sheet of corrugated iron on her head. A black-and-white cat scurries across the road, scales a wall and disappears. A group of men, bare chested in shorts and sandals, sits in what looks like a makeshift bus shelter chewing the fat. We greet each other, hands raised, 'Mornin!' I don't know how much of Bequia's income is reliant on tourism, but the people, although perfectly courteous, don't go out of their way to engage you in conversation. Unlike so many places where tourists represent the possibility of cash, they don't try to sell you anything, or offer to be a guide or driver or try out their chat-up lines. Not that anyone in their right mind would try to chat me up in my current state. But it is refreshing not to be seen as anything other than a slightly eccentric lone female with a very red face undertaking ill-advised exercise in the already hot sun.

'I will run nonstop from here back to the hotel,' I tell myself, firmly, on reaching the museum, safe in the knowledge that it is downhill or flat almost the whole way back. But still my stubborn legs feel weighted down, as if I've got rocks in my shoes, and as I reach the flat bit I feel like any shred of energy I ever had has left me. I see a man in the road up ahead and push myself on, determined to run past him in a breezy show of morning vigour. It takes me an embarrassingly long time to catch him up and I am incapable of speech as I pass, so just raise my hand.

A little further ahead is the bench where the old, very drunk man had been dropped off at the start of my run. I see he is still there, his hat no longer askew but lying at the side of the road, and he is sitting looking very dazed, with blood pouring from his nose and a cut on his forehead. I stop, concerned, but also grateful for the excuse. 'Are you OK?' He looks at me uncomprehendingly. 'I think we need to find you a doctor,' I say. The man I ran past has now more or less caught up. 'Do you know him?' I call. 'He's in a bit of a mess.' He nods. 'Now den,' he says in a tone of voice that tells me that this is not an irregular occurrence, 'What ya bin doin' to yaselv?' I press on. 'Not far now,' I tell myself, but I am spent. I feel sick, wobbly, and have to sit down on someone's garden wall. Bloody hell, I think gloomily, I've just turned 48 years old and I've had it.

6TH JANUARY

SIGHTSEEING ON FOOT:

LITTLE DETAILS WE'D OTHERWISE MISS

*

It is our last morning on the island. In a few hours we will be on our way to Barbados and then, fog or any other inclement British weather allowing, to Gatwick. It is just before 6am and I am quietly tugging on my running shoes in the pre-dawn gloom, avoiding putting the light on and waking Ludo.

Despite the ignominious start to my running year, I've run every morning, going out before the sun is up when it is marginally cooler. Perhaps it is that, or the fact that my cold has got better and I've had more sleep, but the runs have got easier and more enjoyable and I've noticed more around me, little details that are neither here nor there but somehow make me feel like I've become a small, if transient, part of the island for the six days we've spent here.

I've noticed, for instance, that the riot of colour from the flowers in gardens and along the road comes from hibiscus and bougainvillea, morning glory and a pretty weed that I don't know the name of but grows everywhere. The concrete road that runs from the airport along the Atlantic coast and then up and over, dropping steeply down to the harbour on the Caribbean side, is pitted with footprints, mainly cats and dogs but some human. The dawn chorus doesn't come from the island's wild birds – there don't seem to be many of them beyond the gulls and boobies and frigate birds that soar over the bay and the big grey heron that fishes in the pond behind the hotel – but from the chickens and the dogs and the goats, and some mornings are noisier than others, for no discernible reason. And there are other mornings when goats, dogs and people seem to gravitate to their roofs to coincide with the sun rising above the bank of cloud where the sky meets the sea.

I've discovered that the man I saw sweeping his steps the first day is always sweeping something – the steps, the yard and, once, the canvas cloth that shades the flat roof of the building attached to the side of his wooden house. I've drunk in the heady smells of the bakery, which was advertising Christmas buns at the beginning of the week and banana bread at the end of the week. I've been chased by one dog and mobbed by another – a sweet, funny little dachshund mongrel that lies in wait on the corner of an uphill section of road and, when I approach, leaps up, runs to block my way, and then stands on its hind legs, pawing my shins, eyes shining with mischief and delight.

I've greeted a man on his way to his fields, sleepily walking along the road dangling his machete, and waved to another who reads on his porch every morning. The minibus drivers of 'FAITH' and 'LOVE

IS D ANSWER', the ones who do the early shift on the Atlantic side of the island, hooted and waved on the third morning they saw me and continued to do so for the rest of my stay. I've dodged herds of goats coming along the road trailing ropes behind them, on their way to graze by the runway.

Some mornings I've varied the route, running up to the whaling museum, then retracing my steps and on, past the turning to the hotel, up the hill that brings you to the ridge, the top of the island and the first glimpse of the Caribbean. The landmark on the ridge, which tells me I've nearly made it to the top, is a blue-painted wooden shack with 'Heineken' painted in large letters on the side. Fairy lights hang in bedraggled strings from the bar across the road to the telegraph pole opposite, and beneath the telegraph pole is a fine nativity scene featuring a stable, two inflatable snowmen and a Father Christmas that have lost their pertness and gone saggy in the heat. There is also an inflatable dog and a couple of elves and it makes me smile every time I go past it, which is several times a day. Because as well as running every morning, every time we have left the hotel it has been on foot, much to the puzzlement of the staff.

When I'd returned from my run, I'd join Ludo and we'd pad along the narrow strip of sand that lines Friendship Bay, where our hotel is, as far as we could go and then swim back. After breakfast we'd walk up the road that skirts the valley above the bay, its coloured houses and neat gardens still in shadow, past the Heineken bar and the floppy snowmen and pause at the brow to look down on the Caribbean Sea and the yachts parked in neat formation in the harbour below. Then we'd wind our way down to the coast and the little local dive centre to spend an hour or so doing the thing I find more relaxing than anything else: bobbing about several metres below the surface of the sea in the company of fish.

Afterwards we would walk to find somewhere to eat, we'd mooch around the vegetable market, or the tiny bookshop with its surprisingly eclectic collection of books, maps and charts. We'd walk to other bays and beaches, peek nosily at the houses that cling to the slopes, many of which, we were told, belong to foreigners and cost millions of dollars, and idly wonder if we had millions of dollars would we want to live there. Then, at some point, we'd climb back up the ridge, in the hot afternoon sun, dropping back down to Friendship Bay to read by the sea until the sun went down.

It was the evening walks I enjoyed the most, particularly walking back after dinner, which is probably the only thing I miss now we live in the countryside. A post-prandial walk is a good transition from dinner table to bed, a chance to digest a bit and gossip about the evening, none of which, in my mind, works quite so well in a car. We do have one lot of friends who live close enough to us that we can walk to and from their house for dinner, although the first time we tried it we discovered, as we rolled out of their kitchen at 2am, that we were really very drunk, had forgotten a torch, and had forgotten how to get home.

Darkness falls quickly on Bequia and there is little in the way of dusk. Instead, once the sun has set, the sky becomes inky black almost instantly and the few lights from the houses and the boats do little to dim the stars or the moon. The first evening we walked from the hotel over to the Caribbean side, the moon was a perfect crescent, lying on its back like a smile. I don't remember ever seeing it in that orientation before and I kept looking back up at it to check I hadn't imagined it. Over the coming nights the smile got broader until by the time we left it was a proper Cheshire Cat grin. There was little in the way of traffic, so we walked to the sound of the crickets, the scent of flowers and cooking, soft snatches of conversation or music from the verandas near the roadside. Few other people seemed to walk after dark, but it never felt like a strange or unsafe thing to do and it gave us another perspective, another little insight into island life.

Our final walk is a short one, through the hotel garden, with its neatly clipped hedges and shrubs, immaculate lawns and lamp posts that are exact copies of the ones in Kensington and Chelsea, we've been told, proudly, by the hotel owner. The pick-up truck taxi drives us away, along what is now a route I know almost every inch of, the road to the airport. My eyes flick between the familiar little landmarks – the blue gate, the sign to a guesthouse, the house with the puppy, the whaling museum. I say a silent goodbye to the Church of the Seventh Day Adventist, the old men sitting in the bus shelter, the dog lolling in its favourite place in the gutter and almost cheer when I catch sight of the sweeping man with his broom. We bump over a cracked bit of concrete that tells me we are coming to the final, short-but-brutal uphill stretch before the airport and coast in, over the gravel, and come to a stop by the security guards, who take no notice of us at all, but carry on gossiping.

7TH JANUARY

A HOMECOMING WALK

✳

We're back. The plane landed pretty much when it was supposed to, some time before five in the morning, and we began the day marching through the corridors of Gatwick's North Terminal with that rather heady feeling of liberation that comes after a long-haul flight. We breezed through immigration, had the briefest of waits for our bags and before we knew it, were in the car and heading towards the M25 motorway. It was still very dark and the week of beautifully crisp, clear winter weather we had just missed had been replaced by a warmer weather front from the west, shooting the temperature up to a balmy 7°C and bringing waves of dank drizzle with it. But the farther west we got, the clearer the skies became and we crossed the Severn Bridge with the silver-blue light of a dazzling moon dancing across the river below us.

It's still barely light when we drive up to the house, just after eight, to the ecstatic welcome of our three dogs, who leap at the car, leaving streaked muddy paw prints on the doors. 'I'll take them straight out,' knowing the walk ahead is as much for my benefit as it is theirs. I run in, pull on some extra layers, my wellies and a woolly hat and walk to the boundary fence with our neighbour's field, the dogs racing ahead, leaping the stile like steeplechase horses.

We moved to this old stone farmhouse perched on a Welsh hill above the Wye Valley, with its views back to England and the ridge of Offa's Dyke, almost a decade ago. We fell in love with the house for all sorts of reasons; its quirkiness, its feeling of remoteness without actually being very remote at all, but most of all because it is reached, not by road, but up a steep, winding forestry track and there are footpaths that lead from it in every direction. It is entirely possible – I know because I have done it – to leave the house on foot and walk for 15 miles almost without ever seeing a road.

This morning I choose a well-worn route we've done a hundred times or more, but I think of it as a good homecoming walk; one that allows me to catch up with what's been happening in my little corner of the world while I've been away. It starts out across our neighbour's field, without livestock today because his cattle are all inside until the spring grass starts to come through. Today the field looks rather drab and khaki, the grass bleached by winter, limp and sodden, squelchy underfoot. The fence on the western side of the field separates it from the woods – a majestic stand of oaks and beech, their branches bare and sculptural against the grey sky.

It is one of those dawns when it seems the sun can't quite be bothered to both rise and shine, so the dark seems to give way unwillingly to a murky greyness and my beloved landscape feels colourless and lifeless compared to the gaudy vibrancy of Bequia. The path climbs gently, we negotiate a few more stiles and end up at the cottage on the opposite side of our hill. They keep Shetland sheep, which look up as I pass, hoping I might be the one bringing them breakfast. There are also horses: handsome, much-cosseted beasts, their heads appearing over the stable doors as we walk past the yard and down the track that leads to the woods.

This part of the patchwork of woods and forestry plantations that surrounds our house was, I was told, planted by Polish prisoners of war. Again it is a mixture of oak and beech trees, their trunks uniformly the same girth, which backs up the theory that they were all planted at the same time. The plantation slopes down from a lane to a stream at the bottom and there the mix of trees changes. There are more larches and conifers, the ground between them littered with long golden pine needles, whereas the track we follow, traversing the slope, is a thick, mulchy mass of fallen oak and beech leaves. Last autumn, soon after they fell, this path was like a mosaic of golds, reds, russets and rich browns, but now rain and frosts and the passage of people and dogs, horses and deer, have reduced them to a muddy mess.

But I notice, in my longing search for colour, the woods aren't entirely monochrome and lifeless. No longer crowded out and upstaged by the grander broadleaf trees, the hollies are having their moment. They stand among their naked neighbours bedecked in shiny green finery, some still decorated with flaming red berries. Ivy, too, brings a slightly dustier green to some of the trunks, and not all the brambles or ferns have died back so there are still patches of green on the woodland floor. But most vivid of all is the velvety moss that clings to rocks and branches, another sign that the natural world isn't entirely dormant.

There's a badger sett along this track. Occasionally there are signs that it might be in use, but today there aren't any clues to tell me it has been used recently. We drop down, slithering on the muddy track, and cross the stream. On some mornings I'll see roe deer here, a glimpse of a fox perhaps, and there are almost always masses of squirrels which the dogs love to chase, although never with fully committed, murderous intent. A raven calls this morning, but there is no other birdsong, nor the high-pitched plaintive cry of buzzards and even the squirrels seem to be elsewhere. I check for wood anemones – pretty, delicate white flowers which are often the first wild flowers to come out and I have seen them as early as January before – but not today.

We leave the woods via a stile and climb into a field that borders the garden of our friends. If they are around, this walk often gets gloriously interrupted by offers of tea or, depending on the time of day, something stronger, but there is no sign of them this morning. The field slopes steeply upwards and I feel my legs complaining. At the top I pause, looking back over the roof of our friends' house. When the weather is clear there is a beautiful view here out to the Black Mountains, but this morning the mountains are shrouded in an invisibility cloak of cloud.

From this point it is downhill all the way home, through a couple of little paddocks and past our local church, a tiny stone chapel that sits in the middle of a field. Although not church-goers, we were urged by the farmer who lives next door to us to come to the carol service on the Christmas Eve just a week after we had moved in. 'Best way to meet the locals,' he said. It was more than that, and I say that as one of those old miseries who hates Christmas and would go through the rest of my life quite happily if I never had to hear 'Away in a Manger' or that terrible song by Slade ever again.

It was a rather damp, drizzly sort of day, not unlike today, and we walked up through the fields from our house, in our wellies and rather grubby coats. The service started at 4.30pm, but we had been warned to get there early because it would be busy. We arrived just after 4pm and it was standing room only, the pews already overflowing. 'It's like stepping into a scene from a Hardy novel,' I whispered to Ludo.

The church was beautifully, simply decorated with holly and ivy, candles and gas lamps. The lack of electricity meant there was no organ, so musical accompaniment was in the form of a man playing the clarinet and a woman playing the cello. The vicar gave a brief welcome and then the service began. Nine good old-fashioned carols that even I know the tune to, and nine readings, many of them read by the children. A plate was passed around to raise money for a new porch and then everyone piled back outside where we were offered mulled wine, mince pies and sausage rolls to munch in the churchyard. Lots of people were friendly, came to introduce themselves, made us feel welcome, and we wandered back through the dark fields feeling quietly content. 'This feels like a good place to be,' said Ludo.

I walk through the kissing gate by the church, holding it open for each dog to pass, and they canter out into the field beyond. There are scattered crows on the grass, pecking about, looking for worms or leatherjackets. Teg, my Welsh sheepdog – the biggest, youngest and most energetic of the three dogs – sets off at high speed, her sleek copper and white body low to the ground at full stretch, her great plume of a tail streaming behind her. She charges towards the crows, and they take to the air with much indignant cawing, but still she gives chase, barking delightedly at her wickedness. Then she races back and rolls, luxuriantly, in the wet grass. She has always done this, even when she was a puppy. It is almost like her morning ritual, her equivalent of a shower, and she seems to relish it particularly when it is frosty. Back on her feet she shakes, grins and sets off again in the hope of finding more crows.

From this field we can usually look over the rolling hills and woods of the Wye Valley, but the cloud is too low on this side too, so we press on, passing the cattle byre with its sweet fermented smell of silage, skirting around the farm buildings to the gate that leads into our garden. 'Breakfast time!' I say to the dogs and we race to the house. It's good to be home.

WALKING OFF THE JETLAG, A SPARK OF INSPIRATION
AND AN IMPROMPTU TEA PARTY

*

Before Christmas we took delivery of a new mattress. Mattress lore states we should all replace our mattresses every eight years or so and turn them once a fortnight. I think it is safe to say I have never in my life turned a mattress and we worked out, when we both agreed that our bed really wasn't very comfortable any more, that we had been sleeping on the same, unturned mattress for at least 16 years.

So we splashed out – and a new mattress is some splash – and having bounced on every demonstration bed in John Lewis, chose one that felt so unbelievably luxurious compared to what we were used to, I doubted I would ever want to get out of bed again. It arrived on Christmas Eve, and we left for Bequia a week later, so we hadn't given it much of a trial. Having not slept at all on the flight home, I was fully anticipating 12 hours of glorious, perfectly supported, uninterrupted sleep.

I wake not long past midnight. I look at my alarm clock in disbelief. Surely it has stopped. It hasn't. And I am properly awake, in that awful, manic, mind-racing way that borders on madness and makes you feel desperate. And now that I am properly awake I am also properly aware that I'm not comfortable, that my perfect mattress isn't perfect, that it is too soft, or too hard, or too something that makes it more wrong than right and I fret about the huge amount of money we have clearly wasted and remember the years in my transient youth when I slept on thin mattresses, or odd sofa cushions, on various floors with no trouble at all. I toss and turn and wriggle.

I get up, drink some water, have a pee, get back into bed thinking, hoping, that miraculously the mattress might have reverted to being perfect in the meantime.

For someone who travels as much as I do I should be used to jetlag by now, should be better at managing it, but it is a curious, unpredictable thing. Sometimes I don't suffer from it at all, sometimes it seems to drag on for days and there doesn't seem to be a pattern; it's not always worse flying in one direction than another and a time difference of four hours can induce jetlag just as bad, or worse, than a difference of eight hours. Anyway, this is full-on, no holds barred, you-are-not-going-to-go-back-to-sleep-any-time-tonight jetlag and when morning finally comes I know better than to try to attempt a run. Instead I take the dogs for a short, undemanding walk around the hill and do menial-but-rewarding tasks like clean out the chickens and the geese, move the sheep into a different field and put in another load of washing.

After lunch I feel better, less foggy and a bit more energized. Not quite up to running, I decide, but up to walking a route that I want to try out as a running route. So I gather up the dogs and we drive to some woods ten minutes away at the top of the Catbrook Valley. The weather is still a bit murky, but it has cleared since the morning and there is a glimmer of brightness in the sky. The dogs leap out of the car as soon as I open the boot, barking and yapping as if they've just been freed from months of incarceration, and tear off up the gravel track before stopping, as one, and looking back at me as if to say 'COME ON!!!'

I follow at a more sedate pace as they charge up into the trees and back, sniffing and peeing and doing what dogs do. The woods here are older, more mature than the woods immediately around our house and from this track there are expansive views over the Wye Valley which, this afternoon, is looking very atmospheric, with streamers of low, swirling mist curling up over the hilltops and trees.

Soon we cross a small bridge spanning a stream that in summer often doesn't flow at all, disappointing the people who come here hoping to see Cleddon Falls. But now it races beneath our feet and drops away over an incline, bouncing and bubbling over the rocks. There are a few houses here, tucked away on the edge of the woods, and beyond is a path that is part of the Wye Valley Walk, which starts in Chepstow and ends 136 miles later on Plynlimon. This short section of it is rather pretty, running through a tunnel formed by the branches overhead. 'Maybe I should do the whole length of it this year,' I think and my mind starts to wander in that lovely way it can when walking, flitting from whether I would do it in one hit, could I carry enough dog food, would three dogs and me all fit in a one-man tent...?

At a gate we leave the Wye Valley Way, take a path that skirts the garden of a rather lovely house, follows their drive and comes out on a tiny lane. We turn left, almost immediately plunging back into woodland, and walk gently uphill until we get to a junction of tracks. So far this walk is on familiar territory, a route I've walked and run with the dogs many times, especially on wet days, because it is mostly on forestry tracks that tend not to get too muddy or sodden. Starting a run with cold, wet feet is misery.

At this point I would usually turn left, but I want to try the track straight ahead, a narrow path leading uphill between areas of the forest that have, some time ago, been felled, so it has the look and feel of heathland, I can see more sky and there is more daylight than under the trees. I'm pretty sure this will lead me to a spot called Beacon Hill and sure enough, after not too long, I reach a bench at a high point, with more far-reaching views over the trees to the horizon. I know the direction I need to take to get back, it is just a question of finding a path.

I walk on to a gate and the crossroads of tracks the other side allows me to head left, the way I need to go, down a broad, grassy track between the trees. Ahead I can see a clearing and it is flooded with deep, red-gold light. Rays of this light filter through the trees. I gasp, running towards it, and catch the sun making its first appearance of the day in the most dramatic of fashions. A huge, red, perfect sphere hangs just above the horizon and slowly, teasingly, slips away down behind the trees.

I reckon I am still a good half hour or more from the car but, unlike on Bequia, darkness will come gradually, and more slowly now the sky has cleared. I know I need to turn off this path away to the left and, obligingly, not long later, I find a route that starts out being a bit squelchy but navigable, but ends up being a quagmire. The dogs and I pick our way through deep ruts, water and sticky liquid mud. Bella, the smallest of the dogs, gives me The Look, which tells me she is not impressed and is only following under sufferance.

'We made it, dogs!' I shout, triumphantly, as we emerge, mud-spattered onto a familiar forestry track. The dogs, equally relieved, run ahead towards a little group of people walking towards me in the gathering gloom. I hear a voice, a child. 'Mummy, it's Teg!' And as we narrow the gap I see my friends Abbe and Eyal with their kids. We haven't seen each other for a while and we exchange damp, winter coat hugs and wish each other Happy New Year. 'Do you want coffee?' asks Eyal. I look at him, not understanding. It is Sunday afternoon, the sun has set and we are in the middle of a wood. There is no café for miles in any direction.

Eyal smiles, takes off his backpack and takes out a little primus stove, a metal jug and a bottle of water. 'I have Turkish coffee or mint tea...' We stand and chat, sipping drinks that somehow taste so much more delicious when they have been brewed on a little stove in the middle of the woods. So absorbed are we in our conversation that we don't realize that darkness has now completely fallen and stars are starting to appear above our heads. We part, with plans for more walks, perhaps a winter picnic, and they go in one direction and I go in the other.

I love walking in the dark, especially when the darkness is like it is now, softened by the light of the moon that seems to have just appeared, three-quarters full, not on the horizon but already quite high in the sky. How, I wonder, are the sun setting and moon rising connected? Does the moon rise as soon as the sun sets, as if they sit on opposite sides of the same gently revolving wheel? But that can't be the case, I reason with myself, because for the moon to be this high in the sky already, it would have to have started rising before the sun set. And I realize that now is not the time to try to work out this puzzle, my brain addled by lack of sleep and the dogs giving me the 'hurry up, it's dinner time' look.

11TH JANUARY
AN UNEXPECTED TREAT

*

On my walk this morning I catch sight of a peregrine falcon, its sleek outline sharp against a colourless sky. At first glance it appears to be hunting, its quarry one of the doves that roost in our neighbour's cattle shed, but as I watch it doesn't appear intent on killing. It climbs and dives, swoops into the flock to split it up, but even though it seems to get within easy talon's reach several times, it never goes in for the final kill. Perhaps it is a young bird trying out its hunting techniques, but to me it looks like a joyful display of harmless teasing, which ends with the doves settling back on the roof of their barn as the peregrine wheels elegantly away and out of sight. I walk on, the pleasure of what I've just seen buoying up my steps.

12TH–13TH JANUARY
MOUNTAINS, MOONLIGHT AND SNOW

*

An email from my friend Sarah: 'There's another supermoon on Thursday and Mark's getting a gang together to climb the Sugarloaf again. Are you up for it, if the weather's OK?' 'YES!' I reply, without hesitation.

At the end of 2016 there was a flurry of 'supermoons'. They are not unusual – there can be six a year – but the one in November was described by NASA as an 'extra-supermoon'. A supermoon is so-called because it appears bigger and brighter than usual, thanks to the fact that it is at a point in its elliptical orbit when it is closest to the earth, a time known in moon-watching circles by the lovely name of 'perigee'. But the one in November was rare because not only was it perigee, it was also a full moon – something the earth hadn't witnessed since 1948 and won't see again until 2034 – so if we were going to attempt to climb a mountain after dark, this was as good a time as any, even if the forecast was for cloudy skies.

A group of 14 of us met at the bottom of one of the many paths that lead up the Sugarloaf. The Sugarloaf is probably the most iconic, certainly the most recognizable, peak in the Black Mountains. A perfect, volcano-like cone that I'd climbed many times, at all times of year and in every sort of weather, but I'd never approached it from this direction and I'd never climbed it in the dark. It was 8.30pm, the air still and almost unnaturally warm for November. There were clouds, but they were scattered and even when the moon was behind them, so bright was it that it still cast enough light for us to climb all the way to the top, even the last scramble over a rocky outcrop, without needing our torches.

We stood at the trig point, the moon in full view, not seeming any bigger than usual – we would have needed to see it rising for that – but certainly much, much brighter. Someone had brought tea, there were celebratory biscuits and a couple of hip flasks were passed around before we headed down a different path which leads, magnificently, to a pub, just in time for last orders. It was such a beautiful night we took our pints outside and sat, talking in the moonlight, until the barman finally called time.

But this week there has been talk of snow coming, the tabloid headlines shouting about Arctic blasts that will bring death and destruction. 'Thursday night, it's due,' said the girl in the local agricultural store, where I was stocking up on sheep food. 'All the farmers are saying it will be here by the end of the week.' And on Wednesday Mark sends an email calling off the walk, suggesting instead that we meet for the full moon in February.

It's now Thursday and it is certainly cold, but it doesn't feel or look like we are about to be hit by a killer blizzard. It is one of those quiet, benign winter mornings, wishy-washy sunlight and the woods silent apart from the tap-tapping of a great spotted woodpecker. At lunchtime I drive to the farm. Although the farm is at the same height as our house – just shy of 300 metres above sea level – it sits on the top of a hill, exposed to the full force of the weather that comes from the west, over the Brecons and the Black Mountains.

We are all sitting around the table in the farm office kitchen, the wood burner keeping out the chill, when snow starts to fall in big, defiant flakes outside the window. 'Surely it is too wet out there for it to settle?' I say, but it is falling thick and fast enough for the yard and the buildings to already have a light covering. I take childish delight in snow and don't want to miss this. We haven't had a decent fall of snow for four or five years; the last two winters barely got cold enough for frost, so I drag the dogs away from the warmth of the stove and take them out into the fields.

As soon as we leave the shelter of the farmyard the full force of the wind hits us. The snow isn't the lovely, dry fluffy kind. This is wet, chilling rather than thrilling, but instead of turning back as anyone with any sense would and having another cup of tea, I press on into the blizzard, oddly invigorated by how horrible it is out here. I get to the edge of the field from where we can see the outlines of the Black Mountains, the Blorenge, the Skirrid, the Sugarloaf, and on really clear days we can see beyond to the Brecons and the peak of Pen y

Fan. But it is a whiteout and the mountains are completely obscured. Not a night for climbing by moonlight. But then, just as suddenly as the blizzard started, it stops; and barely half an hour later I'm returning to the farmyard beneath clear skies, the snow that had settled already gone.

There is a flurry of emails from various members of the moonlight climbing party. 'It's clearing here. I think we should go for it!' 'No, there's more weather forecast to come in and the road will be treacherous.' 'Don't be such a wimp, the mountain is looking beautiful. It'll be fine...' Ludo and I decide to stick to the decision to stay at home but later, when I take the dogs out for their final pee, I wish we hadn't. The sky is clear, the wind has dropped completely and the moon is magnificent.

'Sorry everyone,' reads Mark's email the next morning. 'I should have held my nerve. A few of us did go up the mountain last night and it was stunning. Apologies. See you next month.' But it is stunning here this morning too. Snow must have fallen at some point in the night, not much of it, but enough to turn the world crisp and white, for my boots to leave crunchy tracks in the grass and for Teg, who has never seen snow, to take glorious delight in rolling in it, dusting her ginger fur with sparkling crystals.

21ST JANUARY

A FAVOURITE WALK WITH AN OLD FRIEND

✳

Amelisa is staying. Many, many years ago, when we were in our late teens, we shared a house in Oxford with two medical students and a goldfish. One of the medical students – Ed, now a respected GP –

played the trumpet in lieu of revising for exams, and the other – Andy, now a cardiologist – showed a healthy interest in affairs of the heart even then, although not medically speaking. There never seemed to be an evening when there wasn't a pretty young thing gazing at him longingly over the remains of yet another dish of tuna, sweetcorn and pasta bake, which, beyond toast and Heinz tomato soup, was all we could afford to cook. The goldfish lived in a bowl in the kitchen where it was regularly experimented on by the boys 'in the interest of furthering our studies'. 'I think I've got it drunk!' Ed announced proudly one evening. 'I put some brandy in its water and it can't swim straight...'

Ed, Andy and Amelisa each occupied one of the three bedrooms and I, for the princely sum of £20 per week (including bills, except the phone), slept in a store room. As store rooms go, this one wasn't bad. It had a window and it was the same length and just a little narrower than a single mattress, but with a bit of brute force we managed to squeeze one in, the sides curling slightly up the walls. I lived there for eight months, working in a hospital during the day and a pub during the evenings and at weekends, and left once I had saved enough to fly to Africa. I lost touch with my housemates. The boys went off to various parts of the country to finish their training, Amelisa to work in Hong Kong, and I didn't see her again until she came back to the UK and a mutual friend reintroduced us some years ago.

She arrived last night with her dachshund Snoopy, who has been coming here since he was just a few months old. His legs could be described by some as stubby – he is long haired, so they are almost completely invisible – but he can walk miles and he has an enormous crush on Teg, despite the fact that she towers above him and gives him very condescending looks down her long, elegant nose.

The snow that fell at the beginning of the week didn't stay long and for the last few days it has been warmer, the landscape has lost its lovely crispness and gone back to being soggy and bedraggled. But that hasn't been the case everywhere. In the middle of the week I left Wales in drizzle to go to London and arrived in sub-zero temperatures, even though it was the middle of the day. I stayed with friends and in the morning got up, before dawn, to run around their local park.

The cold was like a physical force that struck as soon as I stepped out of the front door. The street lights made the frost, heavily encrusting car windscreens and garden fences, glitter and twinkle. There was no one else mad enough to be out at this time and I padded around the park in the dark accompanied only by the unearthly yowling of a fox, a sound that bears a horrifying resemblance to a child in true distress. The animal emerged from a thicket – a dark, lithe shape – and ran just ahead of me for a moment or two before deftly changing course and disappearing into the undergrowth.

It may be a little sad to admit it, but I love listening to the weather forecast on BBC Radio 4, just before the hour. It never fails to amaze me that despite the fact that we live on a not-very-big island, the weather can be so different within just a few miles. And it's not just the weather. As the sky began to lighten above the dark outlines of the buildings around me, I realized that if I were in Wales now it would still be dark and I would have to wait a good ten minutes more for the first light to bleed through, streaking the eastern sky above the ridge of Offa's Dyke with colour.

This morning, as I let the dogs out and go to feed the various animals, the frost is back and I have to break the ice on the water trough. The sky is clear and china blue. Mist sits low in the valley, rising in lazy, smoky wisps to shroud the ridge of Offa's Dyke. The sun is still loitering, out of sight below the tree line then, just as I cross the field to feed the sheep, the sun bursts above the horizon making the frost flash and twinkle like a glitter ball.

This is, I decide, a perfect morning to take my old friend on a walk I particularly love. Rugged up in bobble hats, scarves and gloves, we pile all the dogs into the car and drive a few miles up the Wye Valley road to the bridge that crosses, not just the river, but the border between England and Wales. We don't cross, but stay on the Welsh side, parking up and walking down to a kissing gate by the old toll house to the path that runs alongside the river.

The Wye is tidal up until this point, so sometimes you see the strange phenomenon of the river flowing upstream, but today the tide is going out, the river flowing strongly past us to join the River Severn at Chepstow and then out into the Bristol Channel. There is salmon fishing on this stretch, and it is also popular with canoeists – although it is too cold today. There are always birds – swans, ducks, herons and cormorants – which feed and nest along the river, and just once or twice I've been lucky and seen the flash of unmistakable blue that tells me a kingfisher has just flown by. One friend of mine has seen otter here too, but I never have. This morning, though, it is the beauty of the landscape around the river that makes us pause, the grasses and bare winter branches encased in crystal-like frost.

The dogs run ahead of us. This is heaven for them, no roads, lots of new, captivating smells, the possibility of finding voles hiding in the tussocky grass. For us, it is the peace, the sound of the river bubbling and tumbling over rocks, a robin singing, the beat of the wings of a little gang of mallards flying low over the water. After a mile we come to a dairy farm. Back in September last year, the field we are walking through now was full of people, food stalls, beer tents and music. It was the finishing line for the infamous Monmouth Raft Race, an annual fund-raising event of glorious eccentricity. Teams build rafts, dress up in ludicrous outfits and paddle (if their craft manages to stay afloat, which many don't) from the boat house in Monmouth to here. People line the banks, shouting encouragement, and more stand on the bridges at Monmouth and Redbrook armed with eggs and flour which are gleefully dropped on the rowers below.

At the farm we leave the river for the woods and a track that climbs beneath a tunnel of branches. Squirrels, foraging for beech mast, skitter away up the trunks, much to the frustration of the dogs. Puffing slightly, we meet a wider forestry track which gives us glimpses through the trees of the valley and the river below us. It winds around and drops down, only to climb again, following the Whitebrook that gives this valley and its village their name. The brook, racing to reach the main river, lies between us and the pretty cottages, with their neat gardens waiting for the first warmth of spring to wake them from their winter slumber.

In one garden is a ruin, a rather lovely tumbledown wall and a tall stone chimney, remnants of what was once a paper mill, once the main industry of this area. We cross the brook further up the valley on stepping stones and then, by way of a stile, come to a lane. A short distance up here brings us to Margaret's Wood. This little patch of woodland, managed by the local Wildlife Trust, comes into its own in spring when it is so full of wild daffodils it would have inspired Wordsworth to start writing all over again.

We climb on, then traverse the side of the valley through a short, dramatically dark section of conifers, before coming out into the pale winter sunlight to a slightly damp, mossy bench, where we perch to munch apples. Here there are more views of the fields and woods that slope down to the Wye. This is why I love this walk. In five miles it manages to capture the very essence of this part of the valley, its rolling green hills, tumbling streams, steep-sided valleys sheltering villages and farms, and the woodlands that now are beautiful in their winter nakedness. In spring and summer they are rustling canopies of every shade of green and in autumn the colours are so magnificent I've seen people simply stop their cars on the road, get out and gaze in wonder.

We descend again, cross another little brook by way of a wooden bridge, descend past an old cider mill and then there's the final climb, a heart-racing haul to Pen y Fan, not the mountain in the Brecon Beacons, but a hilltop hamlet with views over the river to England and the ridge where Offa built his dyke. Below us is the bridge where we started. The dogs, with their enviable four-paw drive, chase down the hill, leap a stile into a field and wait impatiently for us to catch them up. It's early afternoon, but the frost persists and we follow their scampering tracks in the grass.

22ND JANUARY
ALONE – BUT NOT LONELY

*

A pink dawn and a light covering of snow. Although barely more than the equivalent of a dusting of icing sugar, it still somehow manages to give the morning's silence that sort of deadened, beneath-the-duvet quality. My feet crunch, the sound magnified, leaving a lone set of dark footprints in the crisp whiteness. I contemplate this morning the gentle satisfaction that solitude brings, the feeling that this tiny, frozen bit of the world at this moment is mine and mine alone.

What is it that makes solitude something special and loneliness something so grim? Why does solitude feel uplifting and loneliness fill the stomach and the back of the throat with a dull, persistent ache? Why is one a joy and the other such misery?

Perhaps, I muse, as the first rays of sun filter through the bare branches above me and the fragile snow almost instantly surrenders to its barely perceptible warmth and starts to pool and trickle, it's because solitude is something you choose and loneliness isn't. I mostly walk alone but I rarely, if ever, feel lonely.

26TH JANUARY

AN INKLING OF SPRING AND AN URGE TO BE PART OF IT

✻

It's not quite light when I leave the house. It is still cold, minus four or five degrees, but dry. The sheep are up on the yard, impatient for breakfast. I feed them, break the ice on their trough, scatter grain for the chickens, ducks and geese. The pigs are awake. I can hear their anxious grunts and squeals. 'I haven't forgotten you, girls,' I say as I pour feed into their buckets and top up their water.

The dogs, meanwhile, are waiting for me, impatient to be off and out. Teg is watching my every move, sitting on the edge of the track that leads from our house down into the woods. 'Come on then,' I tell her and she races away with Badger and Bella in hot pursuit. Something makes me look down at the spot where Teg was sitting.

Poking up through the earth are the first of the season's snowdrops and as I walk down into the woods the sun rises behind the trees, the sky washed with reds and pinks and oranges. And for the first time this year there is birdsong; not a full-throated dawn chorus, but a celebration nonetheless of the start of a beautiful day.

Later and I'm restless. It is not a day to be sitting at a desk. There is a sense of change, of nature stirring. It's not spring, not yet, but it is as if there is a small rebellion going on. Escaping the hibernating cloak of winter are signs that our world is considering waking up. The sun, proud in a cloudless sky, feels warm and I walk with an accompanying shadow that feels like an old friend who hasn't been around for a while.

A robin sings lustily, from the leafless branches of an oak tree, its orange chest puffed out with effort like an over-enthusiastic choir boy. I learned the other day why 'robin red breasts' are so-called, despite their plumage not being red. In the 15th century, when people started giving common names to familiar species, no one in England had ever seen the fruit we now call an orange, so the colour didn't exist. Also 'robin orange breast' doesn't quite trip off the tongue so well...

As I wait for the dogs to cross a stile, a butterfly – a red admiral – flits past as if it too has been made restless by this first warm day of the year.

29TH–31ST JANUARY

ACCEPTING – GRUDGINGLY – THAT WALKING IS NOT ALWAYS FUN

✳

The glimmer of spring was short lived. The last three days of the month have been dismal. We were staying with a friend in Wiltshire on Saturday night, with plans for a big walk followed by an equally big lunch on Sunday. She emailed on Friday to say the forecast was horrible and, sure enough, the bright run of weather we had had for the last couple of days turned to rain by Friday night. But Saturday, which had an unpromising start as I forced myself out for a run in the drizzle, became suddenly bright, the sun broke through and it got warm enough that I finished my run wishing I wasn't wearing thermals and holding my woolly hat in my hand. But it didn't last. We drove down to Wiltshire in driving rain and Sunday morning dawned unwillingly, *dreich* as the Scots would say – part drizzle, part rain, part low cloud.

Determined to stick to our plans and earn our lunch, we donned head-to-toe waterproofs and walked around the nearby National Trust estate. The path took us alongside a lake full of upturned swans. A flock of little white egrets – maybe as many as 20 of them – was perched in a tree on the opposite bank and I caught a momentary glimpse, a flash of brightest blue, as a kingfisher flew away downstream. That was the only bit of colour we saw all morning. A walk that would have been a wonderful mix of hills, woodland and open fields, with the occasional bit of country estate grandeur thrown in – a folly here, a triumphal arch there – became a muddy trudge beneath our dripping hoods and we were all secretly relieved when the cars hove back into view and we could go and sit in a bedraggled huddle and eat roast beef.

At home on Monday I took the dogs out at 7.30am, when usually it would almost be light, but the sun never seemed to come up at all and we remained encased in thick, wet, grey cloud for the entire day. I always feel that when you've had a day of weather like that, nature will come good and make the next day all sunshine and birdsong. It was not to be. I woke this morning before the alarm went off, rain thrumming on the skylight. Even the dogs, usually desperate to be up and out, were reluctant this morning.

I take us across the fields and into woods that I hope will be a little more sheltered and dry, but after an hour and a half we return home looking like the survivors of a shipwreck, Badger and Teg's fluffy bellies caked in wet, black mud. They stand stoically as I hose them off and rub them down with the still-wet towel from yesterday. Beneath my sodden waterproofs the rain has managed to creep in and I am almost as damp as the dogs. Once back in the kitchen, huddled up to the range, it is hard to tell which of us smells worse.

It hasn't really let up all day. One of the joys of being out every day, morning and evening, is noticing that every morning it gets lighter a little earlier and darkness falls a little later, but today it seems never to get light at all. 'Roll on February,' I say as I slosh back from feeding the sheep and the pigs.

February

INSPIRATIONAL BEAUTY UNDIMMED BY THE WEATHER

✻

Of course there is no miraculous change. The weather continues cold and wet for the rest of the week. At the local supermarket checkout, the conversation is dominated by whether lambing has started and how bored everyone is of having permanently wet, muddy clothes/dogs/children or all three. After unloading the shopping, I pull on my waterproof trousers, find the least damp of my coats and follow the dogs along the farm road, water running off the concrete in rivulets and pooling under the hedges. We climb a stile, slither down the field to a track at the bottom, over another stile and into another field where sheep are grazing on the slope above us, unconcerned by the steady drizzle.

The footpath takes us downhill, past a dairy farm and through a muddy gateway to a steep, stony track that continues downhill until we come out on a narrow road behind houses. Just before we turn off this road onto the track that will take us back up the hill and home, there is a gap which allows us to see beyond the houses to the river and the ruins of Tintern Abbey. Even on a day like today it looks splendid and majestic, its old stone the colour of the landscape, as if it has grown out of the earth it sits on, the dark trees on the far bank framed within its arches.

Wordsworth's poem comes to mind – 'Lines Written a Few Miles Above Tintern Abbey, On Revisiting the Banks of the Wye During a Tour, 13 July, 1798' – not the snappiest of titles, and there is no reference to the abbey within the poem itself, but its opening lines sum up not just his impression of this landscape but, more revealingly, how it makes him feel:

> *Five years have passed; five summers, with the length*
> *Of five long winters! And again I hear*
> *These waters, rolling from their mountain springs*
> *With a soft inland murmur. Once again*
> *Do I behold these steep and lofty cliffs,*
> *Which on a wild secluded scene impress*
> *Thoughts of more deep seclusion, and connect*
> *The landscape with the quiet of the sky.*

4TH FEBRUARY

A PERFECT MORNING ALL TO OURSELVES

*

'What a difference a day makes,' sang Dinah Washington, and it certainly has today. This morning it is as warm and spring-like as yesterday was bone chilling and wintery. The sky is cloudless and blue, the garden full of reasons to be cheerful. There are more snowdrops. The daffodil bulbs are pushing up their sword-like leaves through the dark, wet earth. There's a periwinkle, a lone splash of purple in one of the flower beds. The horse chestnut sapling that we planted not long after we moved here has tightly furled, sticky conical buds on the tips of its branches, and the straggling, unruly willow hedge is also in bud. The rhubarb is coming up in the veggie patch, green leaves unfurling and the first hint of those delicious pink stalks rising from the soil.

And there are new mole hills – a scattering of them – in the fields and on the lawn. Small tumps of dark soil that trace the furious tunnelling of a mole – probably a male – in search of a mate.

Teg has a mild obsession with moles and will stand, eyes fixed on a molehill, ears cocked, like an Arctic fox listening for lemmings under the snow. She, too, will do that comical jump – all four paws leaving the ground – land on the molehill and start to dig furiously, earth flying everywhere, then, ever-hopeful, stick her nose into the soil, snorting and snuffling until she realizes her efforts are in vain and runs on, mud all over her face, and tries again at the next one.

She and her brother, Taff, did once catch one. It was when they were puppies, just a few months old, and I'd taken them out around the fields at the farm. They chased at full pelt across the fields, endlessly curious, high spirited and fantastically disobedient. I didn't see what happened, whether one of them had spotted a movement in the grass or whether they had smelt something, but the two of them came racing towards me, looking enormously pleased with themselves, Taff carrying a small black form in his mouth. I got close enough to see it was a mole but there was no way Taff was going to let go of his prize until Teg launched an ambush, and they both rolled over in a flurry of ginger and red fur. Teg emerged victorious, the mole firmly clamped in her jaws, and I knew any attempt at rescue was fruitless.

This morning we want to celebrate the sunshine, soak up its fragile warmth and relish the light, so we steer clear of the woods and head up onto the ridge behind the house. A short climb brings us to a lovely run of three fields, empty of livestock, crows in the trees, buzzards circling, the smell of damp earth and fresh air. We pause by the gate of the last field and look out to where the Bristol Channel cuts through the hills, its dark waters reflecting the sun like a tarnished mirror, the two bridges over the Severn sharp and white against the blue of the sky. It is Saturday, a perfect morning, and yet we are entirely alone up here, just me and the dogs and the birds and the sunshine. This beautiful world all to ourselves.

12TH FEBRUARY

A NIGHT ON MY FEET AND TEA AT SUNRISE

✳

I'm up at the farm. Our first lambs of the year are due and to help out Farmer Tim, I'm doing the night shift. I love being here, the warm woolly smell, the sound of the rhythmic chewing of the cud, the gentle, comforting, nickering exchanges between a ewe and her lambs. As soon as I walk into the shed the sounds and the smells make me feel instantly nostalgic. 'Everything's fed and watered,' says Tim, 'there's just one that might be thinking about doing something. See you in the morning.'

My night starts with a walk, just a short one, along the line of pens, most of them empty ready for the newborns and their mums, but a couple are occupied. Two sets of twins, tiny, all legs and ears, tight curled fleeces soft and dazzling white against the straw.

I sit for a bit, for no reason other than I enjoy being here, watching the ewes and the way they interact. The little squabbles, the minor altercations when one has had the audacity to stand in the wrong place or lie down where another has decided she wants to lie. And as soon as I settle down, many of them do too, plopping themselves down inelegantly in the straw, bellies distended, breathing heavily. Some stretch out completely on their sides, eyes closed, and fall into a slumber so deep I've sometimes been worried they've died.

The ewe that Tim thought might be in the early stages of labour waddles over to the hayrack, jostles her way through the few that are gathered around it already, finds herself a position she likes and starts eating, so it's likely she won't be giving birth imminently. I'm tempted to stay here, warm and snug in the gentle company of the sheep, but I know from experience that they will often hold off going into labour if they are being watched. I creep quietly out and walk across the yard to the office where I have an air mattress and a sleeping bag. The moon has come out from behind the clouds. It is on the wane, a misshapen semicircle, but it still casts a silver-blue light bright enough that I don't need a torch. I snuggle down into my sleeping bag and set the alarm to go off in two hours.

It is the last bit of sleep I get. When I return to the shed, a ewe has just given birth and she is standing in the back corner, licking her newborn lamb. I approach her slowly. Sheep are routinely portrayed as being rather dim creatures, but I disagree. They certainly have an unerring ability to know if you want to catch them and will come up with any number of tactics to avoid capture. However, when they have just given birth they are often – although not always – so fixated with their lamb you can approach them without them bolting away and hiding within the rest of the flock. The lamb is fine, head raised, already thinking about getting to its feet. I put iodine on the umbilical cord to prevent infection and then gently pick the lamb up by its front legs and drag it slowly backwards through the straw towards a pen, all the while making newborn lamb noises. 'Meer, meer.'

It feels mildly ridiculous, but it works. Keeping the lamb low on the ground allows its mother to see and smell it and my lamb imitation keeps her attention. She follows us into the pen and as soon as I lay the lamb down she is back licking it again. I check she has milk and then leave them in peace. The ewe has a blue spot on her back. A couple of months ago all these ewes were scanned. Those expecting a single lamb were given no mark, those with twins a blue mark and those with triplets a red mark. So I know this ewe is expecting another lamb, and now she is in the pen there is no danger that one of the other ewes will steal the first one while she is giving birth to the second one. A ewe about to give birth is so overrun by hormones she can sometimes believe that a lamb that has just been born is actually hers, push the real mother away and encourage the lamb to drink from her, rather than from its mother. This 'mismothering' can mean that when she does give birth to her own lamb she has none of her colostrum left – the source of energy and antibodies vital to keeping a newborn lamb alive.

As soon as I have penned the ewe I see another one is going into labour. She has done the typical thing of taking herself away from the flock to a dark corner of the shed. She is lying on her side, head stretched up towards the ceiling, lip curled and sides heaving. She gets up, paws at the straw, turns around a couple of times and then lies down again. All this is normal and I won't intervene unless it seems to be going on too long or she is visibly distressed, but I won't leave the shed until she gives birth.

In all, six ewes give birth overnight and I don't get out of the shed until dawn is breaking. Although I haven't walked anywhere other than across the yard and around the shed, this time on my feet has, as it so often does, made me feel intimately connected with all the small happenings of the last few hours: the passage of the stars across the sky, the setting of the moon, the wonder of being witness to the very start of a new life. I meet Tim in the yard and we go and put the kettle on, watch the sun rise, our hands wrapped around steaming mugs of tea.

14TH FEBRUARY
LONDON LARKS

*

The last few mornings have been cold again and I've woken to frosts and beautiful sunrises, pale skies streaked with pastel pinks, oranges and smoky blues. I'm hoping that my Valentine present will be the same as last year, when I was serenaded by the soaring melody of the first skylark of the year. But today it is just the caw of crows, flying up around the tractor that is digging out steaming silage to feed the cows. A group of buzzards is in the field below the track, fishing for worms, and somewhere there is a robin singing but it can't compete with a skylark.

Later we go to London, to see a play and have dinner. I can't remember the last time we've been here together and just for fun. No need to rush about to meetings, fighting traffic and crowds, harassed and stressed. We walk from our B&B in Notting Hill to the theatre in Covent Garden, something we would never have done when we lived here unless there was a tube strike and resorting to violence was the only way to get on a bus. But now that we don't live here anymore, it is rather nice to rediscover the city on foot, a visitor rather than a resident, and somehow as a visitor it feels more appropriate to walk, to go down streets I may not have gone down before, to gaze in windows, to people watch in the parks and on the pavements.

The American illustrator Maira Kalman is enthusiastic about urban walking:

> *I walk everywhere in the city.*
> *Any city. You see everything you*
> *need to see for a lifetime.*
> *Every emotion. Every condition.*
> *Every fashion. Every glory.*

She, like Thoreau and Wordsworth, Dickens and Hugo, Nietzsche and Kant, sees walking as indispensable inspiration, a generative force of intellect, awareness and creativity.

The following morning, I have an appointment at Somerset House on the Strand. It is an hour and a half's walk from Notting Hill and when I get there I feel energized and refreshed. Clear headed. Receptive and buzzing with ideas. Meetings can sometimes feel futile – a lot of chat with little constructive outcome – but this one is productive, creative and exciting. I walk back through the streets on a high.

17TH FEBRUARY

A LITTLE BIRD THAT HAS INSPIRED GREAT THINGS

✻

There's my skylark! The dogs and I are returning from our morning walk. The frost has gone and it is rather grey, the landscape monochrome in the early morning light. There is no sunrise visible through the cloud that forms a uniform pale wash from horizon to horizon. But as we descend past the cattle shed I hear that song, that unmistakable trill of sound and I stop, looking up, scanning the colourless sky above me and there it is! A tiny brown form, almost invisible, high above me, wings aflutter, welcoming us to the morning, and to spring.

> *For singing till his heaven fills,*
> *'Tis love of earth that he instils,*
> *And ever winging up and up,*
> *Our valley is his golden cup,*
> *And he the wine which overflows*
> *To lift us with him as he goes.*

Extract from 'The Lark Ascending', George Meredith (1881)

19TH FEBRUARY
AN EARLY MORNING OBSERVATION

✳

A quiet night in the lambing shed last night, no complicated labours, no intervention. There wasn't much for me to do save check the ewes had milk and wait to see the lambs suckle. At dawn I walk out of the door of the office where I spent the night on the floor in my sleeping bag. I make my way across the yard and am halted in my tracks. The eastern sky is a blaze of colour – and this dramatic transition between darkness and light is happening earlier.

Just six weeks ago it was still dark at eight but this morning it is light before seven. And it seems that on mornings like this, clear and bright, the birds are willing to sing again. But, I've discovered, on overcast mornings the woods are quiet, as if the birds are saving their voices for mornings when they will be appreciated. This is what I love about experiencing the world at walking pace: the small but significant luxury of having the time and headspace to notice details that make me feel part of my surroundings. A sense of belonging, rather than passing through.

21ST FEBRUARY

LOVE IS IN THE AIR (FOR FROGS)

✳

There are more indications that spring is thinking about springing. The daffodils are coming into bud, the first purple crocuses are poking through the grass and there are green shoots pushing up through the leaf litter in the woods. The fields are beginning to look a bit more green and a bit less brown. On our walk this morning I notice a couple of frogs, squashed flat, on the track that leads to the cottages on the other side of the hill from us. There are more squashed frogs on the lane.

A squashed frog may not be something that any of us would consider being another happy clue that spring is in the air, but that is exactly what it is. Because something is telling the local frogs and toads that they need to hop back to their breeding ponds – the very ponds in which they were born – and get on with the happy business of spawning a new generation. Unfortunately for them, so intent are they on the job in hand that they will stop for nothing, not even the wheels of a passing car.

As soon as I get home I check the little pond that we dug out the first year we moved here. Within just two years – despite the fact we are on top of a hill with no other significant bodies of water in the immediate area – the pond had become home to all three species of British newt, as well as frogs, toads, diving beetles, dragonflies and water boatmen. And this morning I am delighted to discover the evidence that some of our resident frogs have already made it back and been busy. There is a glutinous mass of frogspawn nestled among the slimy stalks of the marigolds and water mint.

In the afternoon's failing light – which I happily note is now happening closer to 6pm than 5pm – I go and feed the sheep and shut the geese and ducks up in their house for the night. They are in an enclosed run, but hungry foxes are clever, looking for gaps in the defences, seizing an opportunity whenever it arises. I was once given six adorable Aylesbury ducklings, which would trot around in the field in an orderly line, like one of those old-fashioned wooden children's toys that were pulled along by a piece of red string. Their field was enclosed by an electric fence that was on day and night, and only turned off when I went into the field to feed them or muck out their house. One afternoon I forgot to switch the fence back on. The next morning there were six little headless corpses scattered across the grass; a salutary reminder that you can't outfox a fox.

As I walk back to the house, Venus is bright in the darkening south-western sky. It reminds me, as it always does, of an extraordinary journey and the remarkable people I did the journey with. Back in 1999, Ludo and I spent five weeks travelling with four men and their fifty camels over nine hundred miles through the Sahara desert, and although we spoke nothing of each other's languages and came from cultures and backgrounds that couldn't have been more different, over the time we spent together I came to see them as my desert family. It was a brutally hard journey, both for animals and humans, and often we travelled well into the night. There is the common misconception that deserts are vast expanses of monochrome sand, featureless, deadening to the senses, but one of the many things I learnt on that journey was that the desert – well, that bit of it in the northern part of Mali, anyway – is as endlessly varied as the countryside I live in now, although admittedly less green.

It was on this journey that I discovered the joyous, almost hypnotic pleasure of walking, heightened by being in the company of animals and in a landscape that gives the impression that no human has ever passed this way before. It is also where I became aware of the appearance of the first star in the sky, always before it was properly dark, always in the same place, always assuredly bright and twinkly.

Rachman, the leader of our little gang, the senior member of our family, who had spent his whole life since he was able to walk making this journey, called it 'The Shepherd's Star'. For him it was one of the many natural signposts he used to lead him unerringly through dunes, across gravel plains and strange tussocky grasslands to get to the next well, or to a dried-up water course that he knew would have food for the camels, and eventually to the salt mines on which their livelihood for the year is based. For me it became a comforting, familiar presence, an intrinsic part of the natural pattern of the day, like sunrise, and the moment when our shadows had contracted to form an intense dark pool immediately beneath our feet.

The Shepherd's Star would, for a brief spell, hog the limelight and be the only star visible in the sky, but then as the darkness began to descend over the desert like a cloak, the heavens would reveal the full chorus line, a bewildering array of thousands upon thousands of pinpricks of light. As we travelled on through the night we would watch the myriad constellations move with stately majesty across the sky, feeling as if we were the sole visitors to the finest planetarium on earth.

22ND FEBRUARY

A WALK TO BLOW AWAY THE COBWEBS

✻

Our friend Annabelle has come to stay. She lives in Kenya, on the slopes below the towering, snow-covered peak of Mount Kenya. The last walk we did together was there. We climbed, up and up, through the protea plants, sunbirds flitting ahead of us, to a lake where we hoped to catch some trout for supper. The trout outwitted us, which was a shame because the walk had built up quite an appetite. Now Annabelle is on our home patch, we want to take her to climb one of our mountains.

The radio comes on to wake us up in time to hear the weather forecast. I never remember being particularly interested in the weather until we moved to the countryside. Now we are mildly obsessed with it. This morning the dulcet tones of the BBC's weatherman, Phil Avery, warn us of an approaching 'weather bomb'. Storm Doris is storming our way. Who, I wondered, thought Doris was a good name for a storm? Why name them anyway? I do a quick search, discover the naming of storms – and only big, potentially destructive ones get a name – is a relatively recent thing, introduced by the Met Office. The storms are named alphabetically. Doris follows Conor, Barbara and Angus.

But there seem to be few signs of Doris and her impending 'weather bomb' this morning. It is calm and bright and quite warm and so we stick to our plan. The distinctive outline of the Black Mountains is the view on the western skyline from the fields just beyond our house. They would barely count as foothills in Kenya, but I love being in the proximity of mountains, even little ones, and regard it as one of the great joys of living where we do to be able to have a bolstering lunch in the pub, as we do with Annabelle, and then go and climb a mountain before tea.

We emerge from the pub to find that the sky has darkened dramatically and the bare branches of the trees are dancing stiffly in the wind that has apparently whipped up in the hour we've been cosseted by the fireplace eating pork scratchings. We drive to the foot of the Skirrid and when we get out of the car the wind hits us in a breathtaking blast. It makes the dogs skittish. They bark and skip and scamper. 'It's going to be bracing!'

The path climbs up through woodland, sheltering us from the full force of the wind and then, instead of taking the more direct route to the summit, we skirt around to the left on a less frequently used path that winds its way between trees and around boulders, emerging on the lower grassy slopes of the Skirrid, its bulk like some great medieval rampart rising above us. We turn our backs to the mountain to look out across the land, which falls away and then rises again. There is a lovely view of the Sugarloaf from here, but today only the lower slopes are visible, the distinctive angular peak shrouded in dark, brooding cloud.

We wind our way through gorse bushes, not yet in flower, and jump over the little streams that rise up and bubble their way down the slopes in the winter but often dry up and disappear completely in the summer. We are still on the protected side of the mountain, but the clouds above us are whipping across the sky, an ever-shifting kaleidoscope in every shade of grey. And then we round a bend and the full force of the wind hits us, tearing down the slope in furious blasts and we are climbing straight into it.

I choose a brutally steep route that I think then joins a less steep path which zigzags its way to the top, but I'm wrong. This path is not really a path at all, but a sheep track, and it heads almost vertically up the slope, so that for much of the climb we are almost on our hands and knees, hand over fist, grabbing at clumps of grass to stop ourselves slipping, or being blown back down the mountain.

The dogs, of course, are loving it, chasing ahead, whipped into a frenzy of excitement by the wind. Finally, hearts pounding, calves burning, we reach the trig point. These 'triangulation points' are found all over the world, and were used for surveying and mapping. This is one of 25,000 trig points that the Ordnance Survey erected in the UK in the early 1900s. Today GPS has made their original purpose somewhat redundant, but for walkers they are a goal to reach for, a psychological incentive to keep climbing. We gather around ours, the wind up here so strong we can barely stand upright, our hands clamped on our heads to stop our woolly hats blowing away, laughing with the sheer exhilaration and madness of it all. And the dogs stand with us, noses into the wind, their fur rippling, their ears – to borrow a line from AA Milne – 'streaming behind them like banners'.

Brooding clouds, laden with intent, scud across the sky, but beneath them there is an almost ethereal light casting an unearthly glow on the patchwork quilt of Monmouthshire. We turn sideways to the wind to head down, buffeted, unbalanced by its gusting force and I envy the dogs' lower centre of gravity. Finally we are in the woods that hug the lower slopes, breathless and windswept and marvelling at the quiet stillness beneath the trees. We are flushed with the euphoria that comes from being out in wild weather and of not submitting to the 'sensible' option of staying inside.

24TH FEBRUARY

A FALLEN GIANT

✳

Storm Doris swept across the country causing chaos and disruption in her wake. Trains ground to a halt and thousands of people, including me, were stranded at stations wondering how on earth they'd get home. Today it is oddly calm, cold, the sky clear and fresh looking, an almost translucent blue. Frost lingers in sheltered pockets beneath hedges and as I run with the dogs along the track through the woods I'm surprised that there isn't more debris – a few scattered twigs seem to be the extent of the damage. After my previous frustrating, static day spent almost entirely indoors it is liberating to be out here, the cold air making the end of my nose and the tips of my fingers tingle, the rhythmic slap of my feet on the earth easing away the tiredness and stress brought on by yesterday's events.

We run beneath leafless trees and then leave the woods behind to cross a field. In this field is an ancient oak tree, long since dead, but judging by its size it has stood sentinel in this landscape for five or six hundred years. In recent times its branches have shed extraneous twigs and now are stunted, skeletal and black, perfect perches for roosting rooks.

But as I run down the field I see that its dramatic silhouette is no longer there, that this relic of a former age is lying, shattered in hundreds of pieces, on the khaki-coloured grass. I feel compelled to stop at the feet of this fallen giant to somehow pay my respects, to acknowledge that this little part of my world is gone. I am surprised how mournful I feel.

26TH FEBRUARY

A RUN TO FIND MY FEET

✳

I'm in India; a town called Shillong in the far northeast state of Meghalaya, somewhere above Bangladesh. The town is built on a series of hills, steep ones, and I'm running, somewhat laboriously, up one of them. Ahead of me are Alexis and Mark. Over the coming days we will be making a film about this unique Indian state with its matrilineal society. We've worked together many times and we all share the need to get a grip on where we are by going out into the streets.

We were doubtful about being able to run here: as a foreign woman I was particularly sceptical. It would possibly be viewed as inappropriate and would certainly arouse unwanted attention. And it wasn't just local sensibilities that concerned us, but the infamous traffic. But today it is Sunday, still relatively early, the streets are quiet and as I get left behind by my fitter, faster colleagues, the few people I pass don't seem remotely fazed by a lone, red-faced woman panting her way up the hill.

I don't take in much on this first outing; smells mainly, of traffic fumes, burning rubbish, cooking spices, incense. I pass a Catholic church, bright icing-sugar blue and worshippers are gathering, the street choked with cars, abandoned rather than parked. A few beggars sit outside the gates with their bowls. A cat slinks along a wall, a man walks past me downhill, a long pole slung over his shoulder, a jerry can slopping water tied to each end. The air is crisp, cool, thin and dry. We are at over 2,000 metres.

None of the women I see, I realize, is wearing a sari and there is something else too, something that I don't so much see as feel, but as yet I am too jetlagged and out of puff to work out what it is.

28TH FEBRUARY
A WALK TO SCRATCH BENEATH THE SURFACE

✳

Shillong's market is a maze of tiny alleyways and steps, crammed with colour, noise and smells. Unfamiliar fruits and vegetables overflow baskets and crowd the stalls. All of Shillong is here, it seems. Old men read papers while drinking tiny cups of sweet dark tea. Boys with elaborately greased quiffs and mohicans hang out or stalk, self-consciously, through the crowds. There are women shopping, casting discerning eyes over fat red chillies and bunches of coriander.

I walk into a square, a welcome chink of open air after the claustrophobic crush of the alleys. There are rows of vegetables in sacks and baskets or laid out in tempting displays on bits of cloth on the ground. All the market traders are women. Diminutive, quick, their teeth stained red from chewing betel nut, they ooze confidence and savvy. There is much laughter among themselves and with their customers. Crumpled notes change hands and are tucked away beneath what I am coming to realize is the traditional dress – a piece of gingham cloth worn over skirts and jumpers, slung diagonally over the shoulder.

It should be noisy, all these people going about all this business, but the laughter, the banter – even the calls of warning from the men carrying loads so heavy they are actually bent double, their efforts etched into every sinew in their legs and every line in their faces as they ease themselves through the throng – are somehow muted, a constant hum rather than a cacophony.

It is only really later, when I'm out after dark, that the sense I had on the first day – something about the local women that seemed different – becomes a realization.

Shillong is noisier and more garish at night and the streets seem more chaotic. Hundreds of little stalls tempt and beckon. There are cuts of meat laid out on tables, fish brought in from Calcutta, baskets of oranges, piles of pomegranates, grapes, apples encased in bright pink nets. There are plastic jars of sweets, garlands of tiny plastic packets containing nuts and tamarind and some sort of dried berry. The traffic is bewildering. Horns blare, lights flash, motorbikes, dogs and pedestrians thread their way through a tangle of cars and I'm in the middle of it. I dodge and dash alongside the others on foot and it is this perspective that allows me to finally realize what it is that is different.

The women – some in the local dress, many in Western dress, some alone, others in pairs or small groups – exude an independence, a self-assurance that shouldn't be unusual or striking. But in my experience of other parts of India, you don't see women doing this, friends going out in a way we would entirely take for granted. And I would usually feel uncomfortable too, for as someone so obviously foreign, I would be a curiosity, fair game to be stared at or given unwanted attention and scrutiny.

But here, in one of the few remaining matrilineal societies in the world, the local women as well as the foreigner wandering among them are able to walk unimpeded by any constraints or patriarchal sensibilities. The ancient system that the people in this part of India live by gives the women here more than the right of inheritance and of their family name being passed down to the next generation; it empowers them, makes them equal, liberated. It is also the thing that gives this state its unique identity within India and although I had read about it, I didn't appreciate how it manifested itself until I too was out on the streets on foot and after dark.

SPRING

March

___

1ST MARCH

THOUGHTS OF HOME

✳

As I run through the hilly streets of Shillong, India, in the early morning I'm thinking, as I dodge the traffic and the people sweeping the gutters with short, stiff hand brooms, nudging the rubbish into buckets, whether I can quietly celebrate today being the first day of spring. I wonder, as I pass a man carrying water in milk churns tied to a pole and slung over his shoulder, whether back in the Wye Valley the birds are starting to warm up their voices after a winter of silence. Are the wood anemones out yet? Or the celandines?

Here my nostrils are full of traffic fumes and the smell of cooking and spiced chai coming from the little roadside cafés. At home would it be too soon to smell the gentle warming of the earth, the subtle fragrant freshness in the air as things start to grow again and colour comes back to the landscape?

I smile at the two old boys I've seen every morning. They stand on the edge of the track opposite the town's basketball court in tracksuit bottoms, jumpers and blazers, their resplendent moustaches carefully groomed, and undertake a series of dignified exercises and stretches. They wave their arms, jog gently on the spot, tip their heads from side to side.

I run past the man who sleeps in the shuttered doorway of a shop shrouded in a thin tartan blanket, only his flat, cracked, blackened feet poking out to prove it is a person and not just a bundle of rags. Past the women with their baskets of fruit and piles of fish on low wooden tables at the side of the road, chattering and laughing and waiting for a sale. Past a couple of dogs scrapping on the pavement, the sign for the incongruously named Bob Dylan café and around the mini roundabout that brings me back to the hotel, and I realize how much I miss the stillness, the peace and the solitude of my early morning excursions at home. The Welsh language has a particularly beautiful word for this feeling, a word that can't quite be translated as 'homesickness', or 'longing', or 'yearning' for something you love, but sort of encapsulates all of those things. *Hiraeth*.

4TH MARCH

WALKING AS A WAY OF LIFE

✳

We have left the city and are camping in a field at the edge of a small end-of-the-road village perched on the summit of a dramatically steep-sided hill. Here almost no one has a car and there is little point in them anyway. Houses are reached by a network of steps and precipitous paths and most people make a living by cultivating land so vertiginous it seems miraculous that they are able to sow and reap their crops without tumbling hundreds of feet into the valley below. So walking here is not a pastime, or a hobby or a way of taking exercise. It is part and parcel of everyday life, the sole means of getting from A to B.

I have joined a family, including a little boy about five years old, heading to their land to harvest a wild spice called long pepper, which sells for a good price in the markets of Shillong. The track out of the village is stained with vivid red splashes as if it has been the scene of a massacre, but it is the spat-out juice of betel nut, a mild stimulant, which everyone in the village chews night and day.

We make our way on a narrow, well-maintained path cut into the contour of the slope and after a while it descends more steeply, it gets narrower, and I find myself clutching at the trunks of trees to steady myself. We press ourselves against the bank to let a man pass who is carrying a sack so stuffed full it is straining at the seams. The sack is resting on the man's back, held in place by a webbing band that goes around his forehead. He is bent almost at 90 degrees at the waist by the weight of the load, his calf muscles taut, the sinews in his neck rigid with effort. He is small, the sack bigger than him, and I wouldn't be surprised if it is the same weight as him too. 'He's been harvesting bay leaves,' I am told by one of the daughters I am walking with. We have been walking for about an hour at this point, and downhill. He is walking our same route, but up.

One of the things I love about travelling on foot is that it makes me feel very much part of my surroundings, rather than distanced or sheltered from them by the speed, the noise, the cocooning effect of a vehicle. In the West we worry over the general lack of connection with the natural world and it is this lack of connection that is often blamed for a number of ills – some small, some more significant – that afflict life in today's world. As I continue the long, long descent, the bottom of the valley still distant and concealed by a wall of thick vegetation, I wonder whether these people, whose lives and livelihoods are so intimately bound up with the land they live and work on, are happier and less angst-ridden as a result.

The family hosting me has seven children, lives in a small, immaculately clean wooden house, with little in the way of furniture and no modern conveniences like a washing machine or a microwave. There is no plumbing, electricity or running water. There is no television and nor does anyone, as far as I can tell, have a computer. All the older children go to school, the oldest is at university, and they are all bright, literate, confident and chatty. Yet by Western standards they would be considered poor, their house spartan, their living conditions unacceptable. And there's an irony in that, I realize, as their little boy takes me by the hand and shows me the little knobbly fruits on the vines we are here to pick, because so many of us get so much pleasure from doing things like this: being out in the fresh air, earth beneath our feet, doing something physical.

Off-grid retreats, camping, wild swimming, bushcraft have all seen an exponential rise in popularity in recent times. It seems we have a yearning for the simple, for a life more pared down, but this yearning does battle with an equally strong compulsion to acquire more things, perhaps because 'having stuff' is a measure of success in our society. If you have the trappings – a fancy car, a designer handbag, a TV the size of a billboard – you are 'well off'. But would we all be better off if we lived like this family, if our very means of survival depended on a knowledge, understanding and respect for the land around us, if we spent more hours outdoors than indoors, if our feet were our principal mode of transport?

The truth is, I don't know. But I know that right at this moment, having walked almost three hours downhill with the certainty that the only way back is to retrace my steps, carrying a bag bearing the rewards of today's labours, I couldn't feel more content.

5TH MARCH

HALF AN HOUR OF PEACE BEFORE THE WORLD WAKES UP

✳

It is clearer this morning. The low, wispy cloud that hangs over the tops of the hills has broken up and floats in stray, gossamer streamers between the trees. For the first time I get a sense of where we are, perched on a hill in a jumble of other hills separated by plunging, dark valleys, so deep they appear to be bottomless. An orange sun rises mistily in the pale grey sky. It had been a blustery night, gusts of wind playing with the fabric of our tents as if looking for a weak point, but now it is still and quiet – blissfully so, a rare thing in India. I decide to make the most of it and go for a run, to relish the lack of traffic and the peace. The only route is to take the road that leads to the village and stops there. It is uphill all the way, apart from the steep, muddy track that leads to our campsite. At this hour – it is barely 6am – there are few people around.

A girl crouches at the water point where later people will collect water to take back to their kitchens, or come to wash clothes. A small black-and-white dog barks at me, sounding ferocious, but as I get closer it loses its nerve and slinks away into one of the compounds and disappears. There are about five hundred people living here in houses that cling to the hillside below the road and are reached by a tangle of paths and steps. Most of the paths aren't big enough for vehicles and

I've only seen one car in the village, but they make perfect downhill runs for the homemade go-karts many of the children have. They are tiny, rattly wooden contraptions with no means of steering or braking and the kids race them with the glorious lack of fear enjoyed by the very young.

I run slowly up the hill away from the village, fields of what I thought was bamboo but isn't rustling and whispering in the breeze. I pass one other person, a woman, walking with even, measured steps, calm and serene – something about the way she is walking makes me think she is at the start of a long journey. We exchange nods of greeting as I puff past her. I get to an even steeper section of the road and my steps become shorter and slower until I finally concede that I would actually move faster if I walked. Up here, tucked up against a rock face, is a lone house, a wooden shack, and I wonder why it is here, isolated from the rest of the village. I hear sounds from inside – a child playing – but see no one.

Finally I'm at the top of the hill and I pause for a minute or two to take in the grandeur of this green, chaotic landscape. Now the warmth and light of the sun has broken through the mist, there are birds singing – well, making a noise anyway. Somewhere close by is a sort of lisping call, like that of a blue tit, but the sound that dominates and seems to reverberate off the hills is that of a car alarm. Or that is what I thought it was when I heard it yesterday, and it seemed so incongruous and unlikely that I asked if anyone else had noticed it. It's a bird, I was told, a barbet. It is not mimicking the sound of a car alarm, like some birds can, that is just the call it makes. And I'm reminded again of the small pleasures of experiencing a place on foot, rather than from a vehicle. Walking allows all my senses to be engaged by my surroundings,

I have a better, truer sense of where I am, I can hear birds that sound like car alarms...

I relish the run back, downhill, gravity on my side. As I get back to the village I pass a group of lads on their go-karts, going like the clappers, cheeks wobbling, eyes wide with exhilaration. They have an admiring audience of girls, one of whom is holding the hand of a very young child, a toddler in a pink cardigan. She looks at me, no doubt red-faced and at least twice the size of anyone she has ever seen before, and a look of fear, or horror, or both, takes over her face and it creases into a wide-mouthed yell of terror. I run on, as quickly as I can, and get back to my tent just as the first heavy drops of rain start to fall.

6TH MARCH
THE REWARD OF MAKING AN EFFORT:
A TOUGH WALK TO A HIDDEN GEM

✳

I was woken twice in the night by two short, sharp, dramatic thunderstorms. Lightning ripped through the dark, the claps of thunder were so loud they made my heart race and the rain so torrential it was as if somehow my tent had moved in the night and been pitched beneath a waterfall in full flow. It was a dank world, shrouded in thick grey cloud at dawn, but a glimmer of sunlight made us hope it would burn off.

We have another long walk planned today with four of the men from the village. They want to take us to an old river crossing, once the only way two villages were connected. Nowadays these two villages are connected by road and the route we will be taking is not used so much any more. It is, they have told us, a long, steep descent on a very rough, narrow path. We need the cloud to clear and no more rain to fall.

The weak sun has triumphed, the cloud has dissipated and we walk to the edge of the village and take a track that follows the contour of the hillside. The mud path – a rich terracotta red – is smooth and slick. It winds its way along the side of the mountain to a set of steps and crosses a stream. The views are huge, expansive, majestic, but I can't take them in as just walking on this path takes all my concentration. It's so narrow in places that I have to watch every footstep to avoid plunging over the edge. One of our party does slip, tumbling down ten or fifteen feet before mercifully being caught in a tree. He is unhurt, a little ruffled, and very thankful for the branches that stopped a fall that had it happened just a bit further along the path, would have sent him many hundreds of metres down the bare, almost sheer slope.

The sun is getting stronger. Sweat drips down my back. The slick mud has been replaced by stones, equally slippery from the rain, and I inch my way down, feeling nervous and doddery. In front of me are the local men, short, lean, nimble-footed, some wearing plastic sandals with no grip at all, others barefoot. The path cuts through a plantation of bamboo and our guides pass easily beneath the sharp-edged canopy of leaves. We have to bend and walk with our heads down to avoid being lacerated. At no point can we mindlessly put one foot in front of the other. Every step has to be carefully considered, the path at this point barely as wide as my foot and strewn with rocks, branches, roots, creepers, loose stones and patches of mud as slippery as ice. It's exhausting, more mentally than physically.

We've been walking for a couple of hours and we've reached the tree line. The track here is almost non-existent, descending so steeply we almost have to climb down, clutching trunks and branches, sitting on rocks and lowering ourselves gingerly down until we find a foothold. Slowly we slide and curse our way through a thick tangle of vegetation and I become aware of the sound of the river, still invisible, but louder, closer, and not long later I glimpse smooth grey forms beyond the trees. They are rocks, giant boulders sculpted by hundreds of thousands of years of rushing, tumbling water. Finally we have reached the bottom of the valley. The river is clear and clean, the flow at this time of year gentle and babbling. For although we've had some spectacular rainstorms, this is the dry season and the river is low, more a collection of pools, where tadpoles and small fish hide in the shade of the rocks. Butterflies flit in the dappled sunlight filtering through the leaves above our heads.

It is a beautiful spot, but this is not why the villagers have brought us here. They want us to see the bridge. It may seem like madness to walk for a risk-filled four hours just to come and see a bridge which is no longer in use, but as soon as I see it, I know that every moment we have spent getting here has been worth it. It is one of the most beautiful and ingenious partnerships between humans and nature I have ever seen. On each side of the bank, about ten metres above the river, is a rubber fig tree. These trees have a profusion of aerial roots and it is these roots that have been trained across the water, twisting together as they grow to form a living basket that spans the entire width of the river. It is, I am told, probably two hundred years old, maybe more.

I climb up to it and take a tentative step onto the platform of roots, holding onto other roots that have been trained to form a handrail on either side. It is solid and unexpectedly stable. I walk out to the middle of the bridge and look down at the river below and then carry on to the other side. How on earth, I wonder, was this astonishing piece of natural architecture constructed? The oldest of the villagers tells me that when two suitable trees are found a bamboo bridge is constructed between them and the aerial roots, which have huge flexibility and tensile strength, are trained along this bamboo skeleton. Over time they meet and twist together, forming a platform, and the bamboo, now that it is no longer needed, is allowed to rot away.

The walk back to the village is hard. Calves ache, sweat drips and when the village eventually comes into view, perched on a ridge against the horizon, it seems impossibly far away. But it seems a small price to pay to see something so remarkable. In fact, I muse, as I push my way back through the sharp leaves of the bamboo, it felt particularly special because of the walk. If we'd been able to drive, I don't think it would have made such an impression. It was so very rewarding because of the time and effort it took to get there.

13TH MARCH

A WALK THAT REVEALS REASONS TO BE CHEERFUL

*

It is early. Less than an hour ago our plane landed back in the UK. It had been a long journey with almost as much time spent sitting in airports as in the air. Now I'm in a car, travelling west down the motorway against the flow of the rush-hour traffic, feeling disoriented and almost drunk with exhaustion. The trees at the side of the carriageway are still bare and skeletal, the fields a washed-out murky green. I'd hoped to come back to a landscape transformed, bright and fresh, the embodiment of the new season, but instead it looks as tired and jaded as I do. But few things are more restorative than a noisy, enthusiastic greeting from an unruly pack of mongrels, a shower and a mug of tea.

I pull on a coat, stick my feet in my boots and follow the dogs along the river bank. And it is only now that I am on foot that I realize that the landscape I saw from the car was misleading. Through the windscreen everything was still the soft, washed-out monochrome of winter, but now I can see that colour is returning. There are bold, almost garish splashes of it determinedly imposing themselves on the backdrop of winter like graffiti against a grey wall. The willow is covered in yellow fluffy flowers abuzz with bumble bees. The blackthorn in the hedgerows is still leafless but covered in tiny, white, star-shaped blossoms that taste of almonds.

We turn away from the river and into the woods. Poking up through the leaf litter are wood anemones, fresh, white and perky. The precocious periwinkle that had taken upon itself to flower in my garden last month now has company and there is a profusion of stiff purple blooms among the dark green foliage on the bank alongside the path. I pass gardens with hedges of vivid yellow jasmine, but even that is eclipsed a little further on by a low rippling golden carpet of delicate flowers nodding in the breeze. The wild daffodils are out. I'm too jetlagged to think anything poetic, but I walk on with more of a spring in my step.

14TH MARCH
A WALK FOR MIND AND BODY

*

I have that slightly out-of-body feeling today. I slept fitfully but when I was asleep, I slept the sleep of the dead and felt heavy limbed and woolly headed when it was time to get up. I lay in bed and envisaged the walk I might do this morning. I have never done any form of structured, purposeful meditation, but maybe taking these virtual walks in my head has the same effect. I like a day that starts with the question 'where shall I go today?' and lying, eyes closed, letting the idea of a route slide into my mind.

After all those hours in cars and planes to get back home, I still feel rather stiff and unwieldy, despite my walk yesterday. I need a climb, I decide, something to stretch my leg muscles and make my heart pump. I settle on a walk that starts on the English side of the River Wye. It begins with a gentle climb along a lane and then turns off onto a steep, stony track – one of those paths that appears to have been worn down by centuries of trudging boots. It is narrow, wide enough really only for one person, sunk down between damp, mossy banks, low branches of holly scratching across clothing or getting briefly tangled in hair. It emerges from the dark tunnel of overhanging trees and weaves between fields full of fat, expectant-looking ewes, to a lane. By now the sleepy fog clouding my brain has lifted and I feel alert and invigorated. I start to notice the birdsong – not riotous yet, not a full-blown chorus, but another sign that winter is being left behind.

The dogs know this route as well as I do. They know the corner where they leave the lane and join another stony track – flat, muddy, brambles on either side with long, barbed tendrils snagging their backs and tails as they weave their way along, noses quivering. I often wonder what it must be like to experience the world relying more on smell than sight and feel envious of the dogs being so much more connected with their surroundings because they can learn so much more than I can with my infinitely inferior sense of smell. But often I will see something – a fox or a deer – long before they do. Sometimes they won't see it at all, just pick up on the scent and chase madly through the trees or across the grass after an animal that has long since scarpered, and they'll stop dead in their tracks, looking back at me, mildly bewildered.

We scramble over a stone stile and climb up through an orchard. It is too early for apple blossom, but there are fat buds on the twiggy ends of the branches. We traverse a short stretch of woodland, the trees bare, but the leaf litter beneath them full of new green shoots and the leaves that promise bluebells later. Then we are on a lane which follows the contour of the valley. We are high above the river, which is out of sight, hidden by the steep-sided heavily wooded slopes on either side.

But now we are in the open, the climb rewards us with great sweeping views back across the valley and I'm reminded once again how lucky I am that this is my home, that all this is on my doorstep. There is still a bit of a climb and my legs are definitely feeling stretched and a bit achy, in a satisfying way. But it is not long before we start the long descent, weaving our way through oak and beech woods, past mossy walls and the skeleton of a ruined cottage, ducking beneath branches and scrambling over a fallen tree.

Towards the bottom it is muddy and slippery. The dogs race on, unhindered. I pick my way down more carefully to the edge of the woods and find the dogs waiting for me on the river bank. The river's flowing strongly – upstream. This lower part of the river is tidal and the tide is coming in. One particularly cold Christmas we witnessed something extraordinary. Large discs of ice had formed on the surface of the river, like giant lily pads, and the incoming tide was pushing them together, making them jostle and creak. The air had that muffled, deadened quality it gets when there is thick snow on the ground, so the sound of the ice was as sharp and clear as a gunshot. People gathered along the railing of the bridge, their faces taut and reddened by the cold, their eyes bright with delight at what they were seeing. But later when we went back, the tide had turned and the ice had all gone, swept out into the estuary.

There is no ice today, just the usual woody debris swirling about in the brown water. A cormorant takes off from somewhere and I follow its prehistoric outline along the river until it disappears from view. And then I see them: pale pink flowers atop bare, straight stalks poking up through the grass along the river bank. These are lady's smock, although I know them by their other name – cuckoo flowers – so-called because they are thought to coincide with the arrival of the first cuckoo and are a sure sign that spring is on its way. I haven't heard a cuckoo yet but I'm all for believing that these pretty little flowers know that spring is imminent.

17TH MARCH
A CATCH-UP AND AN OLD-TIME CURE

❋

I'm meeting my friend Grace. She and her husband and their young daughter rent a converted barn on a farm in a village a few miles away from us. Behind the barn is a little garden that backs on to a field in which there is a large circular mound of earth. It is a motte, the remains of an ancient castle, its history hazy except that it is known to have been in existence before 1231.

The walk I am doing today, and have done many times, finishes in this field and it has become something of a tradition for us to race up the short, steep grassy slope of the motte to the top, where once would have stood the wooden bailey, for no reason other than because it is there. And if Grace is at home, we wave from the top and she puts the kettle on. But for the last few months her husband has been working in Devon and they have been living down there and the cottage and its little garden have stood empty and rather forlorn. But they are back, just for a week, and when I arrive at their door, even before I see them, I know they are there because the cottage feels alive again.

Grace is exhausted. Her daughter has chicken pox and has been awake all night. 'Are you sure you want to come and walk?' But she's adamant. Her daughter is finally asleep and her husband is staying behind, promising tea when we get back. We walk down the farm lane, across the boggy field in front of the farmhouse to the road for just a short distance before we come to a wide farm track and the dogs can come off the lead and we can talk. It is the perfect way to catch up.

Grace grew up in South Africa, a barefoot, hippy childhood in the mountains. She, like me, takes great pleasure in just simply being outdoors; in seeing and feeling the shift of the seasons. Our conversation meanders, takes on the pace and rhythm of our footsteps, breaks off when we notice something – a tree about to come into leaf, a pair of buzzards circling – then picks up again. We talk, among other things, about how easy it is to lose sight of yourself when life crowds in, in the way it does, a whirlwind of to-do lists and emails, domestic chores, things that need fixing or sorting. How it becomes all too easy to submit to the pressure of the things we believe should be done, should take precedence, and push aside the little things that modern life has made us feel are indulgences rather than necessities.

A question commonly asked in those celebrity questionnaires you find in the colour supplements of the weekend newspapers is, 'What one thing would improve your life?' And the answer, more often than not, is 'more time'. And yet we live in an age where we are surrounded by labour- and time-saving devices. There are machines to wash our clothes, our plates. We can go to the supermarket to buy food someone else has grown for us – or we can get someone else to pick it all up for us and deliver it to our door. We don't need to find fuel to heat our homes or to cook with, we can buy almost everything we need – and lots of stuff we don't – simply by looking at a screen and pushing a button.

We can survive very easily and comfortably without having to make, build, grow or search for anything. And yet the one thing we all yearn for that can't be ordered online and delivered within 24 hours is time. But if we had more time, what would we do with it? Would we use it in a way that would really, properly be of benefit, not materially, but spiritually?

The writer Henry David Thoreau claimed, 'I think that I cannot preserve my health and spirits unless I spend four hours a day at least – and it is commonly more than that – sauntering through the woods and over the hills and fields, absolutely free from all worldly engagements'. To be able to do this, though, he had to live a life so spartan, so without frills of any kind, that in the end it may have done him more harm than good. He died of tuberculosis at the age of 44.

But nevertheless, he was onto something: he understood that fresh air, exercise, a connection with nature all made him feel better, mentally as well as physically. Over a hundred and fifty years after he wrote that, we are starting to understand that all of us benefit from the simple act of walking outside in the natural world. 'That was just what I needed,' Grace said, as we stood at the top of the tump, breathing hard after the run up. 'Tea?'

20TH MARCH
A CROWD PLEASER

✳

A few miles from home is the ruin of what once must have been a very grand country house, called Piercefield. It has lost its roof, but what's left of the façade gives a tantalizing sense of its former glory. Today it is barricaded behind security fences hung with shouty signs: 'Keep Out!' 'Danger!' It is surrounded by parkland, which was landscaped in the style of Capability Brown in the mid-1700s, at about the same time that the Wye Valley was becoming something of a tourist attraction. British artist William Gilpin was one of the originators of the idea of the picturesque – 'the kind of beauty which is agreeable in a picture' – and to his mind, the Wye Valley epitomized this beauty.

Piercefield's parkland, with its woodland walks, grotto and glorious views from the cliffs above the River Wye, was opened up to the public. The poet Coleridge was a visitor, as was the botanist Joseph Banks (the man largely responsible for making Kew the world's leading botanical garden). After his visit he wrote, 'I am more and more convinced that it is far the most beautiful place I ever saw.' And given how much of the world he had seen – he took part in Captain Cook's first great voyage on HMS *Endeavour* – this was high praise indeed.

Part of the parkland was sold off and is now Chepstow racecourse – where a couple of days after Christmas, well-wrapped crowds gather to watch the Welsh Grand National – but the rest of it remains open to the public and there is something rather wonderful about being able to stand on the same spot as Coleridge and Banks with three scruffy mutts at my heels and look out at a view that I suspect, were Gilpin alive today, he would still describe as 'picturesque'.

The parkland, though, is still looking rather drab and washed out and wintery. The paths through the woodland are wet underfoot, the thick covering of leaf litter that later will give way to a carpet of bluebells has turned from a crisp mosaic of browns, reds and coppers to a uniform, squelchy, muddy porridge. The trees, I thought, were still bare of leaves, but then something catches my eye. Just at the end of the branches of a horse chestnut tree the first of this year's leaves have emerged from the fat, sticky buds. They are still small, still soft, like the wings of a newly emerged butterfly, and that fresh, perky, almost iridescent green that is a colour unique to spring. I stroke the leaves with a sort of reverence. It is hardly a surprise – leaves reappear every spring – but the sight of these audacious horse chestnut leaves amid the otherwise bare woodland makes me feel uncommonly happy.

26TH MARCH
THE CHIFFCHAFF RETURNS

✳

I've been away for a few days in France. It was wet and cold – more winter than spring. There was even frost on the last morning, ice on the puddles and it felt like January again. But back at home it is gloriously, colourfully, noisily spring-like.

Yesterday as I walked across our neighbour's fields the air was noisy with the melodic song of skylarks and the bleating of lambs. The woods are full of anemones and violets and the first pungent leaves of wild garlic. Last night the clocks went forward. I leave the house just as it is getting light and, for a moment, just stand and listen to the rising swell of birdsong.

And among the twittering of the sparrows, the lyrical notes of a blackbird, the tits and the robins, and the rolling trill of the chaffinch, there is the unmistakable sound of a chiffchaff calling its name. Chiff chaff, chiff chaff, chiff chiff chaff. These small, rather insignificant-looking birds disappear from our woodlands over winter but are one of the first migrants to come back and their return, in my mind, marks the official moment that spring has properly begun.

27TH MARCH

AN ENERGIZING WALK IN MAD SPRING WEATHER

✳

The weather is more like April today. Short, sharp showers interspersed with dazzling bursts of bright, warm sunlight. It is invigorating, uplifting, inspiring; a day for conversation, for ideas; a day to share. I plan a route, text Polly and we meet outside the shop in a village a few miles away. It is warm enough to push up our sleeves and tie waterproofs around our waists.

We walk fast, the sun on our faces, dogs racing ahead along the woodland path, noses to the ground, in hot pursuit of squirrels they never catch. Well, not anymore. A few years ago, when my Welsh sheepdog, Teg, was still in her young and mildly delinquent stage, we were running through the woods on a bright spring morning and there was a profusion of young squirrels skittering about in a way Teg found irresistible. Small and nimble, but not very worldly, they seemed blissfully unaware that the large ginger-and-white creature blundering towards them might have intentions other than to play.

I'm not sure Teg really had any idea what she was doing, or what her intentions were either; she was simply responding to some deep-rooted instinct. And given the ponderous pace I run, I was grateful to the squirrels for giving her a more lively form of exercise than she gets plodding along with me. But then came the moment when Teg actually caught a squirrel, but with so little conviction and so much surprise that the squirrel managed to wriggle between Teg's teeth and give her a sharp nip on the nose.

I doubled up with laughter, the squirrel was spat out and made good its escape into the undergrowth, and Teg came back to me looking thoroughly dejected and bemused. Since that day both she and Bella, who despite having rather creaky back legs suddenly finds reserves of speed she never knew she had when she sees a squirrel, stop short of ever actually catching one, but never tire of chasing them up into the trees.

While the dogs are taunting rodents, Polly and I are bouncing around ideas, impressions, recounting stuff we've heard or seen, analysing our response to something we both heard on the radio this morning. We've known each other for a decade and I don't think have ever struggled for something to discuss, but there is something about talking while walking that gives a different sort of energy to our conversation. It is almost as if the combination of being outside in a changing, dynamic environment and moving through it, rather than just being in it, does something to the brain to allow it to respond or behave in a different way.

I turn to neuroscientist Susan Greenfield to see if she can shed any light on my homespun theory. In her book *A Day in the Life of the Brain*, she picks up on Friedrich Nietzsche's assertion that 'all truly great thoughts are conceived by walking', which is, she says, somewhat counterintuitive, because the brain has limited resources. It would therefore be reasonable to suppose that doing two things at once would impair the performance of one or the other.

But research has shown this not to be the case when the two tasks are completely different. 'One of the lesser-known benefits of walking in natural environments can be to improve attention,' says Greenfield, 'so cognitive performance is indeed improved when engaged in this other, completely different, behaviour of putting one foot in front of the other.' She quantifies 'natural environments', because it really does make a difference *where* you walk. She cites a study undertaken in Michigan to assess cerebral power – and most specifically attention. Some of the study's participants were asked to walk around the local arboretum and others around the local town. They all took a test before they set off for their walks, and another when they returned. The test scores for what is called 'executive attention' – which allows the brain to keep information active and in focus – rose significantly for those who had walked in the arboretum (their cognitive capacity had been boosted), but didn't improve at all for those who had walked around town.

Researchers concluded that all the stimuli of an urban environment meant the attention of those participants was monopolized by other things. 'A natural environment,' explains Greenfield, 'spares us this relentless reactivity to the outside world and instead shapes our consciousness more subtly in a more voluntary, proactive manner... [with] the additional benefit of restoring a sense of control, of giving you a longer time frame in which to develop and deepen your thoughts.' She goes on to hypothesize that thoughts, ideas, take shape in our heads through a series of steps and that perhaps the physical act of walking reflects what is happening in the brain: 'the mental being enforced by the physical'.

About half an hour away from our cars, the clouds that have been gradually moving in over the blue sky and growing increasingly dark and threatening burst in spectacular fashion. We scrabble into our waterproofs, but to little avail. We are already sodden and we splash back to the cars, rain dripping off our noses and eyelashes, laughing despite it all, because somehow being caught in the rain with someone is funnier than being caught in the rain by yourself.

I drive back home, the car full of the smell of wet dogs, my brain fizzing with ideas. Energized and happy.

31st March
NEW LIFE AND THE GALLOPING ONSET OF SPRING

*

At the farm the lambs that were born in February are out in the fields, growing plump and perky, and the ewes that are due to lamb now are in the shed and have started to give birth. I'm conscious that I haven't been pulling my weight. I've spent the last few days working away in London and then in Manchester and I am all too happy to swap a bed in a city hotel with windows that don't open and the incessant buzz of air conditioning and traffic for a night in the lambing shed.

I arrived last night at about 10.30pm. It was mild, some cloud, but not enough to completely obscure the stars. Tim and his wife Sarah were in the shed checking on the hundred or so expectant mothers and the few that had lambed already. They caught me up on events so far. There was a new set of twins that would need checking a bit later to make sure they were taking milk; a ewe that was a bit restless and might be in the early stages of labour. I made sure there were all the things I might need – iodine, penicillin, lubricant – and bade them good night. Once they had gone I filled the water buckets in the pens, topped up the hayracks, then after a final glance around the shed, I left them in peace.

I get up a couple of times, but all is quiet and uneventful until I check in just after 4am. There's been one set of twins born and another single lamb. There are two ewes in labour and one of them looks like she needs help. I move slowly towards her, but she is instantly alert, knows I'm after her, tucks herself in among the woolly throng and hopes I can't see her. I'm always amazed at how quickly these ewes can move, even in the advanced stages of labour.

I move closer to her and she makes a break for it. I give chase, rugby tackle her to the ground, thinking as I always do that this is no way to treat a pregnant lady. I get her on her side, knee on her neck, say soothing nonsense to her, stroke her face. She settles, allows me to put my hand up under her tail, slide into the warm wetness.

Lambs are delivered front feet first, but sometimes they get tangled and this one has one of its front legs tucked up under its body, and however hard its mother pushes it is not going to come out until I've been able to hook my fingers around the leg and pull it into the right position. It takes a bit of doing – I can't imagine a human putting up with this sort of intervention – but the ewe is now accepting of my help and lies still. I talk to her, hoping I'm being reassuring between my muttered curses as my fingers slip and struggle.

Eventually I manoeuvre the leg into position, get hold of both front feet and pull. This lamb is determined to stay put. 'Come on,' I urge, through gritted teeth, 'it's nice out here.' I feel it shift, the front legs are clear. Holding them with one hand, I push my other hand in and around the bowl of the head, ease it through and the lamb slides out. I clean the mucus from its nose and rub its chest, it sneezes, gives its head a little shake, half opens its eyes. I place it gently by its mother's head and she starts to lick it.

Two hours later I'm just penning up another ewe with her lambs when Tim comes into the shed. 'Come and see this!' he says. Dawn has broken, but what a dawn! The sky is ablaze – streaked pink, purple, orange and gold against a backdrop of deep, velvet blue. The clouds on the horizon are the colour of aubergines, the outline of the trees as sharp as ink drawings against a wild backdrop of colour. We stand in silent reverie until the light creeping into the sky bleaches out the colour and the bleating of a ewe calls us back to the shed.

The dawn heralded the sort of day that makes spirits soar. After a shower, and breakfast, and quite a lot of tea, I go back out to revel in the most perfect of spring mornings. And I realize that in the few days that I have been away, shut up in train carriages, offices, conference rooms and hotels, spring has truly come, all in a rush. There are more cuckoo flowers and red campion. Everywhere buds are bursting, the blackthorn blossom looks like candyfloss and the trees have green halos as their tiny new leaves start to unfurl.

There is birdsong and bees buzzing and butterflies flitting and, climbing through the woods on the English side of the river, I see an audacious spike of blue. It's the first bluebell of the year. It is a day for poetry, if only I knew how to write it, so I steal someone else's and recite it to my thoroughly unappreciative hounds.

> *The spring is sprung, the grass is riz.*
> *I wonder where the boidie is.*
> *They say the boidie's on the wing.*
> *But that's absoid. The wing is on the boid.*
> —Anonymous

April

APRIL SHOWERS, A PICNIC AND AN ARTIST

❋

It is disappointingly murky today. My friend Sarah has come over from Bath and we have plans to tackle a Brecon Beacon, or several of them. We even have a picnic, fuel to keep us going all day. But as we drive west the clouds, low and glowering, put paid to that idea. There are few things more dispiriting than doing a hefty climb in thick cloud with no chance of a view when you get to the top and every chance of getting lost. So as we drive I think of alternative routes that will earn us one of Sarah's chocolate brownies.

April plays games with us. Just as I decide we'll do a low-level route along the river, the clouds break up enough for us to see the little pointed cone of the Sugarloaf, the wedge-shaped Skirrid and the flat-topped sweep of the Blorenge. 'Let's go there!' and I turn left by Abergavenny and head up the mountain road towards Blaenavon.

Blaenavon was once a centre for iron and coal, but the ironworks closed in 1900 and the coal mine in 1980. The landscape here is shaped and marked by its industrial heritage. Sheep graze on the sparse wiry grass that has overgrown the slag heaps, the coal mine is now a museum and the town sits tucked in the shadow of the mountain.

We park at the Foxhunter car park. Foxhunter was a horse owned by Sir Harry Llewellyn and together they won Britain's only gold medal in the 1952 Olympics. When Foxhunter died, he was buried up here on the mountain and when Sir Harry died in 1999, his ashes were scattered over Foxhunter's grave. It is not a bad place to be scattered, among the heather on a mountain that is said (although I'm not sure anyone can prove it one way or the other) to be 'the purple headed mountain' in the hymn 'All Things Bright and Beautiful'. It's too early in the year for the heather to be flowering, so it is more brown and dark green than purple today, but there are skylarks being buffeted on the breeze and lambs bleating and clouds scudding overhead as we take the track that rises gently from the car park towards the trig point.

When I saw the image of the Blorenge, slightly abstract but unmistakable, on the wall of Paul West's studio and called out its name, the way I might call out to an old friend I had spotted at a railway station, Paul looked at me quizzically. 'It's the name of that mountain,' I said, 'isn't it? It certainly looks like the Blorenge.' 'I don't know,' Paul confessed, 'I was walking near a place called Wolvesnewton and there was something about the outline of the mountain, the light, the shape of the fields and the way the road cuts through the valley that made me want to paint it. I have no idea what the mountain is called.'

I came across Paul's work because on one of the many flights I took last year, a painting of his was on the cover of the inflight magazine. There was something about the colour, the symmetry, the energy captured in the image that appealed to me and I turned the page to see if there was any information about the artist on the inner flap. There was his name and the painting, I was informed, was part of a collection inspired by walks he had done in Wales. I looked him up, found his website, wondered if he would think it weird if I got in touch with him. I'm not very good at this stuff. Never sure of the protocol. Was it a terrible imposition to contact him and ask if I could come and talk to him about his work and why he walks for inspiration? Would he expect me to buy a painting? Should I buy one anyway? But what if they are thousands and thousands of pounds? 'Oh for god's sake, Kate,' I told myself sternly, 'just bloody well get on with it and email him. He can always say no.'

A few weeks later I emerge from the Angel tube station in the rather swanky London district of Islington. Paul has sent me detailed directions, including which bus to take and where the bus stop is in relation to the tube station. All of which I ignore and set off on foot. I take a back street that runs parallel to the main road. It is lined with the sort of shops and cafés where you know every item of clothing and cup of coffee is going to be twice the price you imagine it could possibly be.

The people wandering along the street, or sitting at one of the tables outside, vaping, are dressed with the sort of studied casualness that gives the impression that what they are wearing has been thrown on randomly but you know has actually taken hours of careful consideration. I feel like a hick and know I look like one, and when I was younger I might have been bothered, but now I'm rather enjoying the people watching and window shopping and the voyeurism of it all. I lived in London for twenty years, but despite that I always feel a bit like a tourist when I come back.

I get to the end of this little manicured enclave, rejoin the main road and step back into the real world. It's a bit grubbier, there are exhaust fumes, the rumble of traffic, overflowing litter bins, convenience stores with faded plastic signs and rusty security grilles. People stand in ragged lines waiting for buses, clutching shopping bags and looking fixedly at their phones. Others walk fast, heads down, withdrawn into themselves behind invisible armour plating. No one smiles, no one says hello, no one acknowledges anyone else and I seem to be the only person who takes pleasure in the sight of a man cycling up the road, headphones clamped over the wild frizz of his afro, singing at the top of his voice.

I turn into Paul's street, ring the doorbell and hear the bark of a dog. 'This is Poppy,' says the man who opens the door, and the little Jack Russell gives me a brief appraising glance and walks off, her claws tip-tapping on the wooden floor. Paul laughs. 'Don't be offended. She's not very sociable. Come in!'

The flat is neat, but not minimalist. There are books and paintings and vinyl record albums, a turntable playing something folky, plants, inviting sofas. I meet Paul's partner Paula and then follow him out into the garden and the studio – or 'sheddio' as Paul calls it – where he works. Poppy comes too. I have a feeling she is keeping an eye on me.

The subject matter and style of Paul's work had made me assume he would live in the country, wear threadbare corduroy and a hand-knitted jumper with holes in, have paint in his hair and a brush behind his ear. And quite dirty hands. I do this a lot. I can't help it. I build up images of people whose books I've read or paintings I've seen, or I've heard on the radio or talked to on the phone, and always feel slightly let down when they don't look anything like I think they should. And not only does Paul live in a London flat, but he is in crisp black T-shirt and jeans, with shaved head and a neatly trimmed beard. And clean hands.

But any disappointment I might feel that he's not anything like I imagined is swept away by his energy, his infectious enthusiasm, and when we sit down to talk he has records, cuttings, photographs, books ready for me, things he wants me to see, things that excite him, make him curious, fuel his artistic fire. He recalls the week in Wales – 'I've always had a great, great, great feeling about that week we had because we were really lucky with the weather. It was very windy, but we escaped the rain, and all day we'd just go walking through these incredible brick-red fields, marvelling at the geology and how different it was from anywhere else we'd been. On and on through these beautiful rough pastures, the obligatory pub at lunchtime and then carrying on going until evening. We'd go home, cook a meal, sit by the fire and talk about the day and the walking we'd done and then I'd have this overwhelming urge to paint.'

Paul pauses for a sip of coffee. Poppy appears in the doorway, looks at us both and decides she wants to be part of whatever is going on. She jumps up on the bench beside me and lies down, ears cocked, waiting for the next part of the story.

'So, it must have been half past ten at night,' Paul continues, 'and I suddenly remembered this oak tree that I'd seen that day and I just started painting and I didn't stop until three in the morning. Paula had long gone to bed, but I was back there, remembering the sky and the interaction with the trees and the leaves and everything and I've got the colour in my head because I've seen it all day and I've just got to get it all down right then and there.'

Was he, I wondered, always someone who walked? And this brought back a flood of memories of his childhood in Dorset, walking along a disused railway line, sandwiches and a flask, jumping in rivers, sleeping out 'like Huckleberry Finn'. Then the glorious time he went all the way to Bournemouth to buy his first Walkman, came back to Bridport and walked to West Bay listening to *Heroes*. 'I can just remember the moment, the intensity of the music and the landscape and the connection I had with it all and how it seemed to make images build in my head.'

Dorset landscapes feature in some of Paul's work, 'its undulating and beautiful green hills – I never thought I could love another county more. And then I went to Northumberland. It's like a living landscape. You can see it in the deep hedgerows, the furrows in the land, the castles of Dunstanburgh and Alnwick. It's just an incredible place.' He tells me about a walk he does, time and time again, so often that he finds himself being compelled to greet every single tree and gorse bush and bulrush as if they were old friends. The route, from Warkworth to Alnmouth, is only a couple of miles along a dirt track but it often takes him four hours. 'It's just the experience of the fields, the farming districts, the North Sea which flanks the entire walk. It's otherworldly for me. I really love it.'

Do you think, I wonder, that the emotion a landscape inspires in you is then transferred to the canvas, along with the image that has built in your head? 'I hope so,' he nods, 'because that's very much what I'm feeling when I'm doing it.' And there is an undeniable reverence in his paintings and charcoals, and a sort of intimacy too. But they are not chocolate-boxy, not an idealized, rose-tinted vision of the countryside. 'I don't want to be all romantic about the countryside because it can be frightening and unforgiving as well. It's daunting.'

And inspiration doesn't just come in a flash, a single walk doesn't just magically spawn a series of masterpieces. What walking does, he says, is help him unlock a landscape, but it can take time. He describes being really frustrated by the Wye Valley for the first three days he was there, because he couldn't crack it. 'I kept seeing it as curves, but when I tried to interpret it that way it wasn't right. I was missing the essence of it. Then all of a sudden I saw it as a series of straight planes and that was it. I didn't stop painting for five days.'

In that time Paul did a series of paintings of the Blorenge – all exactly the same but each one reflecting the wildly fluctuating colours of the landscape during a windy week in April. 'It was almost too much. Every time I looked down to mix paint I'd look up and the mountain would look completely different. The clouds would roll in. The sun would burst through. The colours changed every second. I don't think I've seen that anywhere else apart from the Wye Valley.'

Sarah and I, standing among the boulders that surround the trig point of the Blorenge, are being treated to a similar April extravaganza of constantly shifting light and shade, which can turn the landscape from moody and brooding to light hearted and sparkling with a mere gust of wind or sharp April shower. From the top we head down, pushing our way through the tough, twiggy heather and last year's bracken, brown and crumpled, soon to be replaced by this year's fresh new growth, which is just starting to break through the mossy turf. We pick up a track that runs alongside a stone wall, curving across the front of the mountain.

Paul's painting shows this landscape to be treeless, and indeed from the perspective he painted, it is. But here, on this sheltered flank, there are trees, mighty ones, oaks and beech, twisted and gnarled by age and weather. The path leads to my favourite spot on the mountain, a sort of scooped-out hollow known as the Devil's Punchbowl. There's a lake that reflects the colour of the sky. Behind it is a grove of trees, a living woodcut of an illustration from Grimm's fairy tales. And behind the trees rises the great dark flank of the mountain, where the distant forms of sheep move across the slope, their throaty calls to each other caught up and carried by the wind, mingling with the coarse croaks of the crows, the harmonizing rustle of the leaves.

I was so entranced by this place when we first discovered it I felt an overwhelming desire to somehow be part of it, to immerse myself within it. 'We should sleep here one night,' I said to Ludo. 'Camping is not allowed,' he said in response, pointing to a wooden sign with the picture of a tent on it over which was imposed an uncompromising red cross. What he really meant was, why spend a night in a tent when your own comfortable, familiar bed is just down the road?

But the idea stuck in my head, for years. Came back every time we did the walk. Until one late summer evening I packed a tent and sleeping bags in a rucksack, along with our supper (bribery, I reasoned, was the way to make this work) and with my very enthusiastic dogs and slightly less enthusiastic husband set off through the heather. It was in full bloom, a haze of purple, alive with the lazy buzzing of bumble bees. The lake was still and glassy, mirroring the evening blue of the sky. A couple of sheep pottered about on the far shore. A blackbird sang its lyrical song, perched on the edge of a branch, a diva bewitching her audience in this most beautiful of auditoriums. Ludo, who is rather more law abiding than I am, found a discreet place in the little grove of trees to hide our tent. We lit a fire close to the water's edge and while the dogs paddled and wrangled over sticks we cooked supper, drank wine and watched the sky darken, the first stars appear. Silence descended, almost tangible, blanketing the landscape.

It wasn't a restful night. Sharing a tent with three dogs – one that insists on sleeping on your head, one that finds the spot in the crook of your knees and curls up (an immoveable dead weight radiating an astonishing amount of heat) and the other restless, too warm and wanting to go out – as well as an increasingly grumpy husband, does not allow for much sleep. Eventually I gave up and joined the restless dog outside. The moon had come up, casting silver-blue shadows across the surface of the lake. We sat together on the short-cropped turf, companionable in our silence, and watched the sky lighten and the day begin.

Sarah's and my arrival at the Punchbowl coincides with a sharp shower, the lake ruffled by the accompanying breeze and pitted by raindrops. Undaunted we sit, in that oh-so-English way, in our raincoats, eating our picnic perched on a couple of rocks, heedless of the rain trickling down our necks. Just as we are finishing, packing our boxes back into our rucksacks, the sun comes out, floods the landscape with golden light in a flash, like a conjurer's trick. We leave the Punchbowl, a long, gradual climb, followed by our shadows, a rainbow arching overhead.

2ND–9TH APRIL
AN ARCTIC INTERLUDE

*

Yesterday I flew to Stockholm, took a bus to a village a few miles outside the city and now I'm sitting in a classroom – in the back row – trying to concentrate, but remembering those endless hours, cooped up at school, legs twitching, my gaze drifting from the window to the hands on the clock that never seemed to move. I suppose the idea of teaching in a controlled, sterile space within four walls is – as well as being practical – to minimize distraction, allow the mind to concentrate solely on declining verbs or wrestling with long division, but it is such a stultifying, oppressive environment. Can any brain really take anything in or work anything out when the body is so inactive, when there is nothing to look at but a blackboard and the slightly greasy plait hanging down the back of the girl in front of you?

In her rather lovely book *Wanderlust*, Rebecca Solnit observes that 'while walking the body and mind can work together, so that thinking becomes an almost physical rhythmic act'. And if thinking is stimulated by the simple combination of movement, natural light, fresh air, would not the same be true of learning? But I digress, because what I'm being taught in this Swedish classroom, by the tall and slightly terrifying Johan, is important. My life may very well depend on it.

I've been invited to take part in an expedition – nearly two hundred miles across Arctic Scandinavia. We will be travelling by dog sled and each one of us will be responsible for our own team of dogs and driving our own sled. We will carry with us everything we need to survive – tents, stoves, snow shoes, shovels, food for the dogs and ration packs for ourselves. We will be entirely at the mercy of the elements and although it is April there are no signs of spring here. Snow lies thickly on the ground, banks up against the walls of buildings and along the sides of the roads in drifts like frozen waves. It is –10°C.

After the classroom, we sort and pack kit: bulky down parkas, waterproof trousers, multiple layers of thermals, hefty boots with removable liners that we've been told to keep in our sleeping bags with us at night so they don't freeze. We learn to put up our tents, to orient them according to the wind that can blast across the tundra with merciless force, to dig out a trench inside the tent so we can sit on its edge to pull our boots on and to use the snow we've dug out to build a wall for added wind protection. With cold, stiff fingers we do battle with unfamiliar stoves, collect lichen and the delicate peels of bark from birch trees and learn how to set fire to them with a knife and a flint. And we meet our dogs, six per team, a ragtag-looking bunch of all shapes, sizes and colours, bred for stamina and strength and not for looks. Then we sleep, or try to, but most of us are too nervous and too excited.

I know the knuckles of my hands beneath my thick gloves are white. I'm gripping the birch wood handle in front of me, every muscle in my body tense and wondering if everyone else is feeling like this. I'm scared. Elated too. Adrenalin pumping. The sound around me is cacophonous. Two hundred dogs, straining at their tethers, barking loudly and incessantly in anticipation, eager to get going. A pale sun breaks through the cloud, lights up the snow, turns it from grey to a pale orangey-pink.

Johan's words replay in my head: 'If you love nature, you have to love it all, whatever the conditions. The Arctic is extremely beautiful, but its dangers are very real. It demands respect. You can't rely on other people. You must take responsibility for yourself, your kit and ultimately for your environment. Do that and you will learn what a truly special place the Arctic is.'

The first team is off, streaming across the snow, up a bank and into the trees. My dogs leap forward, the lead dogs straining so hard that despite the fact I'm standing on the brake and the snow anchor is jammed deep into the snow, my sled starts to inch forward. Our team leader and guide, Amanda, has to grab the dogs to stop them tearing off in hot pursuit. They don't have long to wait. Amanda gives the signal. 'OK?' I give an anxious, not entirely convincing nod, release the brake and with a tremendous jolt that almost tips me off backwards, the journey begins.

There are obvious advantages to travelling by dog sled rather than walking in an environment like this one. We can cover greater distances in less time – our aim is to do 45 miles today – and we don't have to carry our equipment or pull it ourselves; but I had wondered whether the experience of being in this place, one so otherworldly and strange and not a little daunting, would somehow be diminished because I was relying on the legs of the dogs rather than my own to move through it. But as soon as we set off I know my fears are unfounded, because we are not sitting on our sleds, snuggled beneath reindeer skins, whisking effortlessly through a winter wonderland. We are standing on the runners at the back and although we have no direct contact with the dogs – no reins as you would with a horse – we have to keep a sharp eye on the track ahead, look out for hazards, be ready to brake or shift our weight on the runners to enable the dogs to turn. We feel every bump, every rut, the changing texture of the snow.

Amanda told us before we set off that we could only really learn by doing it. 'The main thing to remember,' she said, 'is once the dogs are running they want to keep running. They get in a rhythm and it is much better for them if they don't stop, so you have to get used to drinking, eating, putting extra layers on or taking them off while the sled is moving. And if we are going uphill, you'll need to help the dogs. Use one leg to help push the sled along, like a child's scooter, or on the really steep bits you'll need to get off and run, pushing the sled like a pram. And never let go of it, because the dogs will just keep going and you'll be left behind!'

The learning curve is steep. Every part of my brain and body is intensely concentrating on simply staying upright. There is so much to take in I feel overwhelmed. I'm dimly aware of the landscape around me, but for these first few hours there is no chance to look at it, to take pleasure in it. I fall off the sled more than once, misjudging a rut or a corner, although I manage to hold on to it, and the snow and my padded layers of Arctic kit mean the only thing that gets bruised is my confidence.

After three hours or so we stop. The dogs, panting and grinning, tongues lolling, are given a lump of frozen meat as an energy boost and we break into our ration packs, sitting in the snow, comparing aching muscles. It is surprisingly, unexpectedly physical travelling this way, which is pleasing in one way – I don't feel I'm cheating – but somehow I'm going to have to find reserves of strength I'm not sure I have to carry on for another three or four hours. The dogs are still as eager as they were at the start of the day.

Off we go again, the runners kicking up a spray of ice crystals, following a curving track alongside a wood, its trees stunted by long cold winters, each branch and twig encased in frost. Before long we leave the trees behind and we are crossing a vast, high plateau. It is breathtakingly cold, but so wildly, intoxicatingly beautiful that I forget to be scared, forget that every part of me hurts and I exclaim out loud – a shout of pure, wordless joy – and pray to some entity or other that I am allowed to remember this moment for the rest of my life.

The euphoria is somewhat diminished when we get to the place where we are to camp tonight. It is bleak and blustery and large wet flakes of snow are blowing about. I'm longing for, actually craving, a big mug of tea. But there are so many things to do first, and we are still trying to get familiar with everything, still trying to work out our system. Even the simplest tasks take ages, not helped by wet snow being blown into our faces. We unharness the dogs, put them on the tethers for the night, feed and water them before tackling our tents and doing battle with the stoves. We marvel at how long it takes to melt snow and then for it to boil, but when it does and finally, finally, I get my longed-for cup of tea, it is, without question, the finest cup of tea I've ever had.

Gradually over the following days we all become more adept. Because we are doing everything for ourselves, we learn faster and things quickly become second nature. Johan gives us nightly lectures, passing on the invaluable knowledge he has gleaned from years working in the Arctic. I become more comfortable and confident on my sled, come to love the swish of the runners moving across the snow beneath me, the rhythmic scrunch of the dogs' feet and, most of all, I am now able to appreciate our astonishing surroundings. It is easy to imagine that the Arctic in winter is a rather monochrome place, an expanse of white emptiness, but instead, as each day goes by, it reveals itself to be a landscape of infinite variety and texture. The constantly changing light plays on the trees, the frozen lakes and streams creating pools of colour and casting deep shadows.

Our final night out in the open is the coldest so far at –20°C and Johan has one last challenge for us. 'No tents tonight!' he declares and sets about showing us how to build walls of snow to protect us from the wind. We light fires with foraged lichen and bark, hunt for twigs and fallen branches. I lay out my thermal mat, unroll my sleeping bag and snuggle into it, my hat pulled down low over my eyes and my scarf pulled up over my nose. All around me is the wilderness that just a few days ago seemed so intimidating, even hostile. But now I feel part of it, connected to it. Above me is the Arctic sky, the moon bright, a million million stars studding the infinite blackness and I drift into sleep feeling entirely at home.

11TH APRIL
A COLOURFUL RETURN TO HOME TURF

*

I'm immediately struck by the colour. The colours of the Arctic are subtle, soft, they shift and dissipate. But as I walk out of my front door, dogs crowding around my legs in their eagerness to get out, I am assailed by colours so vivid and varied they almost make me squint. I go to feed the geese, walking towards the first rays of the rising sun that are just appearing above the dark ridge on the other side of the valley. Our fields are no longer the worn-out muddy khaki of winter. While I've been away, the longer, warmer days have reinvigorated the whole countryside. New grass has overtaken the old and I look out over pasture that is now luxuriant, a lustrous green, bright with dew. My footsteps send up droplets of water and leave a shining trail like a snail. The oak, ash and beech trees in the woods below our house are coming into leaf, an artist's palette of different shades. The birdsong is almost deafening.

I let out the ducks and chickens from their houses, scatter grain, refill their water. Duffy and Delilah – my beloved, rather elderly Kunekune pigs, which came here ten years ago when they were eight weeks old – are grunting and squealing at the gate of their paddock, anxious not to be forgotten. 'Morning girls!' I call as I approach them. 'Huff, huff, huf,' they chorus in response. I crouch down between them, scratching the coarse hair on the tops of their heads, and they close their eyes and huff a bit more until hunger gets the better of them. A sharp nudge with their snouts reminds me of my duty. This soppiness is all very well, they're telling me, but what we really want is breakfast.

The dogs and I stride out across our neighbour's fields. The sun has appeared above the horizon – a perfect sphere of red – casting long, low fingers of golden light and throwing pale shadows across the ground. The cherry trees along the farm lane are in blossom, the hawthorn in leaf, house sparrows and dunnocks chirp and flit among the hedgerows, some with nesting material in their beaks. My neighbour's ewes have lambs now, skittering and hopping in the early morning sun while their mothers graze with almost robotic efficiency, gorging on the season's sweet new grass. We climb a stile into the woods that run in a narrow fringe along the top of the limestone cliff that has been carved out over millennia by the river below. We join the well-worn path that weaves its way through the trees, around rocks and over roots. The land falls away dramatically on our right-hand side and were it not for the thick vegetation that disguises just how vertiginous this path really is I might struggle to walk along here. I'm not scared of heights, exactly, just scared (perhaps reasonably) of falling off things.

I have a Canadian cousin – his mother and my grandmother were sisters – a lanky, athletic man of 6ft 6in. Last year when I was working in Canada we met up, spent a couple of days hiking in the forest near the Alaskan border. At one point the trail we were on split. One branch followed the edge of a bank that rose high above a river: a racing, tumbling, foaming torrent of blue-grey icy water. Bald eagles circled, a wide vista of pine forest and mountains opened up before us. The other branch of the trail ran parallel to this one, but away from the edge and through the trees.

I was walking in front, weighed up the options and knew I had to choose the scenic route. There was no reason not to other than it was scary as hell, but I wasn't prepared to admit that to my cousin, who has spent much of his life whisking down mountains at breakneck speed. I walked on, staring fixedly ahead, humming to myself, pretending not to notice that sweat was breaking out on my palms and my heart was thudding in my chest. The path got even narrower, one loose stone, one careless step and I'd be over the edge.

'Kate!' my cousin calls. I stop. Look round. He is pale, fists clenched. 'I'm not sure I can keep going on this trail,' he tells me. 'Oh thank god,' I say, 'it must be genetic. I'm bloody terrified too.' And we turn around and hightail it back to the safety of the trees.

As soon as the dogs and I enter the woods I know they are here. There's that scent: delicate, almost indiscernible, but unmistakable. It's a fragrance that makes you stop dead in your tracks, close your eyes and take great luxuriant breaths in through your nose. It's been almost three weeks since I spotted that first brave spike of blue in the woods on the other side of the river. Now they are on our side, a profusion of them, an intense, rippling wave of glorious colour. The bluebells.

14TH APRIL

A GOOD WALK FOR GOOD FRIDAY

*

I've had a job cancelled. I'm a bit disappointed as it involved going to Zambia, a country I love, for nine days in June. But then I remember that back in January I had once again thought about doing the Wye Valley Walk, as I have every year since we've been here. And I've never found the time to do it. But suddenly here is the perfect opportunity. It is 136 miles from the source of the Wye River in the hills of mid-Wales to where it joins the Severn at Chepstow. Could I do it in the nine days I would have been away in Africa?

A quick calculation and I work out that I would have to do about 15 miles a day. So today is a bit of a test. We are going to do a walk we did not long after we moved here but haven't done since. It is called the Three Castles Walk and is a circular route of 19 miles. That first time we did it we just had Badger, our scruffy little rescue dog with boundless energy. It was midsummer, a bright, breezy day; warm sunshine and the smell of cut grass.

Today we drive to the village of Skenfrith with three dogs and park by the ruined but still impressive outside wall of its castle. The sky is leaden. It's not cold, but everything looks a bit flat and lifeless and it's hard not to feel a little deflated after a day as bright and optimistic as yesterday.

We walk around the castle enclosure, admire the tower, then follow the fingerpost that indicates the way we take past the church and its magnificent cherry tree, frothy with pink blossom. The clouds start to shift, chinks of blue appear, the light lifts. There are cowslips along the track, dappled sunlight in the woods and the dogs paddle in the stream by a ruined mill.

We emerge out into the open fields with views of the Black Mountains, misty outlines against the cloud on the horizon. After seven and a half miles we reach the more substantial ruin of White Castle, with its moat, towers and enclosing walls. We sit on a bench inside the castle walls, munch a handful of nuts, try to imagine the lives of the people stationed here, guarding the marches from the marauding Welsh hordes.

Two red kites circle, their forked tails twisting and turning, surfing the thermals. They are more commonly seen further west than here, or around the Chilterns where a reintroduction programme in the Eighties brought them back to England after decades of persecution.

But gradually the Welsh population is moving east and the English one west and, thanks to one or the other, we are now seeing them around here more frequently.

The distance to the next castle in the village of Grosmont is shorter – six and a half miles – but there is, as Ludo points out as he looks at the contour lines on the map, a 'sodding great hill' to climb before we get there. When I was younger I hated climbing hills. I remember, long before we lived here, coming with friends for a weekend in the Brecon Beacons and climbing the slope behind Llanthony Priory. It is steep and unremitting and my curses got louder and more profane the further up we got. But now I relish a good tough climb, calves straining, blood thudding in my ears, the feeling of triumph when the top is reached and the world is spread out beneath my feet.

I'd forgotten, though, just what a sodding great hill this one is. It looks relatively innocuous when we climb the stile at its base, a broad grass-covered slope with woodland at the top, and it is only when we are about a third of the way up that we realize how steep it is and how far away the woods are. My tactic is to put my head down and march, drive myself forward without stopping until I get to the top, by which time my leg muscles are screaming in protest and I'm panting so hard I feel I might actually pass out. Ludo, whose more measured approach takes longer but means he's rather more alive than dead when he gets to the top, is able to appreciate the view while I'm still trying to regain the strength to stand upright.

The path continues through the woodland, hugging the contour of the hill. Grosmont is far below us, a long descent which stretches the muscles that had had it easy on the way up. When we finally make it to the third castle, Ludo announces that 14 miles is quite enough and declares himself beaten. Luckily for him we are meeting friends here who are going to walk the final five-mile stretch with us. Ludo offers to take their car to Skenfrith and to meet us in the pub. Badger and Bella look rather hopeful that they might get a lift to the pub too, so it is just Teg and me who join our friends on the track out of the village as Ludo waves us off from the car window, Badger and Bella already curled up and fast asleep on the front seat beside him.

My memory of this final stretch of the walk is vague, but I seem to recall it being very pretty, that it followed the river for most of the way and was flat. Memories can be selective, though, and my memory had chosen to forget that almost as soon as we leave Grosmont there is another pretty significant climb. And now I realize that I'm tired too, that the spring has gone out of my step and only a mixture of stubbornness and pride is going to carry me the last few miles.

Teg trots along as if we've only just got started and I decide then that when I do the Wye Valley Walk I want to do it with her. But at the same time, I'm wondering how realistic it is. I'd need to do the distance I've done so far today every day, for nine days, carrying considerably more than I am carrying now. It takes almost two more hours to get to the pub at Skenfrith. Ludo, who confesses that when he got to the car park he wound the driver's seat back and went to sleep for an hour, walks stiffly to the bar while I sink down on a sofa, unsure whether I'll ever be able to get up again. Bloody hell, I wonder, how did we get this old?

A BRIEF, BUT UPLIFTING, ENCOUNTER

❋

We have friends staying for Easter, two couples with two children apiece. They arrived yesterday morning and after lunch we went to the farm to see the lambs and a new litter of piglets. As we were walking across the fields I started to feel rather strange, almost faint. I hoped the feeling would pass, but it got worse. 'I'm not feeling great,' I said to Ludo, quietly, while the others were distracted by the lambs. 'Your lips have gone blue,' he said. 'I do feel really cold', I said, 'and just weird. I think I need to go home. I'll lie down for a bit and I'm sure I'll be OK later.'

I hauled myself upstairs to bed and fell into a sort of stupor from which I didn't emerge until this morning, 15 hours later, leaving Ludo and our friends to fend for themselves and try to work out what was for dinner. Today we are all joining up with more friends for a huge Easter lunch and I've promised – and luckily, already made – ratatouille for twenty and two rhubarb crumbles as our contribution to the feast. Ludo gives me an appraising look and confirms what I already know – that I am in no fit state to leave the house. So I wave them all off, and retreat back upstairs feeling utterly wretched.

Some time later – I must have gone to sleep again – the bedroom door creaks, followed by a pause, a moment of silence and then with a little yelp of excitement one dog, swiftly followed by a second, lands heavily on the bed and the third sticks her long ginger-and-white nose into my face. It's time for a walk. I choose an undemanding route, a loop through the fields around the house, long enough so the dogs don't feel cheated but not so long that I have to finish it crawling on my hands and knees.

It's what meteorologists would describe as a quiet day: still and grey and mild. But this is exactly what I need, a gentle, restorative amble to wake myself up. And it is really not long before I actually do start to feel better, less foggy and discombobulated, less weary. We go through the kissing gate by the little church into a big rectangular field and I hear a sound that brings me sharply to attention, snaps me into life, makes me smile. It is the whooping call of a curlew, ascending up the scale and coming to a trilling crescendo. A call that never fails to lift the heart. I scan the sky and see them, a pair, mottled brown plumage and elegant curving beaks, taking off with brisk, stiff wing beats; a brief glimpse and then they're gone.

22ND–23RD APRIL

WILD FLOWERS AND DYLAN THOMAS

✳

We are feeling frivolous. We have a weekend when neither of us has to work, or has pressing tasks to do, and nothing planned. Bliss. Our friends Simon and Maryann run a restaurant in Carmarthenshire. We work out it has been three years since we've seen them. 'Are you by any chance around?' I asked when I called last night. 'Yes! Come and have dinner tomorrow!'

We don't know this part of Wales very well. We drive to Llansteffan, park beside the broad estuary of the River Tywi and climb up to the castle ruins on the hill above. The sky is Mediterranean blue and it is warm – the first T-shirt day of the year. We follow lanes and tracks and faint pathways through woods and fields. We sit sometimes, on the green, green grass, just to take in these unfamiliar surroundings and feel the sun on our faces. Wild strawberries are flowering, violets, red campion and meadowsweet. We walk for miles, for hours, and arrive at Simon and Maryann's sun-kissed and hungry. We share plates of food, eat with our fingers, drink wines Simon has discovered, made unconventionally and unlike any wine we've ever tasted. And we talk and talk and talk, until our eyelids grow too heavy to stay open. Sleep comes quickly, dreamless, rejuvenating.

The next day we walk again, setting off from a different village, walking alongside the river, then cutting inland before returning to the river. And now we are standing at the open door of a small shed, the window at the opposite end overlooking the glistening mud and silvery pools left behind by the out-going tide. There are threadbare brown curtains, pictures tacked on the white wooden walls with drawing pins, curling up at the edges. Papers lie scattered on a desk and underneath it. There are open books, pens in a jam jar, a striped coffee mug, a beer bottle. A coat hangs over the back of the chair, a crumpled piece of paper in the pocket. It's as if we've just missed him, as if he's just shambled out and forgotten to close the door. This is where Dylan Thomas wrote. It is this view, this landscape, this place, that enkindled the imagination of one of the greatest wordsmiths the world has ever known.

> *Off and on, up and down, high and dry, man and boy, I've been living now for fifteen years, or centuries, in this timeless, beautiful, barmy (both spellings) town, in this far, forgetful, important place of herons, cormorants (known here as billy duckers), castle, churchyard, gulls, ghosts, geese, feuds, scares, scandals, cherry trees, mysteries, jackdaws in the chimneys, bats in the belfry, skeletons in the cupboards, pubs, mud, cockles, flatfish, curlews, rain, and*

human, often all too human, beings; and, though, still very much a foreigner, I am hardly ever stoned in the streets any more, and can claim to be able to call several of the inhabitants, and a few of the herons, by their Christian names.

Now, some people live in Laugharne because they were born in Laugharne and saw no good reason to move; others migrated here, for a number of curious reasons, from places as distant and improbable as Tonypandy or even England, and have now been absorbed by the natives; some entered the town in the dark and immediately disappeared, and can sometimes be heard, on hushed black nights, making noises in ruined houses, or perhaps it is the white owls breathing close together, like ghosts in bed; others have almost certainly come here to escape the international police, or their wives; and there are those, too, who still do not know, and will never know, why they are here at all: you can see them, any day of the week, slowly, dopily, wandering up and down the streets like Welsh opium-eaters, half-asleep in a heavy bewildered daze.

And some, like myself, just came, one day, for the day, and never left; got off the bus, and forgot to get on again. Whatever the reason, if any, for our being here, in this timeless, mild, beguiling island of a town with its seven public houses, one chapel in action, one church, one factory, two billiard tables, one St. Bernard (without brandy), one policeman, three rivers, a visiting sea, one Rolls-Royce selling fish and chips, one cannon (cast-iron), one chancellor (flesh and blood), one portreeve, one Danny Raye, and a multitude of mixed birds, here we just are, and there is nowhere like it anywhere at all.

—*Laugharne*, Dylan Thomas

We take the curving path downhill, skirt around the base of the castle. My trusty boots that I've worn for years – that have walked me hundreds, perhaps thousands, of miles – are, I finally have to concede, more hole than boot. It seems a fitting place to lay them to rest.

27TH APRIL

A SHOCKING WAY TO APPRECIATE A LANDSCAPE!

*

Teg and I are in Snowdonia. We are walking along a track that heads upwards, cutting across the peaty turf and cotton grass towards a crag, a curving wall of dark granite. We have company, a film-maker and visual artist called Natasha Brooks and a camera crew. I am making a series about Welsh landscapes, examining how they shape the lives and livelihoods of the people who live in these remote and often little-known parts of the country. Natasha's films are visual interpretations, not just of the landscape, but of her relationship with it. They are profound, visceral and affecting, the product of someone who immerses themselves completely, totally, in their surroundings.

We climb a ladder stile and follow a sheep track which weaves between rocky outcrops the same grey as the sky. I follow Natasha over a small rise and just below is a lake that until now has been entirely hidden from view. A dark, watery secret hidden within the shadows of the towering rock face above. We take off all our clothes – and up here it is chilly enough to need thermals – and ease ourselves into the frigid shallows, inching our way forward so the water rises over our thighs. It is heart-stoppingly cold, every pore tingles and prickles.

Natasha sinks down, slips gracefully beneath the surface, pushes off into the depths, her pale skin luminescent. I follow her, try not to cry out when the water closes over my body, the sensation extraordinary, terrible and at the same time wonderful, exhilarating and ultimately unbearable.

I return to shore, my skin burning, teeth chattering uncontrollably, but I feel alive. So, so alive. Natasha is still swimming, far out in the middle of the lake, a tiny serene figure encircled by water and rock and sky.

29TH APRIL

NOTHING TO DO BUT WALKING

✳

I love these walks before bed, just Teg and me. Half an hour at the end of a long filming day; no people, no conversation, no obligations. In *A Philosophy of Walking*, Frédéric Gros describes these solitary interludes perfectly:

> *You're doing nothing when you walk, nothing but walking. But having nothing to do but walk makes it possible to recover the pure sensation of being, to rediscover the simple joy of existing...*

The sky above us is midnight blue, the mountains of Snowdonia a dark outline. There's a crescent moon, a multitude of stars. And a cuckoo calling. The first I've heard this year. Simple joys indeed.

May

SKIMMING SWALLOWS AND OCEANS OF BLUEBELLS

✳

The small sleek form of a swallow flew over my head when I went to let Teg out this morning. For the last few years swallows have built nests carefully wedged between the beam and the light fitting in the barn where Teg has her kennel. My daily visits allow me to chart their progress from nest building to incubation, when the adult bird stays put on her nest, even when I come in.

Then comes the morning I find a piece of egg shell; tiny, feather light, the palest cream with dark spots. The eggs have hatched but the chicks are tiny and for the moment invisible, any cheeps or chirps they might make so quiet they are imperceptible. But in a remarkably short time I can see the tiny black domes of their heads just visible above the rim of the nest, the open, yellow-rimmed gape of their beaks when one of the adult birds flies in with food.

And barely two weeks after they have hatched they are overflowing the nest, their heads hanging over the edge, looking down at me and Teg with beady eyes. The adult birds perform a constant relay, flying low over the fields, a deft display of acrobatic prowess, hunting down and catching insects to try to satiate the demands of their swiftly growing offspring. And then they're gone, leaving a small heap of white droppings on the floor and a scattering of old feathers and bits of hay.

It is likely that the swallow that flew out of the barn this morning is one of the pair that nested here last spring. I can see repairs have been done to the old nest – there are fresh patches of mud around the slightly ragged rim and it's been given a spring clean – last year's feathers and grass that lined the nest have been turfed out onto the floor.

In celebration of May Day and the return of the swallows, we thought about heading west, maybe to the coast or into the mountains, but as we drive we can see dark curtains of rain sweeping across the horizon and we decide to stay local where, for the time being at least, it is still dry. We take a path that skirts the edge of several fields, all full of this year's lambs. They have lost the slightly spindly, wobbly appearance they have for the week or so after they are born and now they are fat, bumptious and sturdy, chasing each other around in unruly gangs, then returning to their long-suffering mothers and butting them cruelly in their udders, demanding milk.

We leave the fields, climb a stile to take a narrow track into the woods and step into a scene that so utterly, perfectly encapsulates every facet of spring it is almost a cliché. A chorus of birdsong, the chuntering of squirrels, the bubbling trickle of a stream, sunlight filtering through the tender new leaves of brightest green and casting pools of golden light on the forest floor. And beneath every tree, on every bank and in every hollow there are bluebells; an unbroken sea of them, their colour so intense it appears to rise above the flowers themselves, a delicate mist, a shimmering halo of ethereal blue.

2ND MAY

FOOD FOR THE SOUL - AND SUPPER!

*

It has been one of those days – a messy day – lots of niggling things to do that never quite get completed, given an urgency they perhaps don't deserve only because I am going to be working away for a few days and they are the sorts of things that require me to be at home, at a desk. One of the things I have discovered about living the sort of life I do – peripatetic, unpredictable and often out of my control – is that in order for my brain to engage with the constant stimulation of new places, people, information, experiences, and to be able to fully appreciate them, it needs to have the reassurance of order and organization.

I'm not, I realize, as free-spirited as I like to imagine I am. I've discovered that I feel happier, more stable, when beneath the mildly chaotic, erratic layers that make up my days there is a solid and dependable foundation, a sort of mental anchor. Our house isn't minimalist or obsessively clean – it is full of books and pictures and plants and dog hair – but I can't abide clutter or mess. I find it deeply therapeutic to clear cupboards, empty drawers, get rid of extraneous stuff, and equally feel a bit panicky and overwhelmed when the kitchen table is overrun by unopened post and stuff that hasn't been put away, when the dirty washing basket is overflowing, the animal sheds need cleaning out.

I dread the tyranny of the red numbers that appear on the screens of my phone and computer telling me how many emails and messages need dealing with and have to clear them all before I can go to sleep. I need to know how I'm getting somewhere and how long it is going to take. I don't trust assumption. And when I get back from a trip, whatever time of the day or night, I unpack immediately, put anything that needs washing in the machine and (I can't quite believe I'm admitting to this) tidy the fridge.

And if I've returned in daylight, I'll go and see my animals, stand for a while among the chickens and ducks, wander with the sheep, have a cuddle with the pigs, then gather up the dogs and walk our patch. Only then do I really feel I'm home.

This afternoon I walk because the dogs need it. So do I, but my brain is distracted and this is just another thing I have to do, another thing I have to try to fit into the day. I barely notice the buttercups lifting their cheerful, waxy yellow faces above the grass beside the farm road. I don't hear the birds, or pause to look at the sky. I walk fast, brain whirring, unhappily recalling the list on my desk – a scrawl of black ink and not enough of it crossed off. Thoreau sums up how I feel with his customary elegance:

> *I am alarmed when it happens that I have walked a mile into the woods bodily, without getting there in spirit. In my afternoon walk I would fain forget all my morning occupations and my obligations to Society. But it sometimes happens that I cannot easily shake off the village. The thought of some work will run in my head and I am not where my body is – I am out of my senses. In my walks I would fain return to my senses. What business have I in the woods, if I am thinking of something out of the woods?*

I have to walk a bit over a mile to get to our woods and by the time I have reached the kissing gate by the big old beech tree that marks the boundary between field and forest, I feel slightly less beleaguered, my brain calmer, the to-do list more achievable. I walk beneath the trees. All is still and quiet in their comforting presence. I scramble up the steep path to another area of woodland – flatter and more open – and here nature assails me with a sight and smell that demands – and merits – my full attention.

Just a few days ago it was the bluebells in this wood that were the headline attraction, but they have been joined and in some places superseded by a luxuriant carpet of leaves, smooth and uniformly deep green. Thin stalks rise above the leaves, topped with clusters of white, star-like flowers and the air is thick with a smell so pungent it is almost overpowering. Wild garlic. I gather handfuls of leaves to stick in the cavity of the chicken we are having for supper and flowers to scatter in the salad. A feast for all the senses.

6TH MAY

THE POSSIBILITY OF ADVENTURE

✳

It is a cloudy day, blustery. A day, I decide, to climb, to stand – breathless and buffeted – on a ridge and marvel at the land below with all its colours and textures, spread out like a vast patchwork quilt. Ludo is away, so it is just the dogs and me setting out for this adventure and I know exactly where will suit this whim of mine.

We drive down narrow, winding lanes between hedges. Behind them rise dark masses of rock and turf, rugged and craggy against the pale sky. Finally we emerge, released from the towering presence of the mountains, to skirt along the base of them. Ahead is the distinctive outline of a mountain called Lord Hereford's Knob, immortalized (sort of) by post-punk band Half Man Half Biscuit; and the muse, along with copious amounts of LSD, for Allen Ginsberg's poem 'Wales Visitation'. I have no intention of writing poetry or composing a song, but I like the idea of the sort of adventure Kenneth Grahame describes, not in his much-beloved story *The Wind in the Willows*, but in an essay he wrote entitled 'The Fellow That Goes Alone' for his old boarding school magazine.

> *As for adventures, if they are the game you hunt, everyone's experience will remind him that the best adventures of his life were pursued and achieved, or came suddenly to him unsought, when he was alone. For company too often means compromise, discretion, the choice of the sweetly reasonable. It is difficult to be mad in company; yet but a touch of lunacy in action will open magic doors to rare and unforgettable experiences. But all these are only the by-products, the casual gains, of walking alone. The high converse, the high adventures, will be in the country of the mind.*

I pull the car over onto the verge a few hundred metres from where we start to climb. The path that leads to the top of the Knob is visible from here – a dark channel cut into the turf by centuries of plodding feet. We see a couple of people in bright waterproof jackets making their way ponderously up the slope, but otherwise there is no one else in view, no one to impinge on our quest for lunacy and adventure.

As I make my way steadily, methodically to the top, trailing the dogs that scamper ahead with no apparent effort, I remember doing this walk some years ago with a group of friends, old friends who had come to stay over Christmas not long after we moved here. There was snow, lots of it, knee-deep in some places. We climbed, red faced from the cold and the exertion, our breath coming out in clouds, complaints of aching legs, laughter, snowballs and biscuits when we got to the summit.

This is one of the many things I love about seeing the world on foot, at this pace, and returning to places I have walked before. Landscapes viewed this way, connected and tangible, become like scrapbooks, full of little details and images, impressions and happenings. They may be inconsequential, but that doesn't matter; it is the pleasure that comes from the jogging of memory and being witness to the shifts and changes that can happen over moments as well as months and years that make being out in the natural world so invigorating.

I pass a group of ponies, mountain ponies with wild tangled manes and tails whipped up by the wind. There is a split in the path. If I turn here I can take the longer, flatter route that follows a series of switchbacks to the summit, but I don't turn. I keep heading straight on, straight up, until my head is level with the ridgeline at the top and I can see beyond the face of the sheer slope I have been climbing, to the trig point and the blue-grey expanse of the peaks and valleys that stretch away to the far horizon.

I am close to the Hereford border here, the invisible line that separates England from Wales. If I look one way, back to the wind, out towards England, the land is rolling, gentle, tamed, parcelled up into neat fields and copses. Face the wind and there is the rough, wild adventurous glory of the Black Mountains. And if I keep walking along this ridge, it will eventually drop away, descending to a narrow valley before climbing again to another summit and another view. And so on I go, a solitary figure but not alone: there are clouds and mountains, soaring ravens, trees shaped by the wind, three dogs and my thoughts. It is company enough.

*

Polly and I meet in the car park at the base of the Skirrid. There is no impending storm today; quite the opposite. The sky is a deep satisfying blue, streaked by distant contrails, the horizon clear and sharp, the sunlight bright, and for the first time this year, really, properly warm. Warm enough to walk in T-shirts and to relish the gentle heat soaking into the grateful skin of our arms and faces.

As we come out of the shade of the trees on the lower slopes and take the track that leads along the side of the mountain, we are treated to one of those views that epitomizes the rural idyll, out across the valley with its farms and neat green fields edged with hedges and trees white with blossom. As the land rises on the opposite side of the valley it becomes browner, treeless, a ridge, distinct against the blue backdrop of the sky, the pert peak of the Sugarloaf standing proud above it and beyond the distant, but clear, outline of the Brecon Beacons. And the soundtrack couldn't be more apt either. A cuckoo calls – the first I have heard close to home – somewhere from the woods behind us and another – a rival – calls from across the valley.

We walk on, the coconut scent of the gorse flowers tickling our nostrils. We find ourselves talking – with much hilarity – about age and the looming reality that we are both nearing fifty – indeed, I might be in what could be described as the final approach. How every day a new wrinkle appears that we are absolutely sure wasn't there yesterday. That there is the gloomy realization that our eyelids have drooped, along with other parts of our anatomy. That our necks are beginning to resemble those of poultry, and we have started to make that small grunt of middle age every time we get up off the sofa. We bemoan the fact that we can't drink wine any more because it makes us feel dreadful and that we have to squeeze ourselves into Lycra leggings and trainers and drag our knackered old bodies up hill and down dale in a desperate attempt to keep relatively healthy and be able to fit into our clothes, while our husbands read the papers, drink coffee and eat bacon sandwiches and seem to get away with it.

We become helpless with mirth when we recall conversations with people in their twenties and forget that they are unaware of a world when we had to use phone boxes, the *Encyclopaedia Britannica* and find something to do other than go shopping on a Sunday. And the mildly embarrassed look we get from them in return, which tells us they are desperate to ask whether we have ever, like, actually, really seen a real-life Brachiosaurus.

The view from the summit demands a pause. A moment of reverence for the sheer beauty of the world spread out before us.

On the wander back down, we move on to the very real joys of getting older. Compared to our angst-ridden younger selves we feel more self-assured, less bothered by peer pressure or by what people think of us. We can accept things that were difficult or embarrassing to admit to when we were younger – my fear of parties (particularly fancy dress), my hatred of loud music, shopping and profiteroles. We now know that feeling inadequate or helpless is just part of life, and that those feelings can be overcome. That you can't – and don't have to – agree with or get on with everyone. That feeling worthwhile is not intrinsically wrapped up in how much you earn, what car you drive or handbag you carry. That no one really cares – or indeed notices – if you go to the supermarket in a skanky pair of tracksuit bottoms and slippers.

And with a cheerful promise that we will sink ingloriously and inappropriately into old age together, we head off – Polly to pick her boys up from school and me to go and have an eye test because everything I try to read on my phone is a blur.

GIN IN THE RAIN AND A PADDLE IN THE SEA

✳

Last night we drove down to South Devon to stay with friends. It had been another day of warm sunshine, but as we neared their house, the skies got dark – all of a sudden, in a dramatic, theatrical sort of way – and the rain came down, not in big slow drops that build to a downpour but in an immediate torrent. We ran to their front door, rain bouncing off the stone path, streaking down our faces, to be greeted with gales of laughter and the accusation that whenever I see them it always rains. It was still warm enough to be outside, so clutching large, clinking glasses of gin in one hand and umbrellas in the other we walked to the old pavilion by the river at the bottom of their garden. We stood under the dripping roof of the veranda, amid a watery soundscape and the lovely, earthy smell of wet grass.

The rain stopped at some point in the night and we wake this morning to a world with that bright, freshly washed look and a fragile blue sky, which darkens to a true Mediterranean blue as the sun gets higher. This is a day to be at the seaside. We drive, park at the edge of town, take the coast path. It runs along the top of the cliffs, a narrow, well-trodden ribbon weaving through the gorse bushes and across the coarse, springy turf. Below us is the sea, blue and rippling, sunlight bouncing off the surface.

I always love the idea of walking a coast path and we in Britain are blessed with access to much of our coast. But soon after I start a coastal walk I begin to get a bit restless. I've walked some beautiful stretches of our coast – North Wales, Pembrokeshire, Cornwall, Dorset – but once the initial excitement of being in close proximity to the sea has waned, when the sight and sound of waves crashing on rocks and the seabirds swooping and soaring is no longer a novelty, I find walking on these narrow paths with the sea either on my left or my right restrictive and a little frustrating.

And of course on a day like today when it is almost impossible to resist the pull of the sea and its salty, invigorating air, the coastal paths are busy. We find ourselves joining a line of other walkers, some going the same way as us, some in the opposite direction, and we squeeze ourselves up into the gorse to let them pass. We catch up with the walkers ahead, make polite coughing noises to let them know we are there, mumble 'excuse me' and are greeted by turned heads, a barely disguised scowl of irritation. There is nowhere to pass for a bit and we walk on, the atmosphere slightly fractious because they now feel rushed and we feel held back.

The pace we walk is such a personal thing. It can change every time we set out and is dictated as much by mood as by anything else, so to be coerced into walking at a speed that isn't in step with your mind can be more rattling than soothing. The path ahead widens. The walkers ahead step off the path and pause to let us pass. We thank them, stride on, released from the trap. And the further we walk, away from the town with its cafés and ice cream van, the fewer people we encounter.

Our friends have a favourite spot in mind they want to take us. The path starts to descend steeply, there's a gap in the cliff, a tiny cove, the sand still dark and glistening from the outgoing tide. There is no road near here. The only way to get here is on foot. And, for the moment at least, we have it entirely to ourselves. Our dogs chase ahead, their paw prints scuffing up the smooth, unbroken sand. We follow, run to the edge of the sea, jump and skip in the playful waves, the dogs barking with delight.

20TH MAY

GOING OFF PISTE

✳

Teg and I are back filming in North Wales. This afternoon we have finished relatively early and because the days are now longer and we are in a place that has an enticing combination of mountain and river, I decide to take Teg for a proper leg stretch. There is a map in the car park showing various routes from here, up and across the mountain. I stare at it for a while, trying to hold the pattern of the paths in my head. It looks pretty simple and I imagine that the paths will almost certainly be marked so we make a start, up the slope, a stream babbling cheerfully alongside us.

It is a good, steady plod uphill. I pause to get my breath, turn to look back at the view that has opened up as we've gained height. The magnificent peaks of Snowdonia are visible on the horizon, above them a shifting kaleidoscope of white and grey clouds. We get to a gate and the path curves around the base of a crag. I'm recalling the map, looking for a point where the paths meet and cross. There it is, a bit further ahead, with a fingerpost indicating the way we don't want, towards a lake, and the way we do, which will eventually take us down to the village and the river we follow back to the car.

Teg is enjoying herself. She loves being in the mountains; they are her natural habitat, the place she feels most at home. She criss-crosses ahead of me, picking up scents, scrambling up rocky outcrops, disappearing into dips and hollows then racing back to make sure I am still following her, stops at my feet – briefly, looks up, her eyes bright, smiling – and then races off again.

The path leads us to the edge of a short cliff. The way down is a scramble, a sheer drop of a metre or so followed by a short steep obstacle course through more rocks to get to the bottom of the cliff to pick up the path again. Teg stands on the edge, unsure how she is going to get down. I'm not sure how she's going to do it either. She'd work out how to negotiate the obstacle course, but it is this sheer top bit that is tricky. If she just jumps down, there is nowhere to land other than the jumble of boulders and she will almost certainly break a leg if she tries.

'I'll go first, Teg,' I tell her, and ease myself down the rock face to the narrow foothold at the bottom. Teg is letting out little squeaks of anxiety, worried that I am going to abandon her. I turn around, stretch my arms up to her. 'Just go slowly, Teg.' And she does, lowers herself into my arms, her damp, grateful nose in my ear, and I lift her, lower her gently onto the boulders and she scrabbles through them in a second, and has to wait for me to find my way through them and meet her at the bottom.

The path now joins others, none of which I remember from the map. I take the one I think is right and end up in a bog. Another comes to the edge of a cliff and stops at a viewpoint. Far below in the valley is the village – so we are not lost, we just can't find the way down. We retrace our steps, pick up another path and see someone else walking along it, a man in a red jacket. I wait for him to catch up, ask him if this is the way to the village. He tells me he's not sure, but that is where he is trying to get to too. So we join forces, finally find a path that looks promising, leading down off the hill in the right direction.

He's a shift worker, he tells me, works nonstop for a month and then has a week off. He packs up his van and takes off to see a bit of the country he has never been to before. 'I love walking,' he tells me, 'and this is my first time in Snowdonia. Worth a revisit I think.' Our promising path has by this time petered out. Below us there is a plantation of trees that is work in progress. There are piles of recently cleared vegetation, the charred evidence of a bonfire, newly planted whips, thin and spindly, held upright by tree guards. It is obviously private land, but we can't see any other way to get off this hill. 'Sorry,' I say to the man, 'if we get arrested, blame me.' And we scramble over the fence and make our way over the loose, loamy soil, reasoning that if we just keep heading downhill we'll get to where we want to be eventually.

We reach the edge of the plantation and below us is a lane. But we are above it, on a bank, with no obvious way to get down; so we sit, legs dangling over the edge, and slide somewhat ungracefully to the bottom. The lane takes us between houses and neatly tended gardens to the edge of the village. 'I'm Steve,' says the man, 'thank you for the adventure!' And we part, no longer strangers, but two people briefly brought together by a walk on a mountain and a lost path. An encounter that reminds me how rare it is to have the excuse to talk to someone we don't know. And how much we can miss by simply passing our fellow human beings by.

It is some time before 6am. The view from the window monochrome grey. Drizzle. The very embodiment of Scottish *dreich*. A morning to stay in bed but I know, as I get up, pull on leggings, T-shirt and trainers, that if I don't go out now, it is my last chance to be outside in daylight and fresh air until tomorrow morning.

I'm in Glasgow for four days, recording a series that unusually for me is being done entirely in a studio. Television studios are dark and windowless, the light carefully controlled by engineers rather than left to the whims of nature. It is a strange, intense atmosphere to work in. We are literally shut off from the outside world, with no sense of time passing or the day progressing. Each day we are in this artificially lit space for ten hours or more. There is no chance to stop, to do or think about anything else, or to be alone. When we finally leave the building and take the short walk back to the hotel, we feel a bit befuddled and jetlagged. So the hour I spend early every morning, by myself, padding along the straight, undemanding path that runs alongside the River Clyde and back is as much to reboot my brain as it is to stretch my legs. It is an hour of serenity, a state that philosopher Frédéric Gros describes like this:

> *Serenity comes from simply following the path. And then, while walking, serenity comes because all the hassles and dramas, all the things that gouge empty furrows in our lives and our bodies, become as if suspended... Serenity is the immense sweetness of no longer expecting anything, just walking, just moving on.*

So I take the lift down, walk across the empty hotel reception and out into the damp, grizzly Scottish air. The river is waiting for me. I can taste the sweetness on my tongue.

27TH MAY

ISLAND HOPPING

✱

A couple of days ago we drove to Cornwall, crossed the county border and followed the long, snaking road almost as far west as we could go before falling into the Atlantic. We spent the night in a pub that was once the coastguard's house and the next morning drove to the harbour. Ludo left me there, with dogs and luggage, while he went off to park. After handing over our bags to be labelled and loaded onto the boat, the dogs and I joined the queue that was forming alongside the harbour wall. Queues are generally stoical, rather silent affairs. People shuffle about a bit, looking at their feet, or their phones, sigh and huff if things don't seem to be moving. But this was possibly the most cheerful queue I've ever stood in. Everyone seemed to know each other. There were hugs and 'how are yous?' and 'it's been ages!' and a general air of jollity and bonhomie.

We were on our way to the Scilly Isles – somewhere we had long wanted to visit, but had never quite made it happen. Ludo joined me just as we started to board the ferry, clutching a packet of seasickness pills to get us through the infamously rough crossing. But the sea was flat and glassy, the sun bright, the air still and we sat on the outside deck, the dogs sprawled at our feet, watching for the first glimpse of the islands. They were more rugged than I expected: low, rocky humps covered in close-cropped grass and a few windblown trees, with bays and coves, startlingly white sand beaches and the intensely turquoise water of the tropics. It was hard to believe we were just off the Cornish coast.

The ferry docked at St Mary's on the main island and we got onto a smaller boat going to the island of Bryher, where we were staying. That evening we had dinner in a small stone hut, seated at a long shared table, enjoying a messy, finger-licking feast of scallops and crabs. The couple sitting next to us had been coming to the Scilly Isles every year for thirty years. 'If you like walking and eating, there is no better place to be.'

Bryher may only be one and a half miles long and half a mile wide, but the walk around its perimeter is a gratifying mix of rocky high points, giving dramatic, sweeping views over the sea and the sculpted stacks of rock that lie just offshore. Gulls surf the thermals, luminescent against a deep blue sky. There are grass-covered slopes that the dogs race down, scattering the rabbits grazing in the early morning sun. There are tiny, picturesque coves, pretty cottage gardens, small farms and swathes of wild flowers. There is one short stretch of narrow tarmac lane and I think we only saw one car and a quad bike using it the entire time we were there. We caught boats to go to the other islands and managed to walk on all of them apart from St Agnes.

Each island, we discovered, feels different, has its own personality. Yesterday we spent most of the day on St Martin's. It is one of the larger islands, renowned for the beaches that fringe much of its coastline. There are miles and miles of uninterrupted sand, marram-topped dunes, flowering gorse, palm trees and huge blue spikes of echium. Although many of the people who had got off the boat with us were also coming to walk, there are enough paths, enough diversions that we were soon walking alone. Swallows skimmed low over the grass catching insects, seals bobbed in the kelp beds off the gloriously named Bread and Cheese Cove and we climbed the steep ascent to the island's distinctive beacon, a rocket-shaped edifice with red-and-white candy stripes, working up an appetite for the eating that, according to Scilly lore, must follow the walking.

Until last night we'd had clear skies and uninterrupted sunshine, but overnight a squall came in, rain lashed at our windows and this morning we walk out into a landscape that is quietly muted, all soft greys and eggshell blues. There is a spring tide today and, we've been told, by midday the entire channel between Bryher and the neighbouring island of Tresco will be exposed and empty of water. And so we head down to the beach in the late morning.

It's chilly and damp enough for raincoats, but the weather hasn't deterred anyone from either island from also heading down to the beach, taking off their shoes, rolling up their trousers and setting off across the hard, ribbed sand, paddling through seaweedy pools, scattering tiny crabs, towards a wonderfully eccentric gathering on a sand bar midway between the two islands. A boat has been turned into a bar, someone is cooking a giant paella, there are crab rolls, mackerel in buns. Kids are making sandcastles, dogs chasing each other, or hanging about near the food stalls looking hopeful. We join the throng, two hundred or so people, barefoot on the soggy sand, feet wrinkled, legs slightly goose pimpled, the perfect finale to a few days of walking and eating.

A
SUMMER
EXPEDITION

June

23RD JUNE

A LONG WALK HOME

✱

The last few days I feel I have been permanently on the run, racing against time that has been panting and snapping at my heels. This date has been a set point in my diary for months and every time I look at the entry that says simply 'Wye Valley Walk', I feel a twinge of slightly nervous anticipation. For today is the day I set off by myself to walk for nine days from the source of the River Wye back home, 136 miles away at the opposite end of the Wye Valley. As challenges go it's hardly noteworthy; I'm not trying to follow the Amazon or pioneer a new route through previously uncharted territory. But it feels significant to me for several reasons. The first is I have been meaning – and wanting – to do this walk for a very long time, but perhaps because it is (literally) on my doorstep, it has never been a priority. I've always felt it is something I'll do someday. But someday became a year, and then five years and suddenly it's ten years since we moved here and I think if I don't bloody well get on with it now, it'll be another ten years and who knows what state I'll be in by then? So it feels like an achievement just to have finally committed to doing it.

But there is another factor that has played a significant part in this long prevarication. I want to do the walk alone. Self-reliance and independence are both intrinsic to my self-esteem and I feel the need to test them, to assure myself that I haven't 'gone soft'. But doing battle with the need to challenge myself is the niggling worry that I am being self-indulgent. I'm away from home for work so much, leaving Ludo to deal with the livestock and domestic stuff, that it feels not a little selfish to be heading off again to do something entirely for myself. And even now, on the day I am set to leave, I feel a little uncomfortable and a little bit guilty about what I am about to do.

My friend's campervan pulls up outside the house. Teg, as dogs frequently do, seems to sense that something is up; the beginning, perhaps, of an adventure that she is determined not to miss out on. She comes out with me to greet him, long tail waving in a way she knows is utterly beguiling.

While we are chatting, she makes her way around the side of the van, slips through the sliding door and hops up onto the back seat, stretching her full ginger-and-white length along it, claiming ownership and proclaiming in no uncertain terms that wherever we are going, she is coming too. 'You *are* coming too!' I assure her with a laugh, because walking without human companionship is one thing, but walking without a dog is unthinkable. I bring out two carrier bags, each filled with carefully worked out rations for both Teg and me, and stow them in the back. These are going to be dropped off with the obliging owners of the two B&Bs we have booked en route. The other nights we will be camping and, in the rucksack that I heave out of my front door and into the boot of the van, is a tent, sleeping bag and mat, stove, an extra set of clothes, dog food portioned up into bags, dehydrated meals, sachets of porridge, matches.

The last few weeks I have been compiling endless lists, poring over maps, packing and repacking my rucksack, trying to work out what I need and what would just end up being unnecessary weight on my shoulders. Thanks to the internet I have found a super-lightweight solar panel that I can clip to my rucksack for charging my phone. I don't intend to use it much – I suspect there will be little in the way of signal anyway along most of the route – but I have recently discovered the joy of podcasts and thought an episode or two might be the perfect way to unwind after a long day's walking.

I have found an ingenious water bottle with a built-in filter, so I can refill it anywhere and drink from it straight away without having to use purification tablets. I have a tiny, but comprehensive, first aid kit and 16 photocopied pages from the various OS maps that cover my route. These are numbered and in a plastic map holder that I will hang around my neck. I have always been disparaging of map holders. I don't know why. There is something inherently nerdy about them, but anyone who has packed in the obsessive way I have, has no right to call anything or anyone 'nerdy'. And I am already looking at my map holder with some fondness. 'Is that everything?' my friend asks. 'Think so,' I say, picturing again my packing list, items crossed off as they were stuffed into dry bags with masking-tape labels to remind me what is in each one. 'Let's go then.'

As we bump our way down our track I think back to January, when the idea of walking from the source of the River Wye back home resurfaced, this time with proper intention. I remember the 19 miles we walked on Good Friday, by which time I had made my intention a plan, had dates in the diary, and was testing myself out, seeing what I was capable of. And I recall the exhaustion during the latter part of that walk, the struggle up the hill when we left Grosmont and my feet feeling like bricks as we plodded the final couple of miles back to where we had started. And the sheer heaven of sinking into the sofa at the pub and being handed a pint of cider and a packet of salt and vinegar crisps.

And now, now that I am being driven away from home, the grey road slipping effortlessly beneath the tyres, as one hour passes and then another, as the view through the windscreen changes from woodland and rolling hills to one that is altogether more stark and rocky and daunting, I feel apprehensive. Can I really do this? Alone, apart from my dog? Will my not-altogether-reliable map-reading skills be sufficient? Am I strong enough, fit enough, to cover the distance in the time? To cover the distance at all?

A couple of weeks ago we were in France. May's long warm days had continued into June and the temperatures had continued to rise until, in some parts of the country, it was often over 30°C during the day. Newspapers were full of stories of 'Sweltering Britain', carried photographs of crowded beaches and people wearing as few clothes as they could get away with, paddling in city fountains. Roads melted, train lines buckled, sales of barbecues and paddling pools rocketed.

Over the channel we drove down French roads with the windows down, the warm air blasting our faces, stopping on the edges of shady forests for picnics and to give the dogs a stretch. It's a route we now know well. A few years before we had made a last-minute plan to take a week's holiday. We wanted somewhere to go that was simple and quiet; 'I just want to read books, swim in a river, eat tomatoes and not have to see or speak to anyone,' I said, by way of a wish list. Ludo sighed. 'We need to go in less than a month's time and we have one specific week when we are free. It's peak holiday season and I think the chances of finding what you want – even if I knew what to Google – are remote, if not impossible.'

But, in this case, fortune favoured the belligerent and I managed to find a small, wooden, off-grid cabin which – if the photos were to be trusted – looked like it was by a lake, in a wood and gloriously on its own. Ludo phoned the owners who told us they had just had a cancellation for the week we wanted.

It was better than we could have hoped. The cabin, hand-built by its English owners, was a perfect hideaway. We read, lying in hammocks shaded by oak trees. We swam in the lake, shopped at the local market for stinky cheese, crisp baguettes and tomatoes that tasted of sunshine and dripped red juice down our chins. And we walked. Miles.

We were in the very north of the Dordogne, an area that lacks the tourist draws of beaches or chateaux. Its charm comes from the fact that it is away from the well-trodden tourist trail, rural and authentic. There are neat, sleepy villages of stone houses, most with a boulangerie, maybe a café. And in many of these villages, either in the square or by the church, there is a wooden notice board. On it, behind a slightly foggy sheet of Perspex, is a map of the vicinity with one or several walking routes marked on it. Each route is named and the distance listed. We would find the corresponding fingerpost and head off, following a trail of wooden posts with yellow bands painted around the top.

We walked past fields of fat, sleek Limousin cattle. Small farms with geese and ducks, a donkey, some goats. Carefully tended vegetable plots and little vineyards. Through forests of sweet chestnut, crisscrossed by shady paths, where in late summer those who know where to look hunt for ceps. And everywhere we walked, much to the delight of the dogs, we would come across a pond or a lake, which we discovered later were mostly manmade, built for rearing fish to supply the good local Catholics of years gone by, whose beliefs dictated that they should abstain from meat on a Friday.

As the week went on we found ourselves growing increasingly charmed and Ludo, who spent much of his childhood in France and speaks French well enough to fool the locals into thinking he might be a native, was wondering, out loud, whether we might, one day, end up living here. We found ourselves idly looking in the windows of estate agents, imagining taking on one of the tumbledown stone houses or old watermills that were being offered for temptingly low sums.

At the end of the week the owners of our cabin dropped by to see if everything was OK and to wish us a safe journey home. We told them we had loved being there so much we'd been fantasizing about having a place of our own. 'Really?' they asked. 'Well,' we said, 'you know. In that holiday romance sort of way.' 'It's just that we do know of a lake for sale not far from here. It has a bit of land around it and a small fishing hut that could be turned into a cabin a bit like this one...' Most people when they go on holiday like to come back with a souvenir or two: a local handicraft or a bottle of liqueur that rarely gets finished. We bought a lake.

I have always loved travelling, always loved going somewhere new. There is something energizing about the unfamiliar; it wakes up the senses, enlivens the brain, allows you to do things, try things, experience things that in everyday life you may not notice or bother with. So I've never really understood why people return to the same place time and time again. Why miss out on that glorious liberation afforded by going somewhere you've never been before?

But now we have a lake, and trees, a tiny cabin hidden down a dirt track in the woods, and there is no point in having it if we don't go there. I wondered – worried, even – that I might resent it, that I might find it stultifying, an obligation, but to my surprise I find myself missing being there. I yearn for its simplicity, for days spent cooking on a fire, lying on the grass, swimming in the lake, swallows skimming over its surface catching insects and the kingfisher – our kingfisher, as I like to think of it – darting between the overhanging branches in search of the perfect fishing spot.

And there is the unexpected pleasure of feeling a little more local each time we go there. We have friends to visit, the man who runs the café in the local village greets us when we go in, as does the woman who runs the bakery. There are still plenty of places to explore and discover, but we also have favourite walks, a restaurant that we go back to every time we visit. We know which stalls to head for in the market for the best vegetables or bread or charcuterie.

We know that in autumn and winter the days are short, the countryside quiet, restaurants close, the market has fewer stalls and packs up before midday. Smoke curls up from the chimneys, jays squawk and squabble, rain patters down on fallen leaves. People go away or stay tucked up indoors. But come the summer, doors and windows are flung open, the chairs and tables on the pavement outside the café are full, the market bustling. There's news and gossip and handshakes. In the evenings many of the local villages hold night markets. These will be in the square or sometimes a field. Stalls are set up around the edge selling brochettes, frites, homemade wine, salads, cheese and bread. In the middle there are long trestle tables and benches where everyone congregates, laden with food and bottles. Kids play chase and hide and seek, dogs make hopeful forays beneath the tables and the eating and drinking and conversation and laughter carries on as the setting sun streaks the sky orange and pink, fades and deepens to darkest blue and the stars come out.

We'd been coming to the cabin for three, maybe four, years before we were introduced to what has become something of a summer highlight and if we are there at the right time of year we never miss it. It is the *randonnée nocturne* (night walk) – a tradition, it seems, particular to the Perigord and Dordogne region of France.

Tickets cost a few euros and come with instructions of where and when to meet. Last time it was by the boules court on the edge of the village just a couple of miles from our cabin. A small gang of us decided to go together and we arrived, slightly before seven, to find a sizeable crowd of people of all ages already gathered. There were children in pushchairs, grandparents in wheelchairs, dogs of every description. And what was striking was that it seemed everyone was local. This was not something promoted or organized for tourists. So we felt rather honoured to be there.

Someone gave a signal and the crowd moved off, guided by a handmade sign that pointed towards the woods. People started to string out, gaps opening up between the groups. The atmosphere was festive. There was much chat and banter. The route took us along forest paths and quiet lanes and after a mile or two led us into a field where we were amazed to find a small knot of people waiting for us. They dished out aperitifs and short wooden skewers with tomatoes and salami speared on them.

From here we had to decide whether to carry on along the shorter route or branch off, following the arrow chalked onto the tarmac of the lane, and take the longer, seven-mile route. It was a perfect evening; the warm, mellow conclusion to a hot day and not one of us was in a hurry to get home. We followed the arrow, turned off the lane to walk along the edges of fields, skirting lakes and weaving between the old stone barns and houses in a tiny, picturesque hamlet.

A forest track led us to the outskirts of another village and there, in a field behind the ruin of an old stone house, were tables groaning with urns of soup, baskets of bread, plates of cold meat, cheese and salad. There was red wine in unlabelled bottles, a cask of beer. We joined the queue, shuffled along gathering plates and bowls and glasses as we went, found a gap on one of the tables alongside three generations of one family and feasted.

By now it was almost dark. None of our gang had thought to bring a torch and it didn't seem many other people had either. Not that it mattered. Our eyes had adjusted as the light had diminished, we could still just about make out the route markers and there were plenty of people to follow. And we'd drunk just enough of the rough but moreish wine not to be troubled by thoughts of getting lost or falling into ditches.

It was midnight by the time we got back to the village square and the party was in full swing. The local bar was packed. A mobile disco with crackling speakers and lights that flashed in time with the beat of the music was blaring out cheesy euro-pop. There were flasks of coffee, trays of iced éclairs for pudding, sticky-fingered children dancing and chasing each other around the fountain.

As much as I treasure my solitary walks, walking in a crowd can be an equally illuminating, often transcendental experience. Powerful too. Rebecca Solnit observes that 'walking itself has not changed the world, but walking together has been a rite, tool and reinforcement of the civil society that can stand up to violence, to fear and to repression.' I too have walked – marched – along with thousands of others to try to effect change; been part of a united, urgent force determined that every step we take together will strengthen our message until it echoes off the buildings and through the corridors of power. I've been swept along in a racing tide of pilgrims, all of them eager to the point of being frantic, joined together by a religious fervour and euphoria but ultimately thinking and walking only for themselves.

But our walk through the French countryside along with two or three hundred others was nothing more than an excuse for a community to get together, to share a summer's evening with neighbours and friends. To walk and talk and eat and drink and take pleasure in all those things. It was a celebration. As good a reason to walk as any.

Our visit to the cabin this year was too early for the *randonnée nocturne*, but we walked every day, setting off not long after dawn, before the sun got too hot, choosing shaded wooded routes we knew, as well as venturing further afield. And even though we have been coming to this little corner of France every year for seven years, there was still plenty of enticingly unfamiliar territory to explore, and will be for as long as our legs can carry us.

We walked simply for the sheer pleasure of it, but at the back of my mind was the niggling reminder that these sun-soaked tramps in the rolling hills and forests of Perigord were training. That in a few days after I got back I would be undertaking a walk longer than any I had done before.

Back home, the campervan stops at a junction and turns, following the sign to the village of Llangurig. We've been driving for well over two hours and now we have reached the place where Teg and I are going to spend the night. It is still several miles away from the start of the walk, but there is nowhere closer to stay and Di, the local taxi driver, has been booked to pick us up in the morning to take us to the head of the trail. We find our B&B, unload my pack, bid farewell to my friend, wave until the van is out of sight. Teg looks up at me, her kooky blue and brown eyes scanning my face, sensing my nervousness. 'We'll be all right,' I tell her, with more bravado than I feel, and shouldering my pack we follow our host up the pink-carpeted staircase.

DAY 1
WE'RE ON OUR WAY

✳

The taxi pulls up outside the front door. Teg and I have already been out this morning, just for a brief leg stretch before breakfast. It is a grey morning, damp, the air heavy with moisture – a mist that isn't quite rain, but almost. Part of me is relieved that the heatwave of the last few weeks has broken. Teg, true to her Welsh roots, doesn't enjoy really hot weather, and I suspect I would have found it quite hard work too, but I did wish it wasn't quite so gloomy and dank.

Before we leave, Di, our taxi driver, pink-haired and cheerful, asks if we would mind popping down the road to see Mary. Mary runs the post office cum village shop and asks anyone who is setting off from the village to walk the Wye Valley or the Severn (the two walks start in the same place) if she can have a photo for the community Facebook page. 'I like to keep a record of everyone who's been through,' she tells me, as Teg and I stand outside the shop and she takes a couple of snaps on her camera. 'We may not be on the tourist map, like Snowdonia or Pembrokeshire, but we've had people come from all over the world. There! I think I've got a couple of good ones. Enjoy your walk!'

Di drives us along the narrow roads that wind between the hills to Hafren Forest. She's never done the walk herself she tells me, would like to, though, one day. 'How long is it going to take you?' 'I'm planning to do it in nine days, as long as I don't get lost!' I say it with a laugh, but butterflies flutter in my tummy. I am, I admit to myself, a tiny bit scared.

We pull up in a big parking area which, despite it being a Saturday in midsummer, is completely empty. Di waits until I've got my pack on and I'm ready to go before she drives away with a wave. 'Good luck!' Teg and I stand in the car park, the noise of the engine fading into the distance until there is nothing but silence. 'Right then!' I say out loud, trying to sound confident. Teg trots ahead and I follow her down the gravel path where a sign says, helpfully, 'All walks this way'.

There is a stream at the bottom, a narrow ribbon of clear, shallow, fast-flowing water, chuckling over gravel. This, according to my map, is the upper reaches of the River Severn, Britain's longest river. The Severn and the Wye rise within a couple of miles of each other in the mid-Wales hills, then carve their own way through the landscape, the Severn heading northeast and then south, the Wye flowing southeast, until they meet at Chepstow, by which time the Severn has become a broad, muddy, tidal estuary. I won't join the Wye for a few miles yet, so for the time being it is the Severn keeping me company as I walk along a well-tended boardwalk and then a wide, smooth track. Tall, dark conifers rise up on both sides of the bank, statuesque against the grey sky.

The mist is condensing now, has become mizzle. Teg's fur is covered in tiny droplets of water and I'm soaked. I stop to put on waterproof trousers and to fiddle with some of the stuff hanging off my pack. It has been a long time since I walked with a properly laden pack and I know it is going to take a while, a bit of trial and error, for me to know where I want everything to be and for the load to settle.

I think back to a walk Ludo and I did over twenty years ago in a very remote part of Madagascar, how bulky and heavy and uncomfortable our kit was. We were in the highlands in the middle of the country, had worked out a route that would take us through the mountains. There were, as far as we could tell, no villages or settlements on the way, so we had to carry everything, including a lot of water. We reckoned if we walked for eight hours a day we could do it in three days. It turned out to be almost impossibly gruelling – an endurance test that had us arriving at our final destination bent double, almost crawling, every part of our bodies in pain.

The modern kit I'm carrying today is super-lightweight in comparison, but it takes some effort to hoist my pack off the ground and settle it on my back. 'I'll get used to it,' I convince myself, and press on.

The first hour or so of the walk is pretty, in a manicured, almost 'walk in the park' sort of way, designed for those who have driven to the car park and want a short walk and riverside picnic. But the broad path I'm on starts to get narrower and I come to a junction. The Severn

Walk goes one way but I leave the river and take another path that cuts through the woods to a gate on the edge of the tree line. I've gained a bit of altitude and I'm now walking in thick cloud. I can see barely a metre in front of me.

As I open the gate that leads onto a track crossing an open hill, I hear the sound of an engine: a quad bike. I call Teg to me, put her on a lead in case there are sheep about. The quad bike is getting louder but the cloud is so thick I don't see it until it slows to a stop just in front of me. I'm about to offer to open the gate when the driver, swathed in a muddy wax jacket, a hat pulled down low, cuts the engine and says 'You made it this far then!'

Last night Teg and I had gone to the pub in the village. There were a few people sitting at the tables and a group of men at the bar. The men were all weather-beaten, had the look of solitary grafters who work the land year-round and who, at the end of the week, go home for a wash, something to eat and then meet in the pub to put the world to rights. They nodded a greeting as I walked in and ordered a cider, sitting on a bar stool next to one of them, his big, rough hands wrapped around a pint glass. 'That a Welsh sheepdog?' he asked, nodding at Teg, who had made herself instantly at home and was lying at our feet. 'She is,' I said. And that, it seemed, was enough for me to be accepted into the group, be part of the banter and the butt of the jokes.

Eventually the man who had introduced himself as Dai asked what I was doing there. I told him Teg and I were setting off tomorrow to walk the Wye. 'I own the source of the Wye,' he said, sipping nonchalantly from his pint. 'Wow,' I laughed, 'that's quite a thing to be able to say.' 'It rises on my farm, so you'll be walking across my land tomorrow. Where are you walking to?' 'Eventually to my house near Tintern, but

I'm hoping to get to Dernol tomorrow.' 'You'll be walking past my place too then,' said one of the others. 'I could give you a lift there tonight if you want.' 'That's cheating,' I laugh again, 'but you can give me a cup of tea if I make it there. My husband thinks I'll be lost almost before I start and he's probably right.'

The quad bike driver is, I realize when I peer at the face beneath the hat, Dai from the pub. 'Just thought I'd check up on you, make sure you're OK and hadn't got lost already! Weather's a bit crap.' I'm momentarily overwhelmed by this gruff act of kindness. I'm fine, very happy, I tell him. And I am. He has helped dispel the last of my jittery nerves, reminded me that in places like these out-of-the-way rural communities that get overlooked and forgotten, people look out for each other. 'There's a signpost a bit further down off this main track, says "permissible footpath". It takes you to a point where you can see the source of the Wye. But you won't see a thing today, so I wouldn't bother. Just stay on this track and it will take you out to the road. There's another sign there that will point you in the right direction.' And with that he waves goodbye and disappears into the gloom.

Teg and I trudge along the track until we come to the path Dai told us about. The weather is no better, if anything the visibility is even worse, but I know I won't be able to claim I've walked the Wye if I don't at least make an attempt to see the source. So we turn off, climb up along a rutted, muddy sheep track and follow it for half an hour or so. I'm not entirely sure what to expect, but imagine there might be a sign or a cairn or something that indicates where the source might be.

I get to an area where there are some big rocks. There are lots of boggy little streams and springs bubbling up all over the place and I guess any one of them might be the Wye, but if there is any sort of marker, I can't see it. I scan the slope below me, but most of it is shrouded in mist. Scattered sheep appear and disappear like ghosts. Water trickles through the grass, off my coat and down over my fingers. Teg shakes the rain off her coat, looks at me: 'Shall we go?' So we retrace our steps, back to the main track.

It is not a beautiful walk. Nor particularly exciting. Perhaps if we were able to see more of the landscape, get a sense of the shape and scale of it, I would feel differently, but the next couple of hours are spent on the same, rather tedious, wide gravel track. We walk past a rally centre, mercifully closed today, and pens for rearing pheasants. There are a few scattered buildings, hunkered low against the damp hillside. A farm truck passes us, the driver and his passenger giving us a curt nod.

And it takes me a while to realize that on the right-hand side – following our descent towards a narrow valley that I can see up ahead – is a stream, only a foot or two wide but clearly, from the deep channel it has carved into the turf, a permanent water source. I haven't bothered to look at the map because I know I stick with this track until we get to the road, but now I pause, brush the droplets of water off the plastic and find the track. I look for a thin blue line running alongside it, scan to see if it has a name. 'Teg!' I call. She stops, turns back to look at me. 'That's the Wye!' She looks in the direction I'm pointing, sees nothing that seems worthy of her interest and trots on.

We reach the road and see the fingerpost a few metres ahead on the opposite side. It brings us to a bridge where the young Wye meets another river. Their waters merge and swirl, then flow gently on as one river with one name. Our path takes us initially through woodland. It is a relief to be off the gravel track and on a narrower path, unsurfaced, winding through the trees, chaffinches and chiffchaffs calling from the branches above our heads. The path leaves the woods and meanders along the river bank. I almost feel the need to introduce ourselves to the river, knowing that we will be in its company on and off for the next nine days. Teg makes the introduction for me, wading in for a brief swim then jumping back out onto the bank for a shake and a luxuriant roll in the grass.

We are in more open countryside now. Sheep and cattle graze in the fields on the far bank. A grey heron stands motionless in reeds, its eyes fixed on the surface of the water, poised to strike. Newly fledged swallows are chasing upstream, low to the water, testing their skills like trainee fighter pilots. Above us, forked tail twisting to catch the thermals, a red kite soars. And all the while the river burbles and babbles companionably as we follow the direction of its flow.

We come to a farm, an old stone house painted white, a battered truck parked outside, a discarded pair of boots lying by the front door, but no sign of anyone being about. We follow a way marker into a field, but soon afterwards the path seems to peter out. I look at the map, trying to work out from field boundaries where we might have gone wrong. We backtrack, then follow the line of a hedge up a steep field and find the path again at the top, but on the other side of a barbed wire fence. Fortunately the wire is slack with age and Teg wiggles under it and I manage to scramble over it.

The little glow of triumph I feel at having found our way back on track is short lived. Soon after we reach a cluster of houses and a lane, make another wrong turn and end up walking through a field of yet-to-be-cut grass – it's hay-making time but the rain has made it too wet to cut. The grass is almost thigh-high and both Teg and I get soaked and covered in seeds and buttercup petals. We find a way marker almost completely hidden by a hedge and it points us upwards, away from the river, through open fields. Here there are ewes, recently sheared and looking sleek and smart, and their lambs – three months old or so now – roundbellied and sturdy.

After about five hours of walking we see the village of Llangurig again. I wonder about popping back into the post office to buy something chocolatey from Mary, but the path skirts the town and doesn't go into it and I decide against it, unwilling to add extra miles to a day that is going to be quite long enough.

Soon we are climbing again, steeply. My legs are starting to feel heavy; my pack heavier. And the path at this point is barely discernible and I have to make frequent reference to my map and use landmarks to find the way. I'm surprised. I thought this route would be so popular that the track would be well-worn and obvious. But then I realize that I actually haven't seen anyone else on this path all day. I climb and descend and climb again. The weather has cleared a little bit and I stop to catch my breath at the high point – 479 metres according to the map. I look back over the valley, the sheep, rolling hills and forestry. Wheatears flutter among the rocks and grass, skylarks fill the air with their song and Teg and I stand together, just for that moment queens of all we survey.

We make our way down towards a farm track at the bottom of a valley. It is almost 5pm and I start looking for somewhere we might spend the night. There are no campsites or places to stay around here, so I knew that we would be wild camping. I probably could have pitched my tent anywhere, but despite the fact I have seen no one since this morning and we are crossing what I think is common land, I know

I will feel more comfortable if I have permission from someone.

Teg and I walk along the lane until we get to a house. There is a horse tied to the gate beside the house and a girl is grooming it. On the other side of the lane are a couple of empty fields with a stream running through them: a perfect place to camp. 'Hello,' I say, and ask if the fields belong to her. They don't. She rents them from a farmer who lives further up the valley. 'I'll ring him and you can ask,' she offers, kindly. Edward, the farmer, is equally obliging, 'but there are midges,' he warns. And there are a few, but not many, not enough to detract from the beauty of this place.

The mist and low cloud have cleared, there is soft, hazy sunlight and I pitch my tent near a bend in the stream hidden behind a stand of hawthorn. I feed Teg, make myself a mug of tea and we both lie stretched out on the grass, content with the lovely exhaustion that comes at the end of a day of exercise and fresh air. We have covered 20 miles and reached the place I set out to get to by the end of the first day's walking. I am, I'll admit, a tiny bit proud of myself.

DAY 2

AN UP & DOWN SORT OF A DAY

✻

It was a blustery night with squalls of heavy rain. I was cold too, despite scrunching up and burying myself deep in my sleeping bag. Teg slept curled up on her blanket beside me and barely moved at all. I wasn't sure she would like the confines of the tent, but she was obviously tired enough not to care. At 6.30am I decide to get up. I open the flap of the tent and am greeted by a grey curtain of silent, drenching drizzle and a squadron of hungry midges. Within seconds they have swarmed all over me, unperturbed and unrepelled by my Swedish 'repels everything' repellent.

The matches I keep in the top pocket of my rucksack have gone soggy. I can't quite believe I have been so idiotic; that I didn't think to put them in a dry bag or plastic box. Miraculously I manage to light one and boil water for tea, but I can't get any of the others to light and am forced to eat porridge oats with cold water, while pacing like a mad woman around the field trying to outwit the hateful midges. They are besieging Teg too. She gulps down her breakfast as I pack up the sodden tent. I do a final check to make sure we have left nothing behind and then together we hightail it back to the lane.

There is a bit of brave birdsong from the hedgerows but otherwise nothing stirs beneath the thick, muffling cover of cloud. I walk with my hood up and head down against the driving wet. After about an hour we turn down another lane and something about it looks familiar. A farm comes into view and I remember. Teg and I came here a couple of years ago to get advice from the farmers, Derek and Veronica. They are both well-respected breeders of Welsh sheepdogs and I went to see them before deciding to breed from Teg.

As I approach their barn I see Veronica, resplendent in a high-vis raincoat and red hoody, getting feed for her chickens. 'Hello!' I call, and Veronica looks round. It is clear she has no idea who this bedraggled person is, standing outside her gate swathed in dripping waterproofs. Teg has wriggled through the fence and sashays up to Veronica with her finest grin, tail wagging. 'It's Teg!' Veronica cries. 'Is that you, Kate? You look half drowned!' And she gives me a soggy hug, followed by my favourite word in the English language. 'Tea?'

An hour and a half later, after two mugs of properly strong farmer's tea together with boiled eggs and a plate of bread and butter, we have caught up on each other's news, the rain has abated and I leave, clutching a bunch of elder blossom. 'I was always told that you should plant elderflower near a pigsty to keep flies and biting insects away,' says Veronica, 'so perhaps this will help with the midges!'

Today we will reach Rhayader, a small market town where I am hoping I can replace my matches. But not until I walk for a mile or so on from Veronica's, miss a turning off the lane even though I have been looking out for it and have to double back up a steep hill, muttering curses under my breath. There is a very half-hearted stile with no signs or arrows on it, but it is in about the right place, according to the map. Teg scrambles over and I follow her into the field on the other side and walk downhill, dodging towering thistles and pushing through bracken, until eventually we find a way-marked gate and are reunited with the River Wye.

We cross it at a bridge and almost immediately leave it again, heading over a main road and into a nature reserve. This is a day for redstarts, pretty, perky little birds flitting about the hedges and perching on fence posts, hunting for insects. Red kites too, several of them, soaring overhead in the grey sky, which is slowly beginning to brighten as the cloud thins enough to allow a wash of hazy sunlight to break through.

There are other people out walking – the first I've seen since I set off. We exchange pleasantries, walk together for a bit until they peel off back towards where they've left their car and Teg and I carry on, up and up the hill. I stop to catch my breath and turn to admire the expansive view opening up behind me. We crest the hill and immediately descend through the fields on the other side. We stop for a chat with a farmer who is out gathering his sheep. He's friendly, loquacious, leaning against his quad bike, his dog on the seat keeping a watchful eye on both the sheep and Teg. We say our goodbyes and continue our descent through the fields, the views no doubt magnificent if it hadn't been for the low cloud that has once again triumphed over the sun's earlier attempts to emerge.

Our path joins a lane that passes beneath branches of oak and beech trees. Suddenly I hear a high-pitched scream. My heart leaps, I turn back and see Teg standing on the verge. There is something small and grey and furry in her mouth and a look akin to panic on her face. The small, grey furry thing is a baby rabbit and understandably it is protesting furiously at being held between Teg's teeth. 'Well just put it down, Teg,' I tell her, trying not to laugh. And gently she lowers the irate bunny back to the ground and lets it go, whereupon it skitters off up the bank and out of sight. 'If we get lost and run out of food you are going to be no use at all,' I say, but Teg just wags her tail and walks beside me to the outskirts of Rhayader.

Rhayader is surprisingly busy. It is Sunday lunchtime and after stopping at the newsagent to buy matches I decide to find a café for lunch. The one in the centre of the town is packed with day-trippers. I try to order something at the counter to eat at the table outside on the pavement, but I can't get through the door with my rucksack, am told that I can't bring a dog in and as I'm trying to sort myself out someone else takes the table. I suddenly feel overwhelmed and miserable, as I often do when I've had time on my own and am then faced with lots of my own species.

Ludo and I once did a walk called the Otter Trail, which follows South Africa's magnificent and aptly named Wild Coast. The route takes five days and is carefully controlled so only twelve people are allowed to set off on any given day. There are simple huts to stay in along the route, where we would come together with the other walkers at the end of the day, but otherwise we saw no one. I remember so well the feeling of complete liberation that comes when life is pared down to a few essentials; the self-sufficiency of having everything you need on your back and the seemingly endless possibilities that every day out in the wilderness can offer. And I remember too when we got to the end of the trail, saw cars again, had to find the right bus, deal with people, that I felt just like I do now – claustrophobic and slightly panicked – with the overwhelming urge to flee back the way we'd come and live out my days under a hedge.

Today I flee the café and on the outer edge of town find a quiet hotel with a bar where Teg and I can rest our legs before the next bit of the walk which, if the contour lines on the map are anything to go by, is going to involve quite a bit of climbing. Revived by water and a bag of pork scratchings, we leave the town behind and are alone again. Not far on, the path takes us to a narrow suspension bridge over the river that wobbles as we walk across it, much to Teg's consternation. The water is clear, shallow, flowing fast over the gravel bottom. Teg chases a stick into the water, throwing up a cascade of droplets, sending two grey wagtails twittering off to perch on nearby boulders and scold.

I walk between the lacy heads of cow parsley and tall grasses. Everywhere is the dense, verdant green of summer, trees almost burdened by heavy cloaks of leaves. Here's our climb, a steep, stony track, one that is sunk down between banks as if it has been worn down over millennia by generations of trudging feet. On paths like this I always find myself imagining who might have walked here before and why. Where were they going? What were they carrying? Why were they walking in the first place?

Walking for no particular purpose other than the pleasure of it is a reasonably recent phenomenon – a luxury, really. It certainly feels like a luxury to be here, panting hard, heart pounding, as I stand at the top and gaze out over a patchwork quilt of greens, the enticing outlines of mountains on the horizon. It is a view that could, would, draw crowds, but there is no other way to get here than on foot. It is the reward for putting in a bit of effort, a reward that at this moment is mine alone to relish.

We walk on, downhill once more, to a village with a name I can't even guess how to pronounce. I stand and look at the sign. 'Llanwrthwl'. A gusty breeze heralds a sharp shower and I give up trying to work out how to say it and make for the forest of conifers and the springy turf track scattered with fallen pine needles the colour of tarnished bronze. I am starting to feel tired now, the pack pulls at my shoulders and any energy gleaned from my pork scratchings has run out. I stop, perch on a rock, eat an apple and some nuts, stomp on to the end of the track. I need to get to Newbridge tonight.

Two miles more, the sign at the end of the track tells me, pointing me towards a lane. My hope that these last two miles are going to be a simple, undemanding plod are dashed when a yellow arrow takes me over a stile and on an uphill path that gets fainter and fainter and finally peters out altogether. Trying not to feel dispirited I gaze at my map in the vain hope that there will be some unmissable landmark I have to head for. Anyone with rudimentary compass skills would have had no trouble, but I have neither skills nor, indeed, compass, and have to rely on trial and quite a lot of error before Newbridge finally comes into view.

The campsite I am staying at tonight is not in Newbridge but a few miles further on and the owners are going to pick me up. I call them and we arrange to meet outside the Baptist chapel. I sink down onto a bench feeling done in. My watch is one of those that counts steps. I've done just under 50,000 today – almost 22 miles. The accommodation at the campsite is in cabins built from trees harvested from the owner's woodland. They kindly offer to take me with them to the local pub for steak and chips but I decline, relishing the chance of drying out my tent and having a hot shower. I eat a freeze-dried chicken curry, watch my sodden socks steam on the wood burner and hang out with my dog. As evenings go, this one is pretty perfect.

DAY 3
WHEN THINGS START TO GO WRONG

*

Last night the clouds cleared and the stars were bright in the sky. This morning the sun is soft and hazy behind high, light cloud: perfect walking weather. Teg and I are given a lift back to Newbridge and we pick up our route again, along a road and then onto a well-worn path through a patch of scrubby woodland. But as soon as we leave the woods for open ground the path entirely disappears and we flail about in the waist-high bracken, getting increasingly frustrated and cross, until we get back on track.

We spend the first part of the morning walking through farmland, the river hidden from view in the valley below. We skirt around a house and climb up into the woods behind it, winding through trees in dappled sunlight. Butterflies flit and flutter, birds chirp and trill and from somewhere below us comes the sound of water. The path curves down and I catch a glimpse of liquid silver between the leaves. A short time later and we are back on the bank, reunited with our old friend, the River Wye.

The next few miles are a joy in sharp contrast to the start of the day. The path hugs the river bank. It is flat, easy walking. There is no need to refer to the map and I can just relax and enjoy the company of the river in all its guises. At this point it is quite wide, I imagine quite deep too as it seems to be barely moving. It is languid, lazy, the sun and sky and the trees growing along the bank mirrored on its surface. A raft of Canada geese, I count 15 of them, all facing upriver, drifts almost motionless midstream. A buzzard circles overhead, as if for the sheer pleasure of feeling the sun on its wings, and chiffchaffs chiff and chaff. A little further on I spy a pair of mute swans, elegant and haughty, with their cygnet, still fluffy and grey, the story-book ugly duckling.

The river starts to burble and bubble, there are rocks just below the surface and some of them jut out above the swirling eddies. This is dipper territory. I stop, scan the boulders, looking for these smart little chocolate-brown birds with their white chests. There's a pair, calling to each other. They flit past me, land, take off again, land, bob, dip, dance, disappear beneath the rippling surface of the river, then, all of a sudden, pop up again like corks. So entranced am I by the unfolding story of the river that I barely notice the path is now tarmac, that walking towards me are girls with babies in pushchairs and old men walking stiffly beside ancient, equally stiff spaniels. I've reached Builth Wells.

We've been walking for three hours. Breakfast is called for. I find a café with tables in a tiny courtyard, a bowl of water outside the door for thirsty dogs. I drink two mugs of coffee and devour a plate of scrambled eggs. There's a sausage for Teg. I check the map. The route out of town looks pretty straightforward, but although I know I have turned up the right road, try as I might I can't find any sign of a footpath. I'm on a residential street, an enclave of houses with neat gardens and cars parked in driveways.

A woman with a terrier on a lead comes down the hill towards me. 'Do you know where the path is for the Wye Valley Walk?' I ask. 'It's somewhere around here, but I can't find it!' and I show her the map. 'Well, you are in the right spot, because the castle is just over that hedge, but let's go and ask my husband. He used to be a mountain guide.' Ralph is vacuuming the hall as we arrive on the doorstep. He shuts off the Hoover and comes outside, pats Teg.

'You've got a compass, I see,' he notes, approvingly. I shuffle a bit, embarrassed. I found the compass yesterday, on the ground by a stile. I picked it up, tied it to the strap of my rucksack, thinking that if I got really, truly lost, I'd miraculously work out how to use it. I now confess that I'm clueless. Ralph tells me that I need to turn by the yellow house on the corner, walk a mile along a lane and it will lead me to the footpath. He then, perhaps simply to avoid having to go back to the Hoovering, gives me a quick compass lesson. 'It really is very easy!' he smiles. 'Good luck!'

'Erwood, 6¾ miles', says the fingerpost at the end of the lane and we take the track that climbs up and up until my calves are burning and my heart is thudding in my chest. I stop, frequently, not just because I'm on the point of collapse, but because the views, thanks to a clear china-blue sky, are magnificent: a landscape rolled out like a carpet below me. Hills, valleys, forests and the town of Builth, reduced to miniature by the grandeur of its surroundings. Not far from the top

I meet two people also carrying rucksacks. They are from Sweden, they tell me, and are doing the same walk as me but in the other direction. They started in Chepstow twelve days ago and are on the final day. 'We're finishing in Builth and celebrating with a cream tea!' the woman tells me. 'It's downhill all the way,' I tell them and we wish each other happy walking.

Teg and I press on in the other direction, across open hillside, a clear path through the bracken, watched by idly curious ewes and lambs. The path begins to drop steeply, meets an even steeper lane. Although I was able to dry out my socks last night, my boots have remained pretty much sodden since the first day. My feet at the end of a day's walking look like they belong to a corpse that has washed up on a beach – white, wrinkled and waterlogged. My boots are old faithfuls – well worn in and very comfortable – but the gradient of this slope is making the balls of my feet, pressed as they are against soggy socks, complain.

We cross a little metal bridge and are met on the other side by two paths, both equally feasible according to the map, but neither marked. I plump for the one that heads uphill away from the stream we have just crossed, climb a short but nonetheless breathtaking slope, reach a gate at the top with no way marks on it, climb over it, mess around in a field for a bit trying to find a stile or gate or some clue we are in the right place, conclude we're not, backtrack, take the other path and then finally come across a sign that tells me I'm going the right way.

We've walked about 16 miles, my blood sugar's in my boots, my pack is feeling heavy and my feet hurt. I swear. Quite a lot. Teg looks shocked. But not long later I see the bridge at Erwood down below us and know that our campsite is just a couple of miles further on.

Better still, when we cross the bridge, there is a sign for a craft centre. It is right on the route and has a café. 'Teg,' I tell her, 'we are going to treat ourselves.'

Revived by local apple juice, a pot of tea, a hearty slab of fruit loaf and the knowledge that we have only two more miles to go on a straightforward, flat route, I leave the café with something of a spring in my step, but very quickly realize that springing is something I'm simply not capable of. My feet are now really sore. I can feel myself wincing and tensing up with every step. And this final stretch is on a road. Not only is the tarmac an unforgiving surface to walk on, there are cars – not many, but they drive fast – and Teg, who is not used to traffic, cowers every time one passes.

Up until this point this walk has felt like an adventure. Yes, there have been the frustrations of losing the path. Yes, some bits of it have been physically challenging and I could do without ever having to encounter a midge again, but the pleasure of traversing a beautiful part of the world at a speed that allows me to feel absolutely part of it and connected to it far outweighs all of that. But now that I am in pain, it feels like an endurance test. I've hit a low point. I feel embattled. I stop noticing anything around me. All my concentration is focused on putting one foot in front of the other and not giving in.

We get to the 'rickety bridge' the lady in the café told us about, cross back over the river, negotiate a short section of busy main road and stumble gratefully through the gates of the campsite at Trericket Mill. I put up my tent, feed Teg, dig out my first aid kit and spend a satisfying, if slightly gruesome, half hour popping the enormous blisters that entirely cover both balls of my feet. They have managed to carry me another 20 miles, but we still have a long, long way to go.

DAY 4

COULD THIS BE THE END?

*

I was woken up just before 1am by the pain in my feet. Beneath the plasters all the blisters had swelled and hardened again. By the light of my torch I once more attacked them with a safety pin, squeezed out all the fluid I could, re-dressed them, took two painkillers and tried to go back to sleep.

This morning I hobble about a bit, my feet still painful, but I hope, rather optimistically, that once I get going they'll somehow stop hurting. I've got dry socks but my walking boots are still stubbornly soggy. However, two thoughts cheer me as I'm eating my porridge with freeze-dried raspberries. (Good camping food, this – just by way of an aside. They weigh nothing and make slightly gloopy oats taste a bit more exciting and look like raspberry ripple.)

My first cheering thought is that today is not a very long day's walking – about 15 miles by my calculation – and it will end in the lovely town of Hay on Wye where I am booked into a B&B. So a little bit of luxury (and the possibility of restocking my much-depleted hoard of blister plasters) awaits.

Also, my friend and stalwart walking companion Polly is joining me today. She has already sent a text to tell me that she should be with me at about 9am. This cheering thought is tempered by a slight feeling of guilt. She has juggled childcare, got up at dawn to drive here and also shelled out for a B&B because I lured her with the promise of a beautiful day's walking with a good pub at the end of it. And I'm not sure, at this point, how long my determined stoicism is going to last.

Polly arrives. 'I thought you might be missing green things, so I've brought salad,' she says, waving a box with enough food in it to feed ten people. We walk back to the river and the Wye Valley Walk sign points us along the path that follows the bank. We've barely gone a few steps when I hear a high-pitched *'peep'*. I stop. I hear it again. 'Kingfisher!' I cry. 'Oh, where?' says Polly, 'I've never seen one.' I scan the branches overhanging the river. There's a streak of blue, low over the water. 'There!' The little bird alights on a dead branch just a few metres in front of us. It stays just long enough for us to admire its turquoise and orange finery, its dark eyes scanning the flowing water. Then, in a bright flash – a blink – it is gone.

We stay on the path alongside the river for a mile or so, then cross it by way of a bridge. We carry on towards Glasbury, which doesn't look very big on the map but I hope might have a chemist or, better still, an outdoor shop where I can find some sort of miraculous solution to cure my feet. Because now I have to admit to myself – and to Polly – that I am in agony. It seems so utterly pathetic that something as mundane as a blister is as crippling as this. My boots feel like someone has filled them with ground glass and every one of my increasingly tentative steps sends sharp, shooting pain up my legs. And this part of the route, although unchallenging with no big climbs or descents, isn't distracting or beautiful enough to take my mind off the pain.

Glasbury doesn't have a miracle cure, but it does have a rather lovely riverside café where we stop for coffee. I put on new plasters and an extra pair of socks. I do whatever it is you have to do to gird your loins, heave on my rucksack and suppress a squeak when my nerves register the pain of the first step. I don't like using the word hate, especially in relation to something that gives me as much pleasure, reward and stimulation – both mental and physical – as walking. But I really do hate every moment of the walk this afternoon. It seems that most of our time is spent on – or alongside – a very busy A-road, which makes Teg miserable and me feel a fresh wave of guilt that Polly has come all this way just to walk along a road with a lot of traffic in the company of someone who has gone into a sort of pain-induced trance.

The bridge on the edge of Hay on Wye hovers into view, as welcome a sight as any I can recall. I shuffle towards it, overcome with a sort of gratitude. Our arrival is heralded by the trilling song of a thrush that is sitting on the top of a telegraph pole at the end of the bridge, singing its heart out, as if to congratulate us. I limp on towards the B&B and salvation.

Di, the owner of the B&B, couldn't have been kinder. Hay on Wye is on the route of both the Wye Valley Walk and Offa's Dyke, so I suppose she has seen plenty of sorry folk like me over the years. She brings a huge stock pot to my room. 'It belonged to my ex-husband, who was a chef. Hated him. So I thought it was just the thing for you to put your feet in!' Few things have ever felt so blissful, so utterly luxurious, as sitting perched on the seat of the loo in the bathroom with my feet in that saucepan of hot salty water.

Polly, meanwhile, ever-thoughtful and practical, is on her way to the chemist. She comes back having cleared the shelves of blister plasters. And Ludo, my ever-patient and supportive husband, phones to say he will drive up and join us in the pub for supper, bringing another pair of walking boots to see if they will help. Feeling overwhelmed and bolstered by all this kindness I hobble over the road to the outdoor shop opposite and spend a small fortune on padded socks and gel insoles. I will not, I tell myself, be beaten by a blister!

But later, after Ludo has left to drive back home and Polly has gone to her B&B down the road, I sit on the edge of the bed with my head in my hands. Both feet have swelled up to such an extent I can't get boots on at all. Despair wells up, washes over me in a wave. I walk or run every day, often quite long distances. I do frequent strength sessions with a trainer. I think – or thought – I was quite fit, quite tough. Not someone who gets blisters on the soles of their feet. One hundred and thirty-six miles over mixed, but not overly challenging, terrain should be a breeze but now doubt is worming its way into my thoughts, undermining my belief in myself. Making me question, making me wonder. Have I been deluding myself, thinking that I was capable of this walk? Maybe I'm not as fit or as prepared as I thought I was. Maybe I have underestimated the walk or overestimated my ability. Maybe (and I shut my eyes and hang my head) I'm just too old to do this.

I lie down – my great, fat, damaged feet propped up on a pillow – and fall asleep feeling absolutely wretched, my lovely, loyal dog stretched out on the floor beside me. That day we've covered the shortest distance since we set off – just over 13 miles.

We take our ability to walk so much for granted. From the moment we make our first steps as babies and become toddlers (accompanied, often, by cries of encouragement and congratulation by ecstatic parents), walking on two legs is just what we do. It is how we get around. And it is unique to us humans – no other creature on earth moves the way we do. There are other bipedal animals – the primates, our closest ancestors, can all walk on two legs, although they spend more time on all fours. Birds, rodents, kangaroos – even cockroaches when they are moving at speed – use two legs to move around, but not the way we do. The way we stand, the structure of our skeleton, the interaction between our bones and muscles that allows us to walk with an upright stance and not fall over (much) are some of the key factors that identify us as human. And Claire Lomas's extraordinary story illustrates just how strong the urge can be to walk, even when we can't.

Claire was a successful event rider. A fall from her horse in 2007 left her paralysed from the chest down. For many of us this would be so devastating, so fundamentally life changing it would be unfeasible to believe that life could ever be enjoyed again. (Look how sorry for myself I'm feeling, and I've only got blisters.) And Claire did struggle. It was, she says, a huge knock to her confidence. But her struggle was overcome by her steely determination to rebuild her life.

She discharged herself from hospital after just eight weeks and with the help of lots of rehab and an indomitable spirit has achieved what many would have deemed impossible. She has taken up skiing, hand cycling and racing motorbikes. She also found time to marry her husband Dan, and give birth to her daughters Maisie and Chloe. And in 2012 she did the London Marathon, but not in her wheelchair. She walked it.

She did it with the help of an incredible piece of technology – a robotic exoskeleton which, when worn by someone like Claire with a spinal cord injury, can provide powered hip and knee motion to enable them to stand, walk, turn, even go up and down stairs. Don't be fooled into thinking this robot does all the work – Claire still needed to be at the peak of fitness and it took her 16 days to complete the course. It was the first of many challenges she has undertaken, and her efforts have raised over £600,000 for the Nicholls Spinal Injury Unit, which is working to find a cure for spinal cord injury. One day, and Claire believes it is not far away, people with injuries like hers will be able to walk again.

DAY 5

HOPE IS RESTORED

*

I wake at 6am, the soft rays of the morning sun filtering through the pink curtains. Teg puts one front paw, then the other, on the bed, nuzzles my cheek with her long ginger nose. I look at my feet. They are a more normal size. I stand. Walk to the bathroom. They are still tender, despite a double layer of blister plasters. I lie back down, run through various scenarios in my head, feeling calmer and less despairing after a good sleep. I could stay here an extra day, rest and try again tomorrow. That wouldn't be so bad, I reason. It is a nice place to be. I'd need to make up the mileage, do a bit of logistical juggling, but it should be possible. But what if this is a warning – a sign that actually I should call it a day? Give up altogether. Maybe try again another time. But when?

Whatever I decide, Teg reminds me she still needs to go out. I pull on my new padded socks, the dry boots that Ludo brought with him. I take a step. There is no shooting pain, no need to wince. My feet feel fine. I can't quite believe it. I jump up and down a bit which, had I attempted to do yesterday, would have made me faint. Still fine.

Teg and I walk down to the river. Everything looks beautiful, utopian almost. The colours of the flowers in the gardens and in hanging baskets, the myriad greens of the vegetation along the river bank, the rainbow sparkle of sunlight on the gently rippled surface of the river. I could skip. I do skip, much to the amusement of another early-morning dog walker coming in the other direction. I race back to tell Polly my news. She suggests that we walk the first part of my day's route together, see how I get on. There's a pub conveniently at the halfway point. She'll get a lift back from there to her car and if I'm not able to walk on, I can get a lift back too. 'And you could leave your rucksack here and I can drop it off at your campsite tonight, so you can have a day off from carrying it.'

Maybe it is the relief that my feet feel OK again, maybe it is the treat of walking without the weight of the pack, but I think the route this morning is the prettiest so far. We leave the river early on, climb up through some idyllic countryside. We have left Wales for the time being and are now in the English county of Herefordshire – all rolling hills and woodland and views over a patchwork of fields. There are big swathes of blue sky between the high cloud, the sun warm on our faces.

As ever, we lose the path a couple of times, but never disastrously. There is a gratifying climb up a hill, through beautiful forest, the river just visible between the trunks of the trees, carving its way through the valley far below. We start to descend towards the village with the pub, lose the path once again, but after a bit of to-ing and fro-ing – Teg looking on with slight disdain – we find the pub and join the ruddy-faced, beer-drinking regulars in the bar. My feet still feel OK, the agony of the last day and a half completely gone. Not even a twinge. So I let Polly know where I am camping the night so she can drop off my pack and we hug goodbye.

I take the wrong path not once, but twice, in less than a mile after leaving the pub, but finally find a track that looks right and after a bit of searching find the sign with the picture of a leaping salmon on it that indicates the route of the Wye Valley Walk. It is on a post that in winter would be visible but now, at the height of summer, is buried deep among the foliage of the hedge alongside it. It takes us through woods and then onto a broad grassy ride, like something that might be found in parkland surrounding a stately home, only this one is rather overgrown and unmanicured. I feel wildly happy, euphoric to be liberated from pain, and the lovely sense of anticipation of the journey ahead has returned. I make up a song and sing it, out loud, to Teg.

Up ahead I can see something. I can't quite make it out. Maybe a large sheep? I stop singing and strain my eyes to try and work out what it is. As I get closer I see that it is a big grey dog and sitting on the ground beside it, holding its lead and leaning against a gate, is a man wearing combat trousers and a black hoody. There's a weighty-looking rucksack at his feet. 'Hello!' I call, as I approach, 'would you like me to put my dog on a lead?' 'Yes!' he calls back, standing up. 'My dog might attack it.' I call Teg to me, put her on a lead and walk closer to the man and his dog. There is something about them both, something that – momentarily – makes me feel wary and a bit vulnerable. This is a lonely path, with no houses nearby and from the state of it, not frequently used. I decide my best tactic is to stop purposefully and say something inconsequential and chatty, rather than scuttle past looking scared.

'Are you doing the Wye Valley Walk?' I ask. The man looks momentarily shifty. 'Sort of.' He pauses, perhaps weighing me up. 'We started walking from Dartmouth a couple of months ago,' he continues slowly, and then his words come tumbling out and I learn that he had been planning to walk from Land's End to John O'Groats, had gone to the pub a couple of weeks before he was due to set off to say farewell to his friends. Something happened, his dog attacked one of his friends, took a great chunk out of his thigh and his hand. Put him in hospital for weeks.

'Do you know what sort of dog it is?' he asks me. I look again at the big grey animal, long legged, rangy, wild eyes, passive and unblinking. 'No,' I say. 'It's a Czechoslovakian Wolfdog. Half Alsatian, half wolf. I know I shouldn't have had a dog like this. I lived in a council flat but, well, I got him and he's fine – was fine. He knew my friend. I don't know why he attacked him. The landlord called the police. My friend didn't want to press charges but now the police know, I know they'll take the dog away, destroy him. So I just left. Started walking. We're going to get to the coast of Wales and then head north, up to Scotland. We'll keep going as long as we can.' His hand strays down to the dog's head. 'I figure it's his last walk, so...' and he tails off, looks down at his boots.

So man and dog are on the run: fugitives, outcasts. Entirely reliant on their feet and their wits. 'Do you know what?' I say, after a pause as his story sinks in. He looks at me, questioningly. 'I think you'll both be OK. I don't know why, I just have a feeling.' 'Thanks.' I turn to go. 'There are really nice orchards up ahead,' he adds, quickly. 'I camped there last night. Lots of rabbits for the dog.' 'Good luck,' I say, really meaning it, and Teg and I walk away, the image of the man's hand on his beloved dog's head sharp in my mind's eye. I send a silent plea to the sky that they are kept safe.

The orchards he told me about are not much further on and have an ordered beauty, as formal and precise as an ornamental garden. This is cider country and we walk on wide grass paths between neat, serried rows of apple trees, the blossom gone and the first tiny fruits just visible among the leaves on the ends of the branches. We finish the day on a quiet lane that weaves its way between high hedges and fields mown for hay. There is no campsite near here, but we've been given permission to camp at a National Trust property. There is a field, I've been told, alongside the tea room, where we can spend the night. There are toilets and a kettle too.

We walk down a sweeping drive between rhododendrons and azaleas towards a large house that is now an old people's home. It is the gardens of this once-grand private house that are looked after by the National Trust and I had visions of Teg and me finding some hidden corner of a lawn somewhere, perhaps beside a stream, beneath a weeping willow. I find the tea room, which is actually a small tent. Polly has tucked my rucksack under the table. There is an outside tap, but the door to the toilets is locked, as is the gate into the gardens and the gate to the field where I have been told I can camp.

Momentarily floored, I sit at one of the picnic tables outside the tea tent and wonder what to do. We've walked a fair distance – 20 miles or so – and I know there is nowhere else nearby we can go. I go back to the field gate. It is a wooden, five-bar gate with sheep netting tacked on it, making it hard to climb, but not impossible. 'How are you going to get through?' I ask Teg. For a fairly big dog she can squeeze herself under and through some very small gaps and she manages, with a bit of judicious wriggling, to get under the gate. I heave my rucksack up, balance it on the top bar, scramble up and over and let the rucksack fall into my arms. By the time I've pitched the tent, fed Teg and heated water for my own boil-in-the-bag dinner, I'm ready for bed. There are some very vocal sheep in an adjoining field, but not even their bleating can keep me awake.

THE KINDNESS OF STRANGERS & A NIGHT OF LUXURY

✻

Having fallen asleep so early I'm awake before 5am. It is a grey morning, the light flat, and it is not warm enough to hang about. So I pack up, have a quick breakfast and we are on the road before 6am. We retrace our steps back to the lane and after a mile or two cross a main road. We join a footpath which, according to the map, looks like it weaves through farmland and orchards, so I'm hopeful the walking will be as pleasant as it was yesterday.

But the person who owns this land clearly has no interest in walking, or in encouraging walkers to take this route. The path passes along the edge of a field, but it has been ploughed and planted with barley almost up to the hedge line. We have to pick our way between the crop, a rippling sea of pale gold, and the waist-high nettles in the hedgerow. When we reach the orchards, instead of the path following one of the grassy strips between the trees, we are directed to a narrow, fenced-off section running alongside the orchard and completely overgrown with nettles and brambles. Teg's tail keeps getting snagged on the prickles, much to her annoyance, and when we finally get to the end of the path I'm thoroughly grumpy, covered in welts and scratches and look like I've done battle with a very angry cat.

It has been a while since we've seen our friend the river. At the end of the inhospitable path we get into more open land and pick up a track that takes us back to its bank. The river is below us, out of view for the most part, masked by towering grasses and Himalayan balsam. Teg wants a swim and we find a gap where we can scramble down to a little beach. I sit on a rock throwing a stick into the water for her.

As I watch her doggy-paddling out across its treacly flow, her tail steering her like a rudder, I think about how we've seen the river grow from an insignificant trickle we could cross with a leap, to the broad, confident sweep of water it is now. And how the progress of the river mirrors my own. I remember my nerves on that first morning, the little, niggling worries and doubts that had no real form or substance, but nonetheless flitted around my brain, making me feel on edge and unsure of my capabilities. And now that I have covered more than half the distance, have been lost but not irrecoverably, have camped out alone and in the wilds and not been scared, have, with much kind help, overcome my poor feet failing me, I too feel more confident and more certain that I will, with the river as my guide, get home on foot.

The city of Hereford is up ahead, its suburbs visible across fields long before I reach them. The path and the river skirt along the edge of town. The tower of its famous cathedral, where a copy of the Mappa Mundi is housed, rises up above the trees. I'm tempted to take a detour not, I confess, because of the Mappa Mundi – which is magnificent, but which I've seen before – but because of the cathedral's other great attraction – its café. However, suspecting that Teg won't be allowed in, I carry on, crossing a pretty iron bridge further downstream. I pause to watch a raft of pochard – about fifty smart little russet-headed ducks – diving down among the long tresses of weed that fan out like green streamers, buoyed up by the movement of the water.

We leave Hereford and the Wye behind and plod now, after six hours of walking, into the village of Mordiford where, according to my map, there is a pub. A pub that produces a ham sandwich with proper, hand-cut ham (not that awful, damp, plastic-looking stuff) and tea in a mug. Teg, who has also been given a large piece of ham by the girl behind the bar, decides this is a very good place to be, and spreadeagles herself across the floor with no consideration for anyone who might want to walk past her.

I study the map in an effort to complete the day's walking without any more wrong turns. It doesn't work. It takes three attempts just to find the way out of Mordiford, and Teg loses all faith in me. Finally, I find a man who is out watering his garden and he points me to a path that climbs up through an old orchard, with sheep grazing beneath the trees and mistletoe clinging to the branches. We walk alongside fields of wheat, just turning to a pale, biscuit gold, and in among the robust stalks are delicate poppies of shocking red. Then it's potatoes: row after immaculate row of thick, dark green foliage and clusters of yellow-centred white flowers. We climb a hill, wooded and verdant – a nature reserve – a small, wild oasis amid the carefully cultivated fields of Herefordshire.

We lose the path again as we descend, thanks to really confusing signage, and add a mile, maybe more, to our route before I finally find the right arrow to follow. We are camping on a farm tonight and both of us are quite tired by the time we get there, over 20 miles after setting off this morning. We are greeted with proper, warm hospitality – mugs of tea, Bourbon biscuits and the offer to stay in one of the new eco-cabins they have only just built, rather than pitch a tent. Overhead dark clouds are gathering, threatening rain.

I accept not just the cabin, but the offer of a lift to the local shop where I satisfy a craving for apples (it must be walking through all those orchards) and buy not just the fruit, but a bottle of local juice and a bottle of cider. Teg gets a big chewy bone as her treat and we return for an evening of high decadence. We sit side by side on the sofa, Teg demolishing her bone and me swilling cider and eating boil-in-the-bag curry straight out of the bag, as thunder rumbles and fat drops of rain start to fall on the roof. If there is a heaven, I muse, it might be not unlike this.

DAY 7

FEELING CHEATED

❋

We don't have far to go today and tonight we will be in a B&B, so there is no rush to get going. Instead I sit on the outside step of the cabin with a mug of tea, my bare feet in the wet grass. I listen to the birds and the hum of bees, enjoying the stillness and being still, the sun a warm caress on my face. Last night's rain and the soft morning light make everything sparkle and glitter. Teg is full of beans after her night of luxury and canters around the field in front of the cabin, scattering raindrops and chasing scent trails.

I pack up, lace my boots, lift my rucksack onto my shoulders. It settles easily. After a week of walking it feels part of me, its weight barely noticeable any more. And I feel good, not just physically – it is as if the blisters never happened – but mentally too. I'm clear-headed, undistracted by the 'shoulds' and 'musts' that so often dictate our days. I haven't switched off – I don't feel blank, nor does my mind feel empty, but it feels uncrowded, unburdened, open to suggestion, able to take in and absorb the small happenings of the day. To take pleasure from them.

The path we are to follow is on the other side of the hedge. We leave our tranquil spot, climb the stile at the corner of our field and join a stony track heading uphill. The river curves away in a huge loop and rather than follow it, our route takes the shortcut between the two ends of the loop, climbing up to a crest. At the top we can see for miles and miles, right across Herefordshire's ordered fields to the Forest of Dean and May Hill in the neighbouring county of Gloucestershire.

We descend through pretty woodland full of whispering leaves and birdsong. Ahead of us squirrels dart up the trunks of beech trees, chunter their outrage from the safety of the branches above our heads and out of Teg's reach. We come to the small, picturesque village of How Caple and follow a quiet lane for a mile or two until we rejoin the river. From here, according to the map, we stay alongside the river until we get to Ross on Wye, which is our stop for the night.

It is a long, straight, flat run with fields of wheat and maize on one side and the river on the other. We take our time, saunter, wave to the fishermen on the opposite bank. Teg swims; I paddle. We watch ducks dabbling, a moorhen picking its way across the mud, swans gliding downstream, sweeping gracefully along with the flow of the water. We hear voices and a brace of canoes come into view. 'Any idea how far it is to Ross on Wye?' the rowers call. 'Not far, about three or four miles I think,' I tell them. 'You can see the spire of the church up ahead. Good luck!'

An hour later we see the canoeists again, happily slurping pints in a riverside beer garden. We go to a nearby café and I sit outside with a mug of coffee. We've covered ten miles, have reached our final destination for the day and it is only lunchtime. I have that feeling – a sort of twitchy restlessness – that comes when I don't feel like I've done quite enough, that the day has been too easy. 'We'll make up for it tomorrow,' I tell Teg, and she leans companionably against my legs as I stroke her ears.

DAY 8
BACK TO HOME TURF

✳

We leave the town as the traders are setting up their stalls for the Saturday market. Although Ross sits right on the banks of the river, the walk doesn't follow it. Instead it climbs, then descends, climbs and descends again, over the wooded hills behind the town. The path meanders past hidden cottages and smallholdings. At one point we walk through a small vineyard – neat rows of vines planted along supporting lengths of wire running over the contour of the hill. There are clusters of tiny green fruit just visible between the leaves and twisting green tendrils escaping the confines of their supports. It has the much-cherished appearance of a passion project: that of a person who, I imagine to myself, gets as much enjoyment from coaxing grapes to grow in the Herefordshire soil as he or she does from the sound of a cork being drawn from a bottle and the taste of the fermented juice savoured on the tongue.

It is a true midsummer day – almost a cliché it is so perfect. The sunlight is bright and garish, the sky postcard blue, and it is a Saturday. Until today I have seen only a handful of other people out walking, but now dogs are being exercised, children are being taken out to play, teenagers – doing their Duke of Edinburgh award – straggle along paths in groups, clinging onto their phones and looking at their feet. I realize now what a rare treat it has been to have walked for this long, in countryside as beautiful and accessible as this, and to have seen so few other people. By the time I have made the final descent and am back alongside the river it is mid-morning and the footpath is crowded. I'm at Kerne Bridge which, with its views of the atmospheric ruins of

Goodrich Castle, is undeniably pretty and so popular with canoeists, walkers and families.

I cross over the bridge and take the footpath at the edge of a field of yellow, sickly-smelling rape back to the river. 'Watch out for the nettles!' I'm warned by a group coming towards me, 'they're vicious and they almost block the path.' It's true. The vegetation along this stretch is rampant. Nettles, brambles and Himalayan balsam are all competing with each other, crowding each other out, reaching for the light. It is like something out of a fairytale, and it feels entirely possible that I might, at any moment, push through this spiky barrier of stinging green and stumble upon a turreted tower with Sleeping Beauty in it.

Teg weaves her way through, unbothered by the stings and spikes that are mostly higher than her head. I'm wearing shorts and can't be bothered to dig around in my pack for my trousers, so decide the best tactic is to take the idiom 'grasp the nettle' literally and just march on through. There is a point, when I've been walking for what seems like many minutes and the vegetation shows no sign of thinning out, that I wonder if it is going to be like this all the way to Monmouth. The skin on my legs is tingling – no, burning – from multiple stings and scratches and the only advantage I can see of being on this path is that there are now a lot less people about.

The pay-off for battling on comes not long later. I stumble out of the inhospitable jungle into a green and pleasant land. Grass and buttercups and dandelion clocks. Willow trees with dancing leaves, the river skipping, eddies swirling. The plop and splash of a fish jumping. The sun is high overhead, our shadows foreshortened, defined and dark. Once again there is that heady feeling of liberation and the heightened pleasure of being somewhere hard-won. My stride lengthens, my head lifts, my dog lopes along at my side. All is good in the world. And this is familiar ground. I've walked along this length of the river many times before.

Just upstream from the famous Symonds Yat rock there is a gravel beach and Teg races into the water, barks playfully at the kayakers paddling lazily with the current. I long to follow her and I know I could swim in my clothes, but there are some places and some situations where wearing clothes is to miss the point. So instead I wade in above my knees and enjoy the sensation of the water, cool and soothing against my bare beleaguered skin.

A broken bridge ahead forces us to detour away from the river and we don't join it again until we are at the village of Symonds Yat. There is a pub on the river and next door a tea shop selling ice creams and it appears that all humanity has decided that, on a day like this, this is the place to be. I am caught up, somewhat, in the festive atmosphere and also, I realize, hungry after walking for six hours, so I find a corner of a table in the pub, a place where Teg can tuck herself away from the unbroken flow of feet, and have a late lunch.

The campsite where I am planning to spend the night is not much further on. A friend is also going to be camping there tonight with a group of young people learning bushcraft, and she's invited me to join them. I had envisaged we would be staying in a small woodland clearing with no facilities, so it's a bit of a shock to discover that the campsite stretches along a huge swathe of the river bank and, judging by the number of minibuses and the lines of identical tents, is catering not just for my friend's group, but many more besides. I look at my map. It is not many more miles on to Monmouth. I'd be there in a couple of hours. Maybe Ludo could pick me up? I could stay at home tonight and then he could drop me back in the morning, so I could walk the final leg. There is no phone signal, but I have already decided that I am not up for an evening of ging-gang-goolying and walk swiftly on.

Peace at last. Despite being so close to home, I have never walked this stretch of the river before. Away from the pubs and the tea rooms, it seems no one else much walks it either and Teg and I are alone once more. The bank here is wooded again and our path winds and undulates through the shade of the trees. When it emerges into an open field, the sun is lower in the sky, softer, our shadows longer and paler. I can see the buildings of the Monmouth Rowing Club ahead.

A text pings through in answer to mine and we have a bed for the night. I sit on the steps that lead down to the river, the launching place for canoes and rowing boats, crunching an apple and waiting for our lift. We've walked 18 miles today and have almost done it. Almost completed our journey. Tomorrow when we set off from this spot we'll have just ten miles or so to go. I can't work out whether I feel celebratory or sad.

DAY 9

THE FINAL LEG

✽

Ludo drops me off at the bridge where he picked me up last night. He's working today, so I have all three dogs with me, but my rucksack is at home. It may seem a bit ridiculous, but I almost brought it along – fully packed with the tent and everything – just because it seemed somehow wrong to finish the journey without it. And, if I'm honest with myself, it had become a bit of a badge of honour. It said, 'I'm in it for the long haul, not just a quick saunter to build up an appetite for lunch.' It invited comment and query, gave me licence to say – I admit with some pride – 'I've walked such-and-such a distance today (or since I set off)'. Now, on this idyllic summer morning, I'm just another dog walker enjoying the sunshine. A friend has arranged to meet me at the bridge and walk some of the way with me. And there he is, in a floppy hat, with two of his children, waving a carrier bag at me from the other side of the road.

The dogs are ecstatic to have such young and enthusiastic company and race along the river bank with the children. Sticks are found and thrown into the water, sending the dogs in after them, leaping and splashing. It doesn't take long for the children to wonder why it is the dogs that are having all the fun. Clothes are thrown off, abandoned where they fall, and they too launch themselves into the Wye with squeals of delighted shock as the cool water hits their sun-warmed skin.

I envy them this gloriously untrammelled part of their lives; wonder why, as the years pass, we lose this joyful unselfconsciousness and with it the ability to act instantaneously on a whim without any of the constraints we develop later on in life. We spend a happy, giggly couple of hours along the river, covering almost no distance at all, until they have to head back for lunch. 'We're having sausages. AND ice cream!' And off they scamper, back the way we've come, and the dogs and I continue on, the giggles and shrieks replaced by the rippling flow of the water and the quacking of mallards.

I know this stretch of the river well, have walked it many times in all seasons and all weathers. But every walk is unique, however familiar the route. Today, in the height of summer, we are walking through a tunnel of deep green, the branches overhead arching above us, weighed down by the weight of their leaves. Towering hemlock, ferns and wild grasses jostle for space along both sides of the path. The songbirds are quiet. They've raised their families and now retreat to the hedgerows and thickets to moult and feed up, released from the rigours of parenthood. So our soundtrack is the lazy buzzing of bees and beetles and the scuff of my footsteps on the gravelly track.

'Familiarity breeds contempt', the saying goes, but today it breeds inattentive map reading. I had noted that the route passes through a little hilltop hamlet above the village of Whitebrook and, knowing the way there, take my usual path. It is a steep ascent up a narrow, uneven track with lots of loose stones, runnels and pot holes that makes it hard to get into any sort of rhythm. I push myself on, heart hammering against my ribcage, to the top and cross the green and walk down to find a signpost, the Wye Valley Walk indicated both to the left and to the right, but not from the direction I've come. I stand for a while, pondering how this could be. I look at the map, try to work out where the path is I need to take, conclude it is left from here and then right and assume, therefore, that by cutting across the green I took a shortcut (local knowledge!) and the path actually leads around it, which is why the sign would be pointing right as well as left.

'Glad I've worked that out, dogs,' I say cheerfully, and we turn left and follow the lane, looking for the right-hand turn to take us onto the track. There it is, leading us downhill, which wasn't quite what I was expecting because, according to the map, the path stays quite high above the river. Down and down we go until we meet a lane by a dairy farm – a farm I know – and it is right on the river. Thoroughly confused now, I gaze at the map, turning it this way and that in the hope that looking at it upside down and sideways will somehow make everything clear. Finally, the penny drops. The path I have just walked down is the one I should have taken from the river to the top, instead of taking the path I know and assumed was the right one.

There is only one thing for it. We retrace our steps, up and up, back to the sign and onwards just a short distance and there is the right path, clearly marked, broad and flat beneath the dappled shade of beech trees. I had arranged to meet friends at our local pub for a celebratory cider – imagined I'd be there easily by lunchtime, but I had to text them to confess that I had got lost, practically on my own doorstep, and would be late.

It is hot now, the sun high, squintingly bright, and it is good to be in the cool wooded shade. We meander, enjoying the fact that although we have walked in this forest many times, we have never taken this path before. It reminds me how easy it is to get stuck in our ways – literally in this case – and how a deviation, however slight, can make an adventure of somewhere we think we know well.

After an hour or so we start to switchback downhill and we are back at the river, the pub visible on the opposite bank, a pint of cider waiting for me on the table in the courtyard. It is just three miles or so from here to home. My friends walk with me along the river to the next village. We part, they heading for the café and ice cream, me turning my back on the river and climbing the last hill to get me home.

I cross our neighbour's field to our gate, with its stiff latch and flaking dark green paint. I unlace my boots, peel off my socks, walk barefoot across the grass to the place where we can look out across a richly textured landscape of ridges, embankments, fields and forests. The view that I see every morning I wake up here. The view that made me fall in love with this house and this part of the country. I have no urge to shout or punch the air, or to phone or text anyone to tell them what I've done. This was a very personal quest, something just for me. I don't need congratulations. The quiet sense of achievement I feel, the contentment of completing the test I set myself, is more than enough. And I sit down on the soft, springy turf, my dogs lolling companionably beside me, and relish my luck that a long walk home brings me here.

There is something about rivers that seems to spark in us the desire to follow them. Kevin Parr, angler and author of the book *Rivers Run*, describes the course of a river being a metaphor for life itself, encountering impediments and mingling with tributaries on the journey from source to sea, and tells of the great pleasure he takes in being in the company of the rivers he walks and fishes – a river is one of the most perfect walking companions you can wish for. But there is something else that makes the idea of walking a river so compelling, something about the story it tells, which unfolds with every step you take. In recent times some of the world's greatest rivers have inspired some remarkable journeys and stories. In the mid-Eighties, writer Dennison Berwick walked the length of the Ganges. In 2010, British explorer Ed Stafford completed a walk of over two years following the course of the Amazon. And in 2015, explorer and broadcaster Levison Wood became the first person ever to walk the length of the world's longest river, the Nile.

It was seeing a river on a map that inspired Ursula Martin to start walking too. She was in Spain, the province of Galicia, visiting her sister. She planned to stay a month or two and ended up staying most of a year. She had no fixed plans, was at something of a crossroads in her life. Her childhood hadn't been a very happy one. A difficult home life made her awkward and nervous, so she didn't fit in at school either.

At 19 she had left home, left school. 'I had no direction, I didn't know what I was doing. I had no idea who I was or what I was.' She had gone back to Wales where she had been born, ended up in Cardiff, moved in with a man, worked in an office. When that relationship ended and she met someone else, she followed him to Aberystwyth. She felt she had no control over anything, that circumstances just dictated whatever happened to her next. The new relationship she found herself in was abusive and when it ended she realized, in her words, 'how really messed up I was'. She took time off work, hitch-hiked to Spain. 'If you'd asked me what the hell I was doing at the time, I'm not sure what I would have told you, because I didn't actually know.'

But then she saw the river on the map and a thought popped into her head. 'Why don't I follow it and see where it goes?' She had never done anything like this before. It was curiosity, an adventurous spirit that was emerging now that she had no limits on her time and was free. The 250-mile journey took her a month; was, she says, a journey of discovery, the excitement of finding out what was around the next corner.

And when she finished she felt not just a great sense of achievement – 'I've walked the length of that river! I can point to it on a map and say I've walked that!' – but also the deep satisfaction of getting to know the river in all its guises and the companionship it offered her. Never once, throughout the entire walk, did she feel lonely. Instead it gave her a purpose, it challenged her, left her with a sense of power she hadn't had before. And the confidence to keep pushing herself. So when one of her sister's friends told her that she'd heard about a kayak journey down the Danube, Ursula's response was 'Oh! I think I'll do that next.'

The three-month paddle left her fitter than she had ever been; 'I was crowing about being a smaller dress size!' She decided to stay on, take up an offer of house-sitting in Bulgaria and planned, eventually, to walk back to Britain. But then she became aware of what she describes as a 'funny little pain' in her stomach. A pain she didn't recognize. And because she didn't know what it was, she didn't worry about it. She had, after all, just kayaked the Danube. Her body was strong and tough. And she was only 32 years old. So it couldn't be anything serious. Two days before she hitched back to the UK for a family Christmas, she spent several hours helping a friend carrying and stacking wood. She noticed that if she held the wood against one hip it hurt. She simply switched it to the other side.

It was at her aunt's house that she became overcome by the sensation that she wasn't able to bend, that there was something inside her, a sort of bloating or pressure. 'Go to the doctor,' her aunt advised. He diagnosed a large ovarian cyst and she was sent for a scan. It turned out to be very large indeed, the size of a watermelon. 'So I googled "ovarian cyst", found out I'd be in for some major abdominal surgery, but thought OK, well, I'll just get that done and go back to Bulgaria.'

But after surgery, further tests revealed that what Ursula had was not a benign cyst. It was Stage 1a ovarian cancer. Cancer is described as Stage 1a when it has been diagnosed before it has had the chance to spread to other organs. And it is often curable. In a way, Ursula was lucky. She didn't recognize the symptoms, but because her tumour was encapsulated within the ovary, it couldn't spread. That, she says, is the reason she is alive today.

What followed was a rollercoaster of follow-up treatment and the long, long road to recovery. Walking became her way of healing herself, of regaining the strength her body had lost. 'You can do it with no equipment, no palaver, no fuss, straight from your front door. When you are reduced in the way I was after cancer, you can still walk.' But it wasn't easy. She started by aiming for the postbox 100 metres from her house, writing postcards to friends as an incentive to get her there. It was physically agonizing, but mentally restorative.

'I felt calm when I was walking. The rhythm of my body going plod, plod, and just being outside is so wonderful. My mind felt freer.' But there was another reason for Ursula to get walking again. 'Cancer stopped my life as it was, but didn't give me another one to continue with. I had to make one up and I chose to walk.'

Six months after surgery, she was due back in Bristol for a check-up. She was living in mid-Wales, not far from where I started my walk along the River Wye. The walk along the River Severn starts in the same place and finishes in Bristol. It made perfect sense to Ursula to walk to her appointment. And she did. And when she was given the all-clear, told to come back again in another three months, she walked home, along the Wye this time. A round trip of 400 miles. And that got her brain whirring – questions and thoughts racing. 'What's happening? What do I want to do with my life? What is the point of me?'

And at the same time, struck by the realization that she is one of the lucky few – that ovarian cancer has a 35 per cent survival rate and she is one of the survivors – there was the compulsion to do something, because 'when you've had cancer, it becomes your issue. I really cared, I really wanted to raise awareness, to tell other women about the symptoms so they might spot it in time and survive too.' And she wanted to raise money, for the charities that had supported her. And that was when she knew what she was going to do next.

Once again, she would walk the length of the Severn to Bristol, but instead of returning home, she decided to follow the Offa's Dyke Path, 177 miles from Chepstow to Prestatyn. From there she would pick up the Welsh Coastal Path and follow it back to Bristol in time for her next appointment six months later. But it didn't seem to be enough of a distance to fill the time, so she kept adding routes and paths: Glyndwr's Way, the Cambrian Way, pairs of rivers that, like the Severn and Wye, would allow her to follow one from coast to source and the other back to the sea. More by accident than intent she realized that what she was planning to do was to walk Wales.

Wales isn't a large country. At just over 8,000 square miles, it is marginally bigger than Lake Ontario, but smaller than Clark County, Nevada. But as Ursula totted up the mileage it became apparent she had set herself quite a task. The total was 3,300 miles. If you were to walk that distance in a straight line from London heading due south, you'd get to the equator. It is a long way. And she had no time to do any training, concentrating her efforts instead on working to earn money to fund her walk. She worked out a plan – the mileage she would need to do to make sure she made her next hospital appointment.

The first month she would aim to do ten miles a day, the following five months she would do fifteen a day, although she would have to do twenty on the final day to get her back to Bristol on time. She had no idea if she could do it because, as she said, she had no idea really of what she was attempting. 'I was a plump, unpractised woman in a raincoat and a woollen hat,' was how she described herself as she left the mid-Wales market town of Machynlleth, clutching a bamboo pole topped by a Welsh flag and waved off by a small group of her friends.

Her account of the walk in her blog and later her book *One Woman*

Walks Wales is breathtaking in its honesty. Her descriptions of the pain, of the exertion, of the brutality of the weather, of her fallibility, are raw and often heartrending. I go to meet her, not long after I've completed my own walk, and we sit in the slightly ramshackle office where she rents space to write, with mugs of tea from the café downstairs and doughnuts made at the bakery where she now works.

Remembering the pain I had suffered from the blisters, and the despair I felt at the thought of not being able to carry on, I asked her how and why she carried on when she was told, having walked five hundred miles, that she was in real danger of doing permanent damage to her feet. She was suffering from more than blisters. She had a bruised sort of ache underneath the arch of her foot that spread out to her heel, making her foot tender at the start of a day's walking and by the end sending shooting pain up her leg every time her foot touched the ground. She'd looked up the symptoms: plantar fasciitis, a common condition that can usually be eased by resting, but Ursula couldn't rest.

She was desperate, desperate not to let go of the idea of this walk, the thing she describes as being 'something to fix on to in the aftermath of my illness, a thread I could follow into the future'. But she was struggling to cover more than four miles in a day. There was no way she could walk the distance she had set herself in the time she had allowed. Apart from the debilitating pain in her foot, she was absolutely worn out. 'A lot of walking is an utter empty-brained exhausted nothingness,' she tells me. And the occasional day off wasn't enough to restore her strength. But lurking was the fear, a fear strong enough to make her keep going. 'If I couldn't walk, I had no idea what to do next.'

It was the advice of her brother that helped her continue. She had phoned him, asked him what to do. 'I'm scared the whole thing's collapsing around me and I've put so much effort into telling people about it and trying to raise money and I can't just stop. What a let-down that would be, what a failure, what a disappointment; the whole walk disappears because I can't do it anymore.' And her brother told her to stop worrying about the targets she had set herself, reminded her that they were self-imposed, that no one else was going to worry about whether she did the walk in a few months or a few years. 'Just go for a walk,' he said.

And so she continued, walking slowly along the Conwy Valley, not allowing it to matter what distance she covered in a day. And there were times when she struggled with the difficulty of it, alone with her thoughts in the hot sun or pouring rain, the pain always there. 'Then a car would stop, or someone would recognize me, tell me I was doing really well, that they were inspired or amazed or other superlative compliments that I was embarrassed to hear. It helped to break me out of the hard slog, give me a little boost, know that what I was doing was acknowledged.'

I am staggered, I tell her, by her steely determination to keep going when it seemed so much of the time she wasn't able to enjoy what she was doing, but she refutes my assessment. 'I never not enjoyed it. Even when I hit another low point in the mountains. I was almost halfway to my goal, but winter was coming and I'd climb one mountain and then there'd be another one and another one, and it was physically the hardest part of the whole route. But even then I never thought I wasn't going to keep going. It was a wonderful experience. There would be rain in my face, frozen red hands, deep, deep exhaustion, and I would savour it all because, despite everything, I was deeply, deeply happy.'

And I believe her, I understand, because when I hit my low point, was miserable and hurting, I longed for the pain to end, not the walk. And word was spreading about her and what she was doing. Social media, so often divisive, came into its own. She was offered places to stay by total strangers. People bought her meals in cafés, a pick-up truck came towards her, stopped, asked what she was doing and when she explained, the driver put £20 in her donation tin. 'There you go. My dad had cancer.'

It was just before Christmas when Ursula had completed 2,000 miles. She celebrated by buying a glittery top hat and party supplies in a fancy-dress shop in Llanfairfechan, a small town on the North Wales coast; sat by the sea for ten minutes, took a selfie and felt, suddenly, invincible. She'd walked 2,000 miles and nothing was going to stop her now. But then a missed phone call from an unknown number changed everything. The message on her phone was from a policeman. Her beloved brother – the man who had told her, when she was at her lowest ebb, to 'just go for a walk' – had had a car accident, was in a critical condition in hospital. He couldn't talk, couldn't walk, he was broken and brain-damaged and no one knew whether he would live or die. Ursula's focus shifted. No longer was she thinking about her walk. Every moment was spent with her brother, willing him to recover.

And gradually, gradually, he did. Seven weeks after the accident, he was able to go home and Ursula was, in her words, free to return to her old life. But what was that? It was walking. Walking had been a healing process for her, physically and mentally. Now she was walking to feel better about her brother, about what he had suffered and how it had left its mark.

And there was another challenge. Because the walk had taken so much longer than she had planned she was broke – her savings all gone, despite all the help she had received from friends and strangers. Her sister lent her the money to help her finish but, she admitted, she was tired of trying to live on a budget of less than £50 a week, felt hollow and sad, depleted by her brother's accident. She wanted to hide herself away, but she also wanted to walk because she felt this challenge she had set herself was the only tangible thing she had in her life.

It was the Wye Valley Walk that took her home, 17 months after she set off. She, too, felt torn about reaching the end. 'I didn't want the end to happen. I needed it to happen. I couldn't stop it from happening. I loved this, and yet I needed it to stop.' Sobs welled up as she walked down Machynlleth High Street, friends and supporters waiting, blowing horns and cheering. 'I'd set out on a journey to walk an unthinkable, eyebrow-raising number of miles and I – silly, vague, plump, unprepared, determined, strong, stubborn me – had actually bloody done it.'

Ursula's walk raised £11,000 for ovarian cancer charities. It showed her what she was capable of, what she could withstand. And it gave her something she had never felt she had had before, something that was uniquely hers: an identity. 'I will always be the woman who walked.'

AUTUMN

September

*

I look at my clock. It is just past 5am. Outside the thin curtains that cover the old sash windows of my hotel room, light is seeping into the sky. Dark still, but not middle-of-the-night dark. Teg senses I'm awake, sashays up to the bed and sticks her nose in my ear. A large front paw is placed defiantly on the duvet, followed by another. She stands up on her back legs, leans over me, breathes doggy breath into my face. 'Bugger off!' I tell her. She waves her tail in reply and nuzzles my ear again.

We're in mid-Wales, a village called Devil's Bridge. Tourists have been coming here since Victorian times – Wordsworth among them – drawn by the spectacular waterfalls that tumble down the Rheidol Gorge. Beyond the village, with its tea rooms and gift shops, there are scattered farms and settlements, sheep grazing the soft, voluptuous curves of the Cambrian mountains. And weaving its way between the grass-covered slopes is the Elan Valley, a landscape of breathtaking, heart-racing magnificence which, in 2015, was awarded International Dark Sky Park status. That is why Teg and I are here. We spent last night in the company of two amateur astronomers and a million, billion stars and planets. I was introduced to Saturn and its famous rings. I've seen pictures of it many times, but to see it for real, through the lens of a telescope, is wonderful – emotional, even. We were lucky to have such clear, cloud-free skies. It had been a wet August and there was much hope pinned on September making up for the lack of sunshine.

There seems little point in staying in bed, so I get up, pack and together Teg and I creep out of the sleeping hotel. It's light now, the sky that washed-out blue of early morning, the promise of a fine day. 'I know where we'll go, Teg,' I say, and we take the narrow road between woodland and fields to the Hafod Estate. I discovered the estate the last time I was working in this part of Wales. It was once a hunting lodge but when it was bought by a nobleman called Thomas Johnes in the late 18th century, its land was transformed. Johnes was a great fan of the Picturesque movement and wanted Hafod to be a showcase. He planted over a thousand acres of forest, laid out walks and rides through the woods and along the rivers and streams that ran through his land. He even had a tunnel dug through a rocky outcrop to enable visitors to see the spectacular waterfall – known as the Cavern Cascade – that was hidden behind it.

Today the mansion where he lived has gone, demolished in the Fifties, having stood derelict for decades. The estate church is still there, the stables, a few scattered cottages, but anyone can drive to the car park and set out along one of the marked trails that were once walked by the great and the good of the Victorian era. At this hour the car park is empty, so Teg and I have this wildly beautiful place all to ourselves. A heavy dew has fallen and it is our footsteps that are the first to leave a visible trail through the long grass of the meadow.

The sun is up now, its rays casting soft light, filtering through the branches of the stately larch, oak and beech trees, the legacy of the land's former owner and living embodiment of his Picturesque vision. We walk along a valley, glistening with dew and sunlight, cross a river and climb up a slope of thick, tufted grass and the stalky remnants of wild flowers. And stretched between the blades of grass, the stems of cow parsley and buttercup, are hundreds of cobwebs, all encrusted and sparkling with dew drops. It is a sight worth pausing for. Even Teg, who has been scattering about – nose to the ground in search of voles or whatever else might be hidden in the clumps of grass – is, for a moment, still, apart from the quiver of her pink and black nose.

We walk for hours, savouring the sun and the solitude, the rare treat of having nothing pressing or pending. We explore; follow paths with no thought where they might lead. We climb and scramble up banks, through the trees, then clamber back down to follow the lazy flow of a stream. I remember another early morning walk the last time we were here, noticing, as I followed Teg along a river, a pile of clothes tucked at the foot of a tree on the bank. And feeling a jolt of concern, walking on, wondering. Then seeing up ahead a figure in the water, tresses of brown hair streaked with grey fanning out behind her; pale, naked limbs moving in unison beneath the tea-coloured surface of the river. It was a scene of perfect serenity, a private interlude between woman and water. I immediately felt intrusive and, not wanting to break the spell she had cast for herself, turned away and took another path.

It occurs to me now that I could do the same, slip between the branches of the trees along the bank and lower myself into the shallows, wade out to the middle and drift with the current, but I don't. The urge isn't strong enough and I'm enjoying the walking too much. It is only when my tummy growls that I realize we have been walking for over three hours and neither of us has had any breakfast. We follow the gravel track back to where I left the car, reluctant to leave this oasis of solitude, but equally desperate for a mug of tea and a sausage sandwich.

8TH–12TH SEPTEMBER

OLD FRIENDS AND THE SEA:

WALKING TO CATCH UP

✳

I'm away again, working in Cornwall for a couple of weeks. Ludo has been working locally enough to home that he can come back at the end of the day, but often well into the evening, and for the last month, maybe more, we have barely seen each other. When we do, there is just time to deal with the various issues and bits of admin that clutter all of our lives and then, before we know it, one or both of us is gone again. So to escape the chores and to-do lists that await us at home, I have suggested he comes to Cornwall. 'I'll rent a cottage or something and we can have a long weekend, see friends we haven't seen for ages, eat pasties, go paddling. Do Cornish things.'

The night before he arrives I stay with friends who live in a small coastal town opposite St Michael's Mount. We sit in their garden, which slopes up behind the house and from where we can see the sea over the roofs and between the chimneys of the houses in front. We are drinking gin, ice clinking in the glasses, gallantly pretending it is still summer, but all wearing hoodies and sweatshirts against the keen breeze blowing in off the sea. There are dark clouds gathering on the horizon and before long we are skittering back to the warmth of the kitchen, clutching our drinks, rain drops hammering down in our wake.

The Indian summer we all hoped for, rather felt we deserved, is yet to materialize. After that first magical September day it has been grey, wet and blustery for much of the time. Autumn feels closer than summer. The leaves are already beginning to lose their lustre and look tired. The bracken on the hillsides is getting brittle, the filigree-edged leaves already turning brown. But there is a bumper crop of blackberries and sloes and it is impossible to walk without being assailed by thoughts of crumble and gin.

The next morning the wind has calmed, the rain blown over and I let myself out of the house for a run along the coast path to Penzance. The road is shiny from the rain, the sea and sky a washed-out palette of greys and blues and it is impossible to tell where one ends and the other begins. Herring gulls wheel overhead and strut thuggishly along the sea front, handsome and malevolent. I run through a car park where people in campervans are emerging through their sliding doors, mugs of coffee in hand, to lean against their bonnets and look out to sea. There are a couple of dog walkers, a Lycra-clad cyclist looking at a map, but otherwise there is no one much about on this unremarkable morning.

I follow the South West Coast Path between the sea and railway line. This is Britain's longest national trail, running for 630 miles from Minehead in Somerset along the coast of North Devon and Cornwall and around Land's End before following the south coast to Poole in Dorset. The trail existed long before it was given its designation. The coastguard originally carved out the route, checking the hundreds of bays, inlets and river mouths for evidence of smugglers. Walk its whole length and you will climb four times the height of Everest, but the section I'm on is mercifully flat, if not very pretty.

I turn around at the railway station and retrace my steps. I'm always surprised how different the same places look when viewed from another direction. Surprised too by how calm the sea is this morning. I was expecting the bay to be frothing with white horses – snappy waves, brown with sand, to be pounding the shore – but instead it is benign and glassy, barely bothering to lap or ripple. There are ships moored off Penzance harbour, sandpipers busying about at the water's edge, but St Michael's Mount is almost obscured, ghostly and ethereal in its cloak of mist.

'See you tomorrow,' as I depart my friend's house again, after breakfast and a pootle along the beach with their dog looking for 'fairy glass' – bits of broken bottle that have been tumbled in the waves and roughed up by the sand until they are smoothed-edged, gem-like pebbles hidden among the broken limpet shells and bladderwrack. We missed their wedding and so have planned to get together with Ludo too, and walk from the cove where they got married, so we can see it, and from there along the cliffs to a favourite café for lunch before looping back inland across the fields.

I drive to meet Ludo on Cornwall's north coast. He's brought the dogs and they need a leg stretch before we get to our rented cottage. I've got a map, found a circular walk that should take a couple of hours. The wind has picked up again, is strong enough to lift grains of sand from the crest of the dunes and send them swirling into the air, stinging our faces. We turn our shoulders to the wind, walk as fast as we can through the loose dry sand shifting beneath our feet. Beyond the dunes is wiry coastal grass atop a plateau of rock that ends in a dramatic, sheer drop, plunging down to meet the sea, boiling and foaming at its base.

We follow the cliff edge, swing around with our backs to the wind and look out over Newquay's wide expanse of golden sand below us, deserted save for a couple of tiny figures in brightly coloured raincoats, hoods flapping wildly behind them. We turn again, are offered a brief respite by a more sheltered path running alongside a hedge. It brings us back to the dunes and we run the gauntlet of the whirling grains, arriving back at the car buffeted and breathless. 'I've booked a pub for supper,' I say. 'Good,' says Ludo, 'all this sea air has made me hungry.'

The next day we follow our friend's van down a narrow lane to a car park in the corner of a field. 'Welcome to Cornwall!' they laugh, hugging Ludo in the rain that is blowing in horizontally off the sea. 'Lovely day for it!' But even the weather can't take away the beauty of where we are. Prussia Cove was once home to the Carter family, infamous smugglers, and it is tucked away, discreet and hidden beneath the cliffs. Above it is an estate of a few houses, dotted among the rocks and trees. It is magical, deeply romantic, the perfect place for two people whose lives are so intrinsically linked to the sea to marry.

We leave the shelter of the cove, climb up to the cliff path and are hit by the full force of the wind and rain, but somehow it doesn't matter. We are in holiday mode, we're with people we love and we've never been here before, so the exhilaration of the unknown makes the weather exhilarating too. I've never yearned to live by the sea the way

I know many do, but whenever I visit the coast I am reminded how much I enjoy the sounds of gulls and waves and wind, the salty tang of the air, the uninterrupted expanse of the horizon. And today there is the added pleasure of walking with friends, catching up.

We pick blackberries by the handful, munch them as we walk to stave off hunger until we reach the café, sodden and dripping. We order mugs of tea. There's hot chocolate for the children, piled with marshmallows and whirls of cream. We sit huddled together on slightly too short benches, companionable, ruddy cheeked, bright eyed. Food arrives. We taste each other's choices, eat the things others don't want, share cakes. Steam rises off our wet clothes, fugging up the windows.

Deirdre Heddon (who calls herself Dee) is Professor of Contemporary Performance at Glasgow University. She wrote an essay entitled *Walking and Friendship* that was inspired by an idea she had to celebrate her 40th birthday.

> *I decided to throw something of a peripatetic party and mailed forty invitations to people I wanted to spend more time with, inviting them to take me on a walk of their choice.*

This lovely idea – I wish I'd had it myself – has taken her places close to home and further afield and her walks have been with old friends, new acquaintances and people of all ages, from young children to septuagenarians.

I have been taken on favourite walks, familiar walks, new walks, desired walks, memorial walks, nostalgic walks, short walks and long walks.

Her essay begins quoting the many people who have extolled the virtues of walking alone. But many of those famed solitary walkers – including Thoreau and William Hazlitt, author of the 1821 walking book *On Going a Journey* – enjoyed walking with company too. There are merits and advantages to both, although to quote Bayard Henderson Christy, who in 1920 wrote *Going Afoot: A Book on Walking*, nothing is more important than the choice of companions. I suppose that is true of anything, but walking with the wrong person – or, as I have discovered, the wrong number of people – can turn a walk into a trial.

Walking in a large group is something I have never done, mainly because I am not a 'large group' sort of person. Why have twelve people around a dinner table? You can't talk to them all beyond a quick 'Hello! How are you?' before you sit down. Six is much better – everyone can talk to everyone else as well as all being able to participate in one conversation. And there's less washing up at the end. I would say the same about walking.

I have done two walks with large groups and I confess I didn't enjoy either of them. And yet there are walking groups the world over and for many they offer the relaxation of a walk being guided – no need to bother about maps and getting lost – and the sociability of being with other people who also like walking. But in my experience, too many people mean too many variables. For a start, walking may well be the only thing you have in common. And everyone has their own walking pace, and they vary wildly, so those who like to walk fast feel held back by those who like to take their time and they, in turn, feel rushed or harassed if they think they are holding everybody up. And people have different interests, different things they want to stop and look at, different levels of fitness, different expectations.

But walking, like we are today, with two dear friends, their children and a happy band of dogs is the epitome of the perfect companionable walk, as described so beautifully by Heddon:

> *A feature of the companionable walk is its collaborative, inter-active nature, an activity of mutuality. Whilst walkers might accommodate each other's pace, the ground accommodates particular forms or shapes of companionship, of being-together. There are walks that contain shared memories; walks that allow the sharing of one's memories with another; and walks that prompt resonances and contrast, likenesses and differences. The physicality required by the walk – the walk's materiality – also prompts certain forms of companionship. The path is wide enough to accommodate us side-by-side; or its narrowness forces us to walk one behind the other – which usually prompts silence; or the incline is so steep that talking and breathing become laboured – but at the same time, the incline prompts regular, shared breaks – time taken to look back at the view, sometimes to share a warm flask of tea.*

By the time we've drunk the last of our tea, mopped up the final cake crumbs, the rain has eased and our coats have dripped themselves dry, leaving small puddles on the café floor. The sun remains stubbornly hidden, but there is a glimmer of brightness in the sky. We sally forth across the fields beneath scudding clouds, children and dogs running ahead. We call in to see a friend of our friends who lives in a pretty cottage just off the footpath. We are greeted by more dogs and offers of more tea – 'Or wine! There's wine!' – but we are replete, we say, so instead he pulls on a coat and joins us and together in a cheerful, companionable gang, we walk the fields and lanes back to where we started.

In between walks, Ludo and I feel no compunction to do anything much else. Our cottage has a kitchen full of light, doors that open onto a small garden and a big table where we can sit, read the papers, do the crossword, spread out maps and plan the next day's adventure. We eat in, share a bottle of wine, talk. It is much-needed time together – long overdue.

We are having breakfast when a text pings up on my phone. 'I think we'll need to change our plans. Too windy today to walk on the cliffs. Shall I pop in when I've dropped the kids at school?' The text is from a woman I have never met. She is a writer and some months ago she interviewed me for a Cornish magazine. We hit it off and when I said we were planning to be in Cornwall in September, as well as helping us find somewhere to stay and recommending beaches and pubs and running routes, she offered to take us on one of her favourite walks. But she was right. It is incredibly windy today. I went running early this morning and even away from the coast I was buffeted about.

Fiona arrives and the three of us pore over the map. Like farmers, for whom the weather really matters, the people I know who live near the coast take note of the day's wind direction, tides, weather fronts and take them into account, plan accordingly. She suggests we head down to the south coast, which will be more protected from the wind. The walk she proposes starts in the wooded grounds of a National Trust house, tucked down the side of a valley above a lake.

The paths here are broad enough for the three of us to walk abreast and our conversation is effortless, free ranging; the silences, when they come, are more natural pauses, moments of contemplation. They don't feel awkward, there is no pressure to fill the gap as there might have been had we been sitting around a table or perched politely on someone else's sofa. It strikes me that walking is a gentle, non-confrontational way to get to know someone, a way of sharing time and energy with a stranger that is less pressured, literally less restrictive, than being in a room.

We emerge from the shelter of the woods onto a cliff-top path. It is blustery, waves crash against the cliff face in an explosion of spray and foam. We walk down towards what I think is a beach but as we get closer I see is actually a sand bar between the lake we have been walking alongside since the start and the sea. The dogs, excited by the wind and the sand, skitter away, chase each other, race towards the waves then retreat, hastily, as the water roars down, thuds onto the sand, hissing as it's drawn back down the beach by the power of the following wave.

We curve around the bottom of the lake and follow its shoreline back inland. After lunch we drop Fiona back to pick up her kids from school. Despite it being the first time we have all met our goodbyes are casual; there's no finality about them. They are the goodbyes you use with friends who you know you will see again.

It's our final day in the cottage. Early tomorrow morning I will drive to another part of Cornwall and meet up with the people I'm working with for the rest of the week and Ludo will drive home to Wales. Today it's just the two of us. Ludo wants to visit the studio of the sculptor Barbara Hepworth. I've been before but will happily go again. Art has so much more meaning and resonance, it seems to me, when it can be seen in the home, studio and garden of the person who created it. It was in 1949 that Hepworth bought a studio in the middle of St Ives, saying, 'Finding Trewyn Studio was sort of magic. Here was a studio, a yard, and garden where I could work in open air and space.'

She turned the garden into a gallery with bold, structural planting to perfectly complement her striking, unmistakable works in bronze and stone. Before she died in a fire at her studio 25 years after moving to St Ives, she had stated in her will that she wanted her house and garden to be a museum for her work. It has been set up with the lightest of touches, so that as we walk the paths that twist and turn around the garden, pausing to gaze at and run admiring hands over the lines and planes of her evocative sculptures set among the dark green foliage, it feels almost possible that we might bump into her, head encased in a flowing scarf and a tumbler of whisky in hand.

We carry on walking through the narrow streets of St Ives, pause at a bakery and buy a pasty, which we share as we watch the surfers in the bay. We finish the day on the beach. It is still windy, but more stiff breeze than howling gale. This beach, on the outskirts of Hayle where we've been staying, is not an intimate cove or picture-postcard bay, but altogether wilder. There are miles of uninterrupted buff-coloured sand, glistening and hard-packed by the retreating tide. We walk for an hour or more, throwing frisbees for the dogs, taking off our boots and running, laughing, into the sea. We return, flushed and windblown, salt on our lips and in our hair, eat the leftovers in the fridge, finish the wine. We feel tired, that satisfying sort of tiredness that comes at the end of a day of fresh air and exercise. Before we go to bed we give each other cards and small presents, the final element of today's celebration. We've been married for 25 years.

KILLING TWO BIRDS WITH ONE STONE

*

It is my first day at home in weeks. I return to a pile of unopened post and irksome admin as well as the usual chores that are mundane but somehow satisfying at the same time. There's washing to be done, the chicken shed needs mucking out, the sheep moving to another field. There's not much in the fridge and we're running out of dog food. I have a meeting scheduled and the dogs need walking and on days like this time seems to race away. 'How,' I mutter to myself as I race back with a car full of shopping, dump it in the kitchen, haul a load of washing out of the machine, peg it out on the line, load another, return to the kitchen to unpack the shopping, 'am I going to fit it all in?' The dogs are twitchy and restless. They need to go out, but there's not enough time to give them a walk before I need to leave for my meeting. Unless...

I park next to Ruth's car. We shake hands, say our hellos. 'Thank you so much for doing this,' I say. 'Not at all,' she says. 'It's a great excuse to get out of the office.' I open the boot of the car. The dogs jump out and disappear among the trees and we follow them.

Ruth has kindly agreed to combine our meeting with a dog walk and we've arranged to set off from the edge of the woods midway between her office and my house. It is a rather pleasant late September afternoon. Soft sun, gauzy cloud, the smell of autumn in the air. The meeting is to explore ways we might work together. We need to find out what each can offer the other, establish our aims and goals and come up with ideas. It proves surprisingly productive and constructive, despite the fact that we are not in an office and there are no computers, or handouts, or flip charts or PowerPoint presentations.

I shouldn't be surprised, really. The idea of having meetings while walking is not new. Steve Jobs and Mark Zuckerberg are well-known proponents of the walk-talk meeting, but they are not trailblazers in this respect either. Aristotle and Plato were doing it over two thousand years ago, but we humans do have a habit of reinventing the wheel.

Nilofer Merchant is a highly successful business woman who has made a name for herself as a motivational writer and speaker. She was ranked as one of the top fifty global management thinkers in 2015 and 2017, thanks to her reputation of taking 'wild ideas' and making them mainstream. She did a TED Talk in 2013, wearing a sassy pair of cowboy boots, and opened with the line 'What you are all doing now is killing you.' We sit, she told her seated audience, on average over nine hours a day. More hours than we sleep.

She quotes Dr James Levine, one of the leading experts in obesity in the US, who says sitting is the new smoking. Our sedentary lifestyles are having a marked and dramatic effect on our health. Too much sitting contributes not just to obesity, but to heart disease, certain cancers such as colon and breast cancer, and Type 2 diabetes. It is of such real concern that Public Health England prescribed walking meetings as a way of combatting the number of hours we spend sitting down. 'Get out for a walk, get some fresh air for a meeting,' urged Public Health England chief Duncan Selbie in a speech in 2017.

Nilofer, too, did a lot of sitting, but all that changed when someone

– like me – had a dog that needed walking and asked if Nilofer would mind having their scheduled meeting while taking the dog around the park. 'It changed my life,' she announced to the audience. 'And I took the idea and made it my own.' Her meetings now all take place while walking and she claims to regularly cover twenty to thirty miles a week. She trots out a lot of rather pat comments – 'fresh air drives fresh thinking', 'the amazing thing about getting out of the box is that it leads to out-of-the-box thinking' – but they are not without basis.

There have been a number of academic studies looking at the effects of walking on the way we think. One, undertaken by Ruth Ann Atchley, David Strayer and Paul Atchley, published in 2012, set out to discover what the effects of a four-day hike – without mobile phones or other electronic devices – would have on the participants' cognition and creative ability. Before setting off, those taking part were given tests designed to assess their creativity and problem-solving abilities. After four days of walking in the wilderness, they were tested again, and the results were astonishing. Their scores were 50 per cent higher than before they set off for their walk.

My meeting with Ruth does exactly what we hoped: spawns ideas that leave us both feeling galvanized and excited. I can't say whether we wouldn't have come up with the same ideas had we been sitting in an office, but it was infinitely nicer to be outside. And the dogs have had a good run at the same time. Everyone is happy.

The flamboyant 'Godfather of Funk', musician George Clinton, wrote the title track for Funkadelic's 1970 album *Free Your Mind… and Your Ass Will Follow*. But perhaps what we all need to do is take his advice and switch it around – Free your ass… and your mind will follow.

October

THE SMALL BUT DELICIOUS TRIUMPH OF OVERCOMING A DEMON

✳

I've set myself a test. A few years ago, I did a 20-km run called Offa's 'Orror. Organized by the Chepstow Harriers, it is described as 'challenging'. It is all off-road, on tracks and paths through fields and woodland, some of them – many of them – breathtakingly steep. I'd trained hard. A month before, I did a cross-country half marathon through the Forest of Dean in a fairly respectable time (for me) and, more importantly, really enjoyed it. I had never done an organized run on this scale before, with several hundred complete strangers. I almost always run by myself. I prefer to. It is not just that I am self-conscious about my ability – or lack of it – it is also that I find running, like walking, a time to think. Or rather, not think.

More often than not, I run first thing in the morning, before I do anything else. I don't clutter up my head by looking at my phone or computer, I don't drink or eat, I just go. And over the course of the run, in between the slightly indignant questions to myself – 'Why isn't this getting any easier?' being the most frequent one – thoughts will pop into my head, some fleetingly, others stick around for longer and develop. But I never consciously decide what to think about, I don't have a mental checklist. And sometimes the things I think about while I'm running are things I never give another thought to, yet sometimes they will be thoughts that become actions. The main thing, though, is it doesn't matter. What matters is that when I finish a run, red-faced and mud-spattered, I feel physically and mentally capable of taking on the day.

So running for a reason other than kick-starting the morning in the fresh air and returning clear-headed and – let's be honest – feeling virtuous, has never really been on my agenda. I'm not interested in turning something I enjoy into something competitive and I am more than aware of my limitations – I'm never going to be a Paula Radcliffe. So I'm not entirely sure, even now, why I thought I would take on Offa's 'Orror. It certainly wasn't because I thought I'd try to win it, come home with a cup or a medal, or whatever the winner gets. It might simply have been because someone said it was hard – up there with the toughest half marathons in the country – and some belligerent part of me thought, 'How hard can it be?'

The short answer is 'very hard'. I don't know why or how I could have imagined it to be anything less, except that I was buoyed up by how much I'd enjoyed the Forest of Dean half marathon. Also, Offa's 'Orror was on my doorstep. I'd run much of the route while I was training, so I felt completely prepared and quietly confident.

We all talk about and experience 'off-days', days that for no particular reason anyone can pinpoint things don't quite work out or don't go according to plan, and I'm not sure 'getting out of bed on the wrong side' explains them either. I got out of bed on the same side I always do on the morning of Offa's 'Orror, laced up my trusty running shoes and drove the few short miles to the village over the river where the race was to start. It was a rather drizzly, dank April morning.

As there had been before the Forest of Dean half marathon, there were people in the car park stretching and bouncing about, some of them sporting the slightly extraordinary compression socks I had never seen or heard of before. I wondered, as I looked down at my own very ordinary, bought-in-a-pack-of-three sports socks, whether they might be the reason I was yet to break a land speed record. A shout by someone with a clipboard gathered us together for a pre-race briefing. I felt a flutter of excitement. I can do this. Am doing this. And then we were off, racing out of the car park and straight up the first of many, many hills.

I didn't come last, but I think I was second last.

Sometimes doing something hard, something challenging, is truly uplifting. You feel buoyed up by the effort and the hardship and the adrenalin coursing through your body. But sometimes it is utterly dispiriting, and this was one of those times. It wasn't because I came straggling in at the back, it was more because I hadn't enjoyed any part of it, had never found my rhythm. The whole thing had been a slog. And the saddest thing for me is that I had been running in a place I know and love, a place famed for its natural beauty, a place that has inspired world-renowned poets and writers and artists, and I hadn't appreciated it at all. Had barely noticed where I was. Had battled rather than embraced. And far from feeling euphoric, I crossed the finish line exhausted, broken and with my confidence in shreds. I could see no reason for or advantage in putting myself through anything similar again.

But that was five years ago. I haven't forgotten the misery I felt after Offa's 'Orror but I do think I need to get over it. And although I enjoy my morning runs with the dogs, thinking about something and nothing, there is something about having a goal, something to aim for, that is an added incentive to get up and go out – even if it's raining or cold, or your head is telling you, very persuasively, that an extra half hour in bed will make you feel just as good. And nor, I now realize, do I want to be a quitter, be beaten or put off by one bad experience.

I turn to my friend Ophelia, who greets the idea with her characteristic infectious enthusiasm. 'There's a lovely run called the Bath Hilly Half,' she tells me. 'You can either do the half marathon distance or the Ultra 10km.' 'What's an "Ultra 10km"?' I ask, suspiciously. 'I think they call it that because it is just as hilly as the half marathon and is actually more like 12km.' Right. 'I think you should do the 10km,' Ophelia advises, 'because you know you can do that distance – you do it all the time – and the most important thing is that you enjoy it and get your confidence back.'

So that is why this morning I leave the house early, without the dogs, with a plan to run 8 miles – just over 12km – the theory being, according to Ophelia, that if I practise doing a greater distance than the race, the race will feel comparatively easy and all the more enjoyable for it. She has put together a training programme for me that will have me doing regular 10-mile runs in the weeks preceding the event. And getting enough practice running up- and downhill is no problem at all. I live on a hill and the only way home, once I have left the house, is up.

This morning I have two psychological barriers to overcome. The first is the distance – I haven't run this far for a while. The second is the route. Part of it is along Offa's Dyke – my old nemesis – and I haven't run there since the race. But it is dry and mild, the sun is just peeping over the ridge I will soon be running along and there is a robin singing in the crab apple tree outside the kitchen door. I pad down our track to the lane and down the lane to the road, trying not to think that everything I've done so far has been downhill and I will be doing it all again, but in reverse, at the end of the run.

I cross the road and the footbridge over the river. The next bit is flat, along the old railway line, glimpses of the river and Tintern Abbey through the trees. Blackbirds peck beneath the hedges, squirrels scurry across the track and up tree trunks. I'm doing OK, enjoying myself, keeping my pace steady, conserving energy because up ahead is the quarry hill. This steep gravel track that runs up alongside the quarry is just under a mile long and takes me from the river up to Offa's Dyke on the top of the ridge. I settle into a rhythmic plod, eyes fixed on the ground a few feet ahead of me, chanting a childhood rhyme in my head in time with my footsteps.

One. Two. Buckle my Shoe.
Three. Four. Unlock the Door.
Five. Six. Pick up Sticks.
Seven. Eight. Open the Gate.
Nine. Ten. Start Again.

Just when I think my lungs are going to burst and my legs crumple beneath me, I'm there, I've done it, reached the point just below the crest of the ridge where I turn onto Offa's Dyke Path. I remember this next section being flat – or flattish – but I've remembered wrong. It is even steeper than the hill I've just climbed and my exhausted legs stutter. I allow myself to walk the short distance until the path flattens out. This next bit is fun, undulating and weaving through the trees, hopping and skipping over rocks and roots. I hear the croaking call of a raven and another answering it. The white rump of a jay disappears into a thicket and I'm running in the wake of a deer, its two-toed hooves leaving neat imprints in the soft mud of the track.

I come to the Devil's Pulpit, the glorious viewpoint that looks down through the trees to Tintern Abbey and the river below – a sight I never tire of and if I ever do, I know it will be time to move on. From here I take the wrong track, reach a dead end and have to retrace my steps. Back on the right path I'm doing well, have a second wind, my legs feel strong. But the next section is a steep scramble downhill over wet rocks and I steady up, take it slowly until I'm on more level ground.

Before long I'm back at the footbridge and facing the long final haul up the hill that will bring me home. I focus my mind, try to think 'I can' rather than 'I can't'. Part of the way up, on one of the steepest sections, there's a telephone engineer up a pole. 'How you doing?' he asks, in lovely, friendly, lilting Welsh tones, which makes me smile even though I think I'm about to die. 'Knackered!' I gasp, waving limply, and shuffle on a bit further before I admit defeat and stumble to a walk.

From the bottom of the forestry track to our house at the top is half a mile. I am determined to run this last bit, however slowly. I set myself goals – 'I'll get to that tree' – and when I do I pick another tree a bit further ahead and keep going. As I get nearer the house, three dogs come racing down the track to meet me and, with much waggy-tailed encouragement, accompany me to the top and through the kitchen door where I collapse on the floor in an exhausted, happy heap.

5TH OCTOBER

A WALK TO PAY HOMAGE TO THE MOON

✻

I've been out all day and I am driving up the track to the house just as the sun is setting. The sky is clear. There are no clouds to make this sunset worthy of a fanfare, no streaks of vibrant colour across the darkening sky. Just a lengthening of shadows and a gradual fading of light.

I run in, pull on my wellies and old coat to do a last check on the animals before the light goes completely. I walk towards the field where the sheep are and pause, confused. There is a light on the horizon, a glow. It could be the last remnants of sunlight, but I'm looking east. The pale shimmer low down in the sky behind me has been left by the setting sun. I check the sheep, lock up the geese. The glow is brighter. My neighbour swears he saw a UFO once, just two fields away from where I'm standing now. He's a down-to-earth, no-nonsense farmer, not given to flights of fancy, but when I made some flippant comment about little green men and alien abductions, he looked affronted. 'I wasn't the only one who saw it,' he tells me, 'three or four other people reported seeing it too.'

A narrow rim of gold peeps out behind the hill. This is no alien spaceship, but almost as strange. It is as if the sun is rising again immediately after it has set. But it's not the sun. It's the moon. But not a pale, silvery moon casting a blue light and throwing ghostly shadows. This is a perfect, red-gold disk – huge, magnificent – a sight that makes me feel both small and somehow magnificent too. It is a true Harvest Moon, the first full moon after the autumn equinox. Its name dates back to the time before we had artificial light and farmers worked by the light of this moon to bring in their harvests. And like all full moons, it rises as the sun sets and will stay visible in the night sky until the sun rises again tomorrow.

We don't have a harvest to bring in, but it seems a shame not to make the most of this beautiful night. I shut the chickens and ducks up in their sheds, say goodnight to the pigs, gather up the dogs and we go for a moonlit walk before supper. We walk down the farm road and through the gate that leads into a big sloping field with an old ash tree in the corner. We climb the slope and, at the top, turn back to look at the moon in all her glory. No wonder we humans have worshipped the moon for most of our history. Some ancient religions thought of the moon as being male, but to me she is unquestionably female. The sky is so clear, the sun's light reflected from the moon's surface so bright, that I can make out the craters and waterless seas. (There's no sign of any aliens though…)

7TH OCTOBER
METEORS AND OWLS

✳

There is a meteor shower forecast for tonight. An evening sky full of shooting stars. 'We should go up the Skirrid to see it!' I say excitedly to Ludo, 'I'll text a few people and see who's up for it.' I am ignoring the fact that it is cloudy and Ludo is looking less than keen. It soon transpires that no one else is particularly keen to climb a mountain on a cloudy night to not see any shooting stars either.

Undaunted I go out into the garden at 7pm – the time, we have been informed, of peak activity. It is very dark, even the brightness of the Harvest Moon has been dulled to a faint glow behind the clouds. Just to make a point I stay out there, even though I know I'm not going to see a thing. I climb the stile into the neighbouring field, walk out into the middle to get an uninterrupted view of the sky. Nothing. Not a single star is visible, shooting or otherwise. But then, from the woods, comes a sound synonymous with autumn. 'Keeee-wick! Keeee-wick!' It is a tawny owl, calling to her mate. 'Woohoooo,' he answers. I eavesdrop on their exchange for a bit longer, savouring the sound and the deep silence that follows, then wander slowly back to the house. Even a short foray outdoors in the dark can bring unexpected delights.

THE ART OF BEING NOT QUITE LOST

*

What is it that makes it so hard sometimes to determine whither we will walk? I believe that there is a subtle magnetism in nature, which, if we unconsciously yield to it, will direct us aright.

So wrote Henry David Thoreau in a time before we relied on satnavs or apps on our phones to take us in the right direction. As I have already confessed, my navigation skills are not always very reliable and maps, much as I love them, love looking at them, can often add to my sense of confusion. A friend of mine in the SAS takes young recruits out on exercise, setting them navigation tests across the Brecon Beacons. He says a common mistake these beginners make (and I find myself nodding in recognition) is that they will look at the map, look at the landscape in front of them and try to make the landscape fit the map.

I can't tell you how many times I have done this, convinced myself the stream, the line of telegraph poles, the field boundary I can see on the map all tally with the way they appear in the landscape in front of me. But often it is wishful thinking and I overlook the carefully charted details that prove that I am not actually where I think I am, however similar the map and landscape may appear.

This morning I am in London. I spent the night here last night after a day of meetings and appointments and I have more today. Conscious of my training schedule, I have brought my running kit with me and at first light I am loping along a pavement in Paddington, aware how muddy my trainers are. This is not their habitual terrain. I am making – I hope – for Hyde Park. I know this bit of London well enough to know roughly where everything is, but the layout of the streets, the squares, the mews, the cul-de-sacs and crescents can mean, in my case, there is an element of luck getting to where I want to go.

I make my way down a network of narrow streets, around a square, over a pedestrian area and as the roar of traffic gets louder I'm hopeful I am approaching Bayswater Road. 'Yes!' I congratulate myself, as I pause to wait for the traffic light to turn red so I can run across into the relative tranquillity of the park.

There are other runners out, all looking rather spry and springy. There are smart London dogs, trotting along on leads or chasing tennis balls across the grass while their owners look at their phones. Commuters walking to work, bags slung over their shoulders, marching, headphones clamped over their ears. Nannies pushing babies in prams. And a pair of horses trotting smartly, in perfect unison, along the sand track that runs along the outskirts of the park, muscles rippling beneath carefully groomed coats.

I could just run around the perimeter, follow the line of Park Lane down to Hyde Park Corner and turn right, run parallel with Knightsbridge and Kensington High Street, but that would be boring. The appeal of Hyde Park is the seemingly endless number of enticing paths that cross and criss-cross it at every angle. So I just run, wherever my mood takes me. And pretty soon I have no idea where I am.

I think I may have got to Kensington Gardens, but I'm not altogether sure. But I'm not concerned because not knowing where I am is not the same as being lost. I'm not out in uncharted wilderness in a blizzard or thick fog. This feeling is not panic-inducing but liberating. It feels almost frivolous and a bit of frivolity in life is no bad thing. And before long I find myself back at Bayswater Road. It might have been thanks to the 'subtle magnetism of nature', or simply because I saw a Number 94 bus on the other side of the trees.

14TH OCTOBER

A SPUR-OF-THE-MOMENT WALK AND A MYSTERY

✱

October is turning out to be like the September we hoped for: days of soft golden sunshine and gentle warmth. But this is not an Indian summer – the smell of the air, the quality of the light, the morning dew all belong to autumn. Acorns crunch underfoot in the woods, there are shiny red berries on the holly bushes, the leaves are turning, some dropping, and with them the first conkers. I picked up two yesterday, put them in my pocket. I love their rich colour, but more the feel of them, that smooth glossiness like sea-washed pebbles, and I roll them between my fingers as I walk.

Today is another beauty. I take the dogs out for a quick pre-breakfast stretch. We walk towards the rising sun, its rays filtering through my lashes, giving the impression I'm seeing the landscape through a kaleidoscope. The dew fall has been so heavy that when the dogs run through the grass they send up iridescent showers of spray.

'We should see if Jo and Jonathan are around,' I say as I come back into the kitchen to the smell of toast and coffee. 'It'll be beautiful up their way today.' A flurry of phone calls and we have a plan. Jo is away, but Jonathan and their son Hugh are both at home and keen to head for the hills. Mutual friends who live near us are also around, also want to come and we all, together with assorted dogs, converge in Jonathan's kitchen an hour or so later for pre-walk coffee.

Jonathan and Jo live in a beautiful old Welsh farmhouse tucked into the side of a mountain above the village of Crickhowell. Crickhowell is something of a walking hub for the Black Mountains and on a day like today we imagined that many others would have felt similarly impetuous and come to walk one of the many routes that start in or near the village. We walk straight from the house, taking the lane that leads to a stony track, which in turn leads up and out onto the open hill.

I love this walk. It is an intrinsic part of what has become something of a post-Christmas tradition. Jonathan and Jo have a smokery and sell their smoked foods all over the country. The run-up to Christmas is their busiest time of year and they can never come to any of the parties or festivities before Christmas as they are always working. So, instead, their lucky friends are invited over once Christmas is finished and life less frantic, to have a huge walk and afterwards help finish off the leftovers. But I've never done this walk at any other time of year.

We climb and climb, up through the heather. Its flowers have turned brown now, but Jonathan says that back in August it was as if the whole hillside had been painted that soft, misty purple. The sun is warm, warm enough that coats come off and get tied around waists. We get to the top, puffing, faces shiny, and gaze out. The outline of the Table Mountain is clearly defined against the blue sky. We can even see the figures of a few walkers moving around on the summit, but what's striking is that we can see no one else. On this most perfect day in this wild, irrepressibly beautiful landscape that is open to all, there is no one else here apart from us.

It's a mystery we try to get to the bottom of later, in the pub. But no one can come up with a logical reason why on a day like today, so few people would be out and those that are have all felt compelled to take the same route. So instead, we toast our luck that we've had such a place exclusively to ourselves and get stuck into a well-earned lunch.

17TH–23RD OCTOBER

A WALK IN A FORGOTTEN PART OF THE WORLD THAT DESERVES TO BE REMEMBERED

*

I land in Kigali. I've never been to Rwanda before. The genocide that decimated the country and horrified the world ended in 1994, but I think I was still expecting to see a country scarred and damaged by the years of atrocities. Yet there is no sign, no hint. It is as if the whole country has been wiped clean or built again from scratch. And in a way it has. And it is immaculate, almost unsettlingly so.

On the journey from the airport to the hotel, I try to work out what it is that makes it feel somehow unreal, like a theatre set. Then I realize. There is no rubbish anywhere. No bits of shredded plastic hanging in trees or bushes, no discarded packets or cans at the side of the road. I can't think of another country I've been to – including my own – that is as startlingly clean as this. One reason, I discover later, is that in 2008 plastic bags were banned – the use of them, the selling of them, the production of them, the importing of them. It is shameful that the rest of the world hasn't seen what this small African country has achieved and immediately followed suit.

It is late afternoon when I get to the hotel and there is maybe an hour of daylight left. I meet up with my colleague Jonny, who has already arrived, and suggest we walk into town. We are only here for the night and really only passing through Rwanda, but I still need that walk to anchor me here, to help me make the mental shift from home to this new, very different place.

Kigali is hilly, unsurprising really given that the whole of Rwanda is mountainous. We wander down the streets, trying to find some sort of centre or hub – a market perhaps – although it is probably too late in the day. There are people about – women in colourful cottons and men in neat suits, or slacks and polo shirts – all as tidy as their surroundings. It all feels rather subdued and well-mannered, lacking the raw edgy energy of most African cities I have visited. We are offered quiet greetings, no one tries to sell us anything, there is no hustle or banter. This fleeting first impression leaves me intrigued and a little frustrated. I would need much longer here to feel I had scratched beneath the orderly surface.

We leave Kigali the next morning, drive on a series of pristine tarmac roads, past tea plantations, small tidy farms and immaculate villages. We pass through rain forest that stretches as far as the eye can see on both sides of the road and, in every direction, the horizon is crowded with the peaks of mountains. After an unexpectedly straightforward border crossing we have left Rwanda for its somewhat notorious neighbour: the Democratic Republic of the Congo (DRC).

We meet up with John, a local man, born and brought up in a village not far from here on the edge of an area of mountains and forest and swamp that in 1970 was declared a National Park, called Kahuzi-Biega. It is here John takes me for a walk that I will remember, I hope, for the rest of my life.

It is morning. The sky pale grey, the sun hidden behind cloud. We drive a short distance down a dirt road, the mud the colour of old terracotta: deep, earthy red. We pull in and stop behind an open-backed truck. The men standing beside it are wearing khaki uniforms, berets and caps. They are armed, some with rifles, others with machetes. We are beckoned to follow them and they push through the branches of the trees that line the road and into the thick forest beyond. We walk in single file. No one speaks. Our footsteps are silenced by the mud and leaf litter beneath. Occasionally an unseen bird calls. The air is still, humid. On all sides the trees press in, a thick impenetrable wall of green. Above us the canopy is so dense it obscures the sky.

John stops suddenly, turns to point out something on the ground. It is a pile of shredded bamboo. 'They have been here,' he whispers. Further on there are more piles of discarded bamboo shoots. Every part of my body is now alert. I've never felt anything like it before. The anticipation has raised the hairs on my arms, given me goosebumps. I try not to think, try not to imagine what might be about to happen. John stops dead in his tracks again. I almost bump into him. His whisper is urgent. 'Did you hear that?' I've heard nothing, but my nostrils pick up a scent. It is unmistakable. I feel my eyes go wide, my heart beat racing. 'We are close.'

Moments later John pushes through a curtain of foliage. My breath catches in the back of my throat. Tears spring into my eyes. I walk a couple more paces then drop to my knees, hardly daring to breathe. 'Meet Chimanuka and his family.' And I sit, dumbfounded with delight, in the presence of 19 eastern lowland gorillas.

These animals, which are unique to the DRC, are only here because of the astonishing bravery and dedication of the men that I am with. I can only sit here, watching the gorillas play and tussle, groom each other or just laze and scratch, because of the years and years spent habituating them so they no longer fear human contact.

In a country ravaged by decades of exploitation and corruption, war and anarchy, there are still those who will risk everything for the things that are truly precious and truly irreplaceable. 'But,' John tells me, when we have walked back to the road – and I'm still trying to take it in, still trying to believe what I have seen – 'we need tourists to come. This park used to bring in lots of tourists and the revenue supported not just the park but the people who live in the communities around it. Communities like mine. We are doing our best to keep the gorillas safe, to protect them from poaching, but when people are hungry, when they have nothing, when they are desperate, they will do anything. That's why we need the tourists to come back. To save the gorillas. To save us.'

28TH OCTOBER
PROGRESS

❋

Home again, in a more familiar forest. This one not dense, green and humid, but with its own sparse, autumn beauty. The trees aren't bare yet, nor have they reached their crescendo, their firework display of colour, the finale before winter. But the leaves are more gold and brown than green and some have fallen, the beginnings of a mosaic of beech and oak leaves on the earth beneath their branches.

I'm running again. I ran earlier in the week, in Yorkshire. I was working there for a few days and drove up straight after landing back from Africa. After two long stints in a plane and another in a car, I was desperate to be back on my feet, despite being exhausted.

I intended to run six miles but ended up doing eight because – well – usual thing. But I haven't run for four days and today I'm taking things up a notch and attempting ten miles. I'm doing the same route as before – over the river, along the railway and up quarry hill, but instead of dropping down the steep, stony path I carry on along Offa's Dyke until I get to the next village.

There is plenty to distract me this morning. There have been lots of little changes in the two weeks I've been away. I had the joy – and privilege – of meeting naturalist Richard Fitter before he died. Fitter wrote the seminal field guide to British birds in the Fifties, as well as one on wild flowers, but he also kept records for fifty years of the dates when he saw the first celandine bloom, or the first frogspawn of the year, or the swallows return from their migration. This dedication to phenology – the science that examines the correlation between climate change and when natural events, such as returning migrant birds or the blooming of wild flowers, happen – helped us understand not just that the climate was changing but how it was affecting the growth or behaviour of many of our favourite plants and animals. So I always think of him when I notice something like the first bluebell coming out or when I hear the first skylark of the year.

Today, as I'm panting my way up quarry hill, I hear the barking roar of a stag. The rutting season has started and the sound of male deer announcing their virility and general irresistibility to any females that happen to be in the vicinity reverberates through the trees. But, more importantly today, I manage to complete ten miles and get all the way up the hill to home without having to walk. The training is paying off. Thank goodness. There's just two weeks to go.

November

A WALK TO FIND A SOLUTION AND, WITH IT, PEACE

*

Something's come up and it is making me anxious and unhappy. It was an incident that happened some time ago. One that was both confusing and upsetting, but I thought had been resolved. But now there are repercussions and my mind is in a maelstrom. I feel both blameless and culpable, wronged, but also in the wrong. And I simply don't know how to deal with it or how to react.

Protest my innocence, or accept responsibility? I'm not very good at these things. I worry and worry over them, constantly replaying scenarios or conversations in my head, losing all perspective and proportion. So I get up this morning after a night of miserably turning over a hundred 'what ifs' and 'if onlys', feeling jangled and still with no clear idea what to do. Anxiety is curled up in a knot in my stomach like a small, malevolent animal. I go through the morning routine like an automaton – checking and feeding animals and then calling the dogs and setting out for their walk.

Animals have an unerring ability to know when something is up. The dogs sense I am out of sorts this morning and do their best to amuse and distract. And nature has put on her best show for me too. A low mist lingers in the valley, and smoky wisps curl among the trees in the wood, lit up by shafts of hazy morning sunshine. The leaves that are left on the trees, clinging on until they are sent swirling down by the next gusty autumn day, are a harlequin of copper, red, brown and gold. Jays squawk, ravens chuckle and grouch at each other, like guttural old men who have spent a lifetime smoking rough tobacco.

We walk for an hour and by the time we return home the creature curled in my stomach is still there, but its presence doesn't weigh so heavily, and it no longer absorbs my thoughts. I can think around it instead of feeling hamstrung by it.

Later, I'm at my desk, typing. Notebooks, to-do lists, a mug with cold dregs of tea crowd the surface. Teg has a tried-and-tested ploy to let me know she is ready for another walk. The door creaks as she slinks in and up to my chair. She pushes her slender head under my arm and lifts it, so I can no longer type, and looks at me beseechingly with her kooky eyes. I'm powerless to resist.

And this walk – through the woods, down the hill, along the stream to the ponds where the dogs throw themselves in with unabashed enthusiasm – turns out to be more productive than the last few hours sitting at my desk.

Rebecca Solnit writes, with characteristic fervency, about the lack of time and space modern life gives over to simply thinking:

> *Thinking is currently thought of as doing nothing in a production-oriented culture, and doing nothing is hard to do. It's best done by disguising it as doing something, and the something closest to doing nothing is walking.*

And this form of 'doing nothing' – combined with the comforting sensation of unharried movement and fresh air – conjures up, apparently from nowhere, the solution I know will banish the anxiety monster completely.

I suspect the solution was always there, but it was obscured by the fog anxiety causes and this walk on a chilly autumn afternoon has cleared that fog. In my head, as I follow the dogs back up the hill, I compose the email I will write, playing with phrases so that my words will reflect as truthfully as possible my sentiments. As soon as I get in I type it, fast and unwaveringly. I press send. The small, malevolent animal slips away.

For some people, though, anxiety isn't so easily banished. It is something far more deep rooted and complex. Jonathan Hoban had a loving upbringing but, he tells me, he was a very sensitive child, was very badly bullied at school and constantly felt unsafe.

'I was always self-doubting, giving myself a hard time, and I suffered permanently from high anxiety.' He'd try to block everything out and shut himself away at home, listening to loud music through headphones. And when that didn't work, he started drinking. He was an alcoholic by the time he was 15.

He went on to have five years of therapy, which included him training to become a counsellor himself. Initially he worked with people with addictions like his own, people who had been enrolled in drug programmes, and because he knew exactly where they were coming from, recognized the demons that plagued them, he was able to help get them back on track. And in the course of helping them he realized that this was what he was destined to be: someone who could help people fix themselves.

But sometimes, if someone came into his therapy room and they were suffering from extreme anxiety, Jonathan's instinct was to take them out, take them to the park. 'A room can get filled with negative energy, it gets trapped and as soon as you take a client out of that environment you can see immediate relief.' Someone who is anxious will have high cortisol levels – the hormone that is released in times of stress. The hormone that combats stress is oxytocin. There are various ways to stimulate the release of oxytocin. Hugging is one of them. But if you are feeling anxious and not quite able to deal with people, going for a walk, outside, in the fresh air, communing with nature, releases oxytocin too.

So walking really does make a physiological difference to our state of mind. It is therapeutic. But as a therapist, is it professionally acceptable to take your clients for a walk in the park? And would someone in a fragile mental place feel able to talk to a therapist as freely as they need in an open space, in public?

There is an on-going debate – has been since the very early days of psychotherapy – on the best way talking as a cure should be conducted. It was not unusual for Freud to analyse his clients while walking the streets of Vienna. But gradually what became accepted and established as the professional and ethical place for a therapist to work with a patient was in an indoor space – more often than not the therapist's office.

But as British psychiatrist Jeremy Holmes wrote in an article in *The International Journal of Psychoanalysis*, conducting therapy in a room can be counter-productive. Yes, it is a safe, contained space, 'but this is counterbalanced by a deep existential sense of the limiting and restricting nature of the therapeutic environment, which mimics the finiteness and vulnerability of life itself'. His is just one of many articles and academic papers on the pros, cons and pitfalls of taking therapy outside, but was there anyone who was actually putting the idea into practice? Jonathan told me about a man he had been in touch with in New York with the rather splendid name of Clay Cockrell. 'You might be interested to talk to him,' Jonathan suggested.

6TH NOVEMBER

MORNING:

A TINY BUT PERFECT WINTER WALK TO START A DAY

✻

I leave the house just before dawn, slightly rushed, wondering if I've left early enough to get to my meeting on time. The darkness envelops me as I walk out of the door. I love this deep, velvety lack of light. It is one of the great luxuries of living here. There are faint pinpricks of light from houses across the valley, but there are no street lights, none of that sodium glow that blights the night skies above our towns and cities.

I look east. There are pale streaks across the blackness heralding the sun, which will rise in another half hour or so. In the southwest, above the branches of the old silver birch, is a different sort of light, fragile and luminescent, coming from the waning moon. And somewhere, invisible in the dark, perched in a tree nearby, is a robin, singing.

I've walked just a matter of metres from front door to car, but the moonlight and birdsong give me reason to stop rushing, stop worrying about possible traffic jams. Compel me to pause and to savour. It is such an insignificant thing, really. Nothing out of the ordinary. Robins sing in the dark and the moon shines. But it is an uplifting moment nonetheless. A lovely start to the day. Slightly regretfully I shut myself into my car and drive away.

EVENING:

A RUN TO STRETCH THE LEGS AND STIMULATE THE SENSES

*

I get back home in the last gasp of daylight. I've done lots of driving and talking and sitting today and I feel sluggish. And the Bath Hilly Half is at the end of this week. I dash into the house and put my running kit on. Moments later I set off down the farm road. Nature is settling down for the night. The last rooks are heading back to their roost in the ash tree. A small group of starlings flies in tight formation swiftly across the fields and disappears. The wintery glow left by the sun seeps out of the western sky, but the light lingers for a while yet. It is only when the lane starts to descend between high banks at the edge of the woods that it is hard to see where my feet are landing. But my eyes are adjusting as the light fades and I'm surprised how much I can see even now the sky is almost completely black.

I turn off the lane onto our track. The trees alongside are dark shadowy shapes with no definition. I hear a noise up ahead, catch sight of something pale crossing a few metres in front of me and disappearing into the trees. A deer. Silence has descended. All I can hear is my rhythmic breathing, keeping time with the beat of my feet on the earth.

I round the bend and push myself on for the last few hundred metres. It is a wonderful feeling to be out in this cosseting darkness. All my senses feel alive and alert. I don't feel scared. Not a bit. I feel primeval, a creature of the forest.

But I do slightly hope that Ludo has started to cook supper.

THE BREACHING OF A PSYCHOLOGICAL HURDLE

✳

The day has come: the day of the Ultra (little-bit-more-than) 10km. The day when I will either obliterate the mental scars left by my last attempt at running in a public event or add a few more.

Back in early October when I decided to do this, I sent an email to Polly, trying not to sound too pleading, but hoping to encourage her to do the run too. Although we walk together frequently, we have never run together.

She, like me, enjoys running by herself, enjoys the solitude. But I know she has done events like this in the past and my thinking – entirely selfishly – is that a person who has tended to my revolting blistered feet and put up with my bad-tempered mental anguish over the 15 miles of the Wye Valley Walk we did together is exactly the person to have with me now. And Polly, overlooking this flagrant abuse of our friendship, sent an email back to say she had signed up.

So here we are, in our Lycra and trainers, in her car, driving to Bath. I have not slept well, nerves making me jittery and restless. Polly, it turns out, hasn't slept well either. Because her ankle hurts. A lot.

An open packet of painkillers in the cubby hole by the gear stick is evidence that she has already had to take measures to deal with it. 'Are you sure you should be doing this?' I ask, properly concerned and for once actually not thinking of myself. 'Oh yes,' she says, breezily waving – in a dismissive sort of way – the slice of toast and peanut butter she is eating while driving. 'It'll be fine. I'll just take it slowly.'

We are standing in a queue to get our numbers. 'Everyone looks very fit and whippet-like,' Polly mutters. I look at our fellow runners.

Add up the BMI of the lot of them, I think, and it will still be in single figures. I feel very middle aged and slightly fraudulent.

Who the hell am I kidding? I can't do this. But we're at the front of the queue now and, instead of being told, kindly, that the organisers don't think it is wise for me to take part, which is what I have convinced myself is going to happen, I am handed a number and wished 'good luck!' without a hint of irony.

It was cold but sunny when we left the Wye Valley. Now it is just cold. The run starts and ends on Bath racecourse and we walk out onto the turf in front of the grandstand and stand in a shivering huddle. A bitter wind carries with it a sharp shower of stinging rain drops.

It is Remembrance Sunday, just before 11am. We, like people up and down the land, will observe a two-minute silence in honour of those who lost their lives fighting for our country. We stand still, heads bowed, alone with our thoughts. And when we look up again from our quiet contemplation, we can see we are about to be given the signal to start the race. The atmosphere becomes instantly charged, prickling with anticipation. 'Three. Two. One!' And we are off...

I'm back on the springy turf of the racecourse. I've run – and walked when the route got really steep – just over six miles and there's not far to go now. 'Come on!' I urge myself, out loud. 'You can do it. You can do it. You can do it.' I'm on the final furlong. I can see the finish line up ahead, the small knot of people who have generously braved the cold to cheer us on for the last few metres. My legs feel heavy, done in; I'm pretty sure I'm lumbering rather than running, but my mind is singing.

I am euphoric, flushed with delight and with a sense of achievement. And there's a deeper feeling than that, something very personal. I am overcoming a self-imposed 'can't'. I had allowed a negative experience, an 'off day', to become an established part of my psychological make-up. In my head I was a person who 'can't' do this: take part in a physically challenging race, up and down hills, through mud and puddles, along with a crowd of strangers. And if asked why I felt that way, I knew I couldn't explain it, not even to myself. I like physical challenges. I run up and down hills, through mud and puddles, all the time. Perhaps it is the presence of the other people, the fear of not being as fit or as quick, of being judged inadequate. Of just not being good enough. But today I've discovered that, actually, after all, I *can* do this. I have no idea whether I'm among the front runners or at the back of the pack and I don't care.

I cross the finish line and God! It feels absolutely fantastic!

18TH–23RD NOVEMBER
A FACT-FINDING MISSION:
IS WALKING REALLY GOOD FOR THE MIND?

*

At Jonathan Hoban's suggestion, I'm in New York, wandering around in a haze of jetlag and traffic. I've been to this city before; a couple of times for work, a couple of times to see friends. It is a place that seems to incite rapture among many. 'Oh, I *wish* I was in New York!' came the reply to an email I sent this morning, but I don't get it. Its charms elude me.

This is my third day here, and I've retreated to a bench in Central Park. I've avoided the subway and taxis, taken advantage of cold, bright weather and walked everywhere. I've been running too, but I find the grid pattern of the streets, although easy to navigate, restricting and stifling.

There are moments – fleeting ones – of appreciation. On my first day I walked the High Line in both directions. This is an elevated park – complete with trees and shrubs, sculptures and, inevitably, a coffee shop – built on an abandoned railway line. It stretches for just under a mile and a half and being able to walk above street level, out of the canyon of buildings, is a welcome relief. It is windy, and the wind is surgically cold, but I embrace it because it makes me feel like I really am outside. In the elements. I look out over the expanse of the Hudson River, across the tangle of buildings and down the length of the cross streets. It is more open here, I can see the sky without having to crane my head so far back I feel dizzy.

It is, undeniably, an architecturally impressive city. At a meeting yesterday on the 33rd floor of a block on the corner of Madison Square, I stood in front of a huge window in reception, gazing with unashamed awe at the sight beyond the glass. It was mid-afternoon. I was looking east and the sun, low and golden, was illuminating the buildings, making the rather dead grey of the concrete, the steel, the plate glass come alive. The grid of the streets was invisible from this perspective, the towering array of buildings, of all shapes and sizes, gave the impression of being placed randomly, growing out of the shadows towards the sun like trees in a forest.

But down at street level the forest analogy is lost. The natural world has been banished, covered by concrete and tarmac, pushed aside and bulldozed to make way for a rigid, manmade plantation. Today I walk for an hour, maybe more, and find myself getting increasingly uncomfortable, shoulders hunching, walking faster and faster. Shop windows are dressed for the holiday season. Thanksgiving is in a couple of days, Christmas not long after. I'm aware of sparkle, glitter, twinkling lights but I don't take anything in. I'm blanking my mind, retreating into myself in an effort to pretend that this is not where I really am. I feel almost panicked and turn off Madison Avenue, walk a block, hit 5th Avenue, race along the boundary fence until I find a way in and then, finally, I breathe.

Central Park. Trees. Grass. Birds. Very fat squirrels. Very pampered dogs. Paths that don't run in a straight line. I find a bench, tucked away up a narrow track between flower beds, the shrubs sparse and brown, rustling in the breeze. I sit and look out around me, allowing my mind to come slowly back to life and take notice of my surroundings.

There are trees, resplendent, the gold and red and copper of the remaining leaves shining in the sun, iridescent, so much more beautiful than anything in the shop windows. The sky is the brittle blue of almost-winter and I realize with relief that from this vantage point I can't see any buildings, it is as if an illusionist has done something clever to magic Manhattan momentarily away. There are big rocks below me, children scrambling, posing for photos.

Along the meandering paths are people in woolly hats and winter coats meandering too, leaves falling, spiralling down from the trees above like confetti. There's conversation, laughter, as if they too feel released and relieved to be away from the constraints of the streets. In a city where there is so little green, so few chances to see the horizon, this feels not just like an oasis, but a lifeline. Space. Peace. Solitude. I find the effects of these almost instantaneous.

My panic has subsided, my mind has re-engaged and I feel able now to reflect on why walking here – something I usually find so soothing – has today made me feel so out of sorts, unaccountably sad. The light has something to do with it. In the narrow canyons between the buildings the light at this time of year seems to have that permanent end-of-day quality. It gives a mournful feeling to the day that isn't overcome by the holiday atmosphere, by the families, the friends, the couples walking arm in arm, crowding the pavements, taking selfies and photos of the Christmas trees, the lights, the ice rink that has been set up in Bryant Park.

Among these jovial crowds stalk the locals – focused, fast-walking, fast-talking, apparently to themselves, and then I realize everyone is on the phone, talking through headsets hidden by hats and scarves. Conspicuous among them, within this crush of humanity and temples of consumerism, are the Haves – those people whose bearing, poise and impeccably quiet good taste scream wealth and privilege – and the Have-nots. These people – men and women, black and white, old and young – are on every block. Some are missing limbs, others mumble and pray, some sit silent and crumpled with despair among their few possessions, carefully written cardboard notices explaining their circumstances propped up against their knees.

I pass a man lying, prostrate, on his front on the pavement while another tenderly removes the shoes from his aching feet. A girl sits with studious dignity, leaning against the wall of a textile house where the towels in the window are displayed in such a way that you know they are not going to be $19.99 for three. She is writing in a notebook, seemingly oblivious to the crowds that pass her without a glance. The Post Traumatic Stress Disorder handbook is open and resting on the tatty duffel bag beside her. A few doors down a man in a wheelchair recites his military history '...two tours of Iraq... nine months in Afghanistan...' And a little further on a woman sits saying nothing, gazing fixedly at her lap, sending out waves of misery. And all the time my feet continue to slap rhythmically along the pavement, my mind in turmoil, battling with the injustices of our species so starkly evident here in Manhattan. My throat is tight. Tears tickle the backs of my eyes. And despite all the people, all the noise and the colour, I feel terribly, terribly lonely.

Against this backdrop one man has taken on the daunting task of trying to make the people who live here happy. He is tall, strawberry blond, broad and capable-looking in brown leather jacket and scarf, holding a large cup of coffee in one hand and a furled umbrella in the other 'because it might decide to rain on us'. We meet, as he suggested, by the gold statue at the Columbus Circle entrance of Central Park at 11am. His name, I tell him, is marvellous. 'Why thank you!' he smiles, and we start to walk.

Clay Cockrell grew up in rural Kentucky, a happy, uncomplicated childhood filled with stories told with great relish and skill by his grandmothers and great aunts – tales of their own childhoods, or bizarre things that happened at the grocery store, or just everyday events – and Clay loved listening to them. Couldn't get enough of them. Always wanted more. 'I guess I was just good at listening and somehow other people picked up on that. Friends from high school would come and talk to me, tell me stuff, and I loved it. And then there was *The Bob Newhart Show*.' *The Bob Newhart Show* was an American sitcom that ran for six years during the Seventies and featured Bob Newhart playing a psychologist dealing with crazy patients, friends and family. It was, Clay tells me, extremely funny, but it also made him think 'I could do that for a living'. Not, he clarified, be a comedy actor, but a therapist.

We have, by now, skirted one of the smaller lakes on the edge of

Central Park, crossed a road, picked our way around a large pile of horse manure and are following another broad path beneath the last of the autumn leaves. There are a few people about, joggers and dog walkers, rain starts to fall gently, pitter-pattering on the leaves and forming dark polka dots on the tarmac. Clay unfurls his umbrella with a flourish and I ask how he turned what appeared to me to be a childhood whim based on his grandmothers' stories and a TV show into his profession. Because that is what Clay is – a therapist – but one who does things a little differently.

He moved to New York because his actress wife felt the opportunities would be greater for her there than in Kentucky. Acting is a famously precarious profession, rarely paying any sort of regular salary, so it fell to Clay to be the reliable breadwinner. By this time, he had gained a Master's degree in psychology, but more importantly he had had clinical experience, working first with adolescents struggling with substance abuse and then in a psychiatric emergency room.

The work was rewarding, but he struggled with the reality that many of the people he saw while working there were simply not going to get better. 'My job was to evaluate them and move them on to the right resource, just like any emergency room. I realized I didn't want to do that for the rest of my life.' Instead Clay saw his professional future helping people who were struggling with their marriages, or with their job or with depression or anxiety – people he described as 'high-functioning but needing a little help, not someone hearing voices or seeing aliens'.

Anyone who has ever watched a Woody Allen film will assume, as I did, that for New Yorkers a visit to their therapist is as much part of their normal routine as their commute to work or brunch on Sunday.

And so, I ask, wasn't he, like his wife, trying to break into a highly competitive and already saturated market? 'Absolutely,' he nods, 'but I started small, took a job in an insurance company and slowly built up a private practice on the side, one day a week, then two, but my big break came thanks to my wife.'

He had a client who worked on Wall Street who kept missing his sessions or turning up late. He struggled to get away from work on time or for the amount of time he needed to travel to Clay's office, have his session and return to work. Clay's wife suggested that Clay go to him. Clay tried to explain to her that it simply wouldn't work, that it wouldn't be appropriate to give someone therapy in their office, and she said, 'You could go outside. You could just walk for the session.'

That simple suggestion launched not just Clay's career. It turned him into a modern-day pioneer of the way Freud used to conduct his therapy sessions: outside and in the open air. The Wall Street guy agreed to Clay's suggestion – 'it was far more convenient for him' – and his therapy session took place while walking around Battery Park. And he started, as Clay put it, 'making connections with some of his issues', which in the whole six months Clay had been seeing him in his office he had never been able to do. 'He was struggling with his job, stress, anxiety, time management and I think the walking helped him realize that he never took time for himself; that simply making the decision to go for a walk by the river and talk to someone was relaxing. It made him more at peace and then he was able to think about how he could change his life, what he needed to do.'

Seeing the positive effects that talking while walking had on this particular client, Clay offered walking therapy to other clients and saw similarly positive results. He was frank with me: 'I thought, well

OK, this could be clever, a bit of marketing, something that makes me different,' and he took the domain name *walkandtalk.com*. The *Wall Street Journal* contacted him, then *Good Morning America* and 'boom!' he says, smiling at me with an expansive wave of his coffee cup, 'it took off'.

That was 12 years ago and the majority of Clay's clients do what I'm doing now, walk with him around Central Park. He has a favourite loop that takes us alongside lakes, under trees, across more open ground. The paths are smooth, there are no uneven tracks or steep gradients to break the gentle rhythm of the pace that we have fallen into. We are not alone, but the other people – walking, pushing prams, riding bikes, throwing balls for their dogs – pay us no attention; our conversation is as private as it would have been had I asked to conduct this interview in an office. And Clay has developed, whether by accident or design, a way of talking and walking that allows both for conversation and contemplation: easy, even paced, almost hypnotic. It is clear now why this form of therapy that Clay stumbled on by accident is more than just 'a clever little bit of marketing'.

As a species we've been walking for hundreds of thousands of years, but recently, in less than the last hundred years, many of us have become dependent on other speedier, less physically demanding ways of getting around. Clay looks pensive. 'I think we'd forgotten that connection to the earth and the power of walking and we're kind of remembering it now. As far as our mental health is concerned, we are now aware of the connection between exercise and mental health and we know that people do better when they have some form of exercise, even one as simple and fundamental as walking.'

And he sees it all the time. 'I saw a new guy last week. He's anxious.

Fist in his pocket. Really hunched over. Very nervous. Lots of fast talking and fast walking, but after about half an hour he has released his fists, his posture's improved, his gait has slowed. He is physically more relaxed. And when you change the way you behave, you begin to change the way you think. When you're walking you're breathing differently, you've got more oxygen going to your brain, you're outside, you can think more expansively, more clearly, more creatively. You can think about the things that are making you anxious and depressed in a new way; a way that is more progressive, perhaps because you are doing something proactive, you are physically moving forward.' 'So would you say that what you are doing is encouraging and enabling people to literally get back on their feet, take action, move on?' I ask. 'Absolutely, that's it. Simple as can be. This is not rocket science.'

It may not be rocket science, but walking therapy has undeniably contributed to improving the lives of not just the New Yorkers who have sought Clay's help, but people from much further afield too. Clay now advises other counsellors and therapists in the States and all over the world, on the practicalities and legalities of offering walking therapy. Jonathan Hoban was one of them. He tells me about a client who was going through a difficult time at work, was physically and emotionally burnt out and suffering from exhaustion, anxiety and headaches. After trying traditional therapy in an office, Jonathan suggested they try walking instead. Afterwards the client wrote:

What a revelation, to walk in beautiful surroundings in the changing seasons uplifted the soul, stopped the headaches and was not nearly as intense. I found myself looking forward to my weekly walks and even factored in times to walk around the common each weekend.

Subsequently my activity levels increased and I felt better physically, but most importantly I found that I was able to work through the very complex issues that had culminated in a long period of anxiety and depression and complete burnout. Walking therapy enabled me to reach a point where I felt that I was in control of my life once more.

And I think back to the day at the beginning of this month, the day when my brain felt scrambled, consumed by a tangle of confusion and anxiety. And I remember the feeling of blessed relief and release that came from those walks I did that day. And I know how powerful and how healing the simple act of putting one foot in front of the other can be.

THE END
OF THE
YEAR

December

A WALK OF FORTITUDE:
A CELEBRATION OF HUMAN SPIRIT

❉

I've been thinking about a young man called Sam Doyle. Back in May, Sam asked a friend to drop him off on the beach at Blackpool. He waved goodbye, shouldered his rucksack, turned north and, keeping the sea on his left, started walking.

Sam grew up not far from Blackpool, the second oldest of seven children. It was a tough childhood. The family didn't have much money and Sam, who is dyslexic, didn't do well at school. As soon as he'd done his GCSEs he left, signed up for the army. He set his sights on joining the Parachute Regiment once he'd completed his training, but he failed the medical and was offered a position in the fire support team of the 3rd Regiment Royal Horse Artillery.

After more training in Germany and Kenya, soon after he turned 21, Sam and his regiment were deployed to Afghanistan. They were to be sent right down to the south of the country, near the Pakistan border, an area where the Taliban were known to recruit and train. They were excited, excited to put into practice all the hard work, all the training.

Their mission, Sam was told, was to win the hearts and minds of the local people so that they would feel less inclined to join the Taliban. And that, Sam thought, made the mission more exciting because it was for a good cause. Except when he said 'good cause', his voice was ironic and his fingers drew inverted commas in the air.

His regiment was sent to relieve the American Marines who had taken control of a small compound with a building – that had once been a shop – in the middle of it. They were there for three months, sleeping in tents, living on rations, going out on patrol every day, talking to the villagers, trying to establish if and where there were any Taliban hiding out. And in the three months they had no contact, they were never mortared, never shot at, 'but you wake up scared every day. You can never relax. Monday to Sunday. It's the frontline. You're trying to find the weakness in the enemy and they are doing the same to you. If you close your eyes for a second at the wrong time they will seize that opportunity.' He was given two weeks leave – R&R – halfway through the tour, but he spent those two weeks panicking about the friends he had left behind, knowing that they couldn't really afford to be a man down. He was relieved to get back.

And then they were on the move, pushing further south, following and sustaining the clear-up operation done by the SAS and the Americans, keeping the enemy at bay. And naturally there were casualties, members of his regiment injured and killed, others suffering from combat stress and shellshock. But there was something else that afflicted many of them too, including Sam. Guilt.

'People believe that combat guilt is when you've lost a close friend that's right beside you when he is killed, but it's not just that. I felt guilty because I don't think we had a right to be there. I felt guilty for the devastation I was causing, the tyranny I was playing a part in. Those people didn't need their hearts and minds winning. I loved them. They were the most beautiful human beings I have ever met. We were so welcomed. They didn't care what race we were, if we came with big rifles or guns or intimidating helicopters and tanks. They would still offer us grapes. They would offer us accommodation, they would share tea, shake hands, talk to us.'

After seven unremitting months of being constantly on the alert, scared senseless, under fire, anxiety levels sky high, the tour was over. Sam was sent to Cyprus where he, like everyone else, was evaluated by medics and if they were deemed fit to continue, they rejoined their regiment to wait for the next deployment. But Sam couldn't switch off, just like that. He was anxious, still constantly alert, like a caged animal.

'I knew there was no calming down. Everything I had seen out there was so abnormal, so unnatural. It is so unnatural for a human being to see another one suffering. I was struggling to understand the logic of it, to understand why we were actually there. It was the graphicness of it all. On my very last day I watched a twelve-year-old boy dying in front of me. I will remember that for the rest of my life.' And he looks down at his hands, eyes glassy and blank.

But despite all this Sam wanted to go back to Afghanistan, because he simply didn't know how to cope with life away from the frontline, didn't know how to channel his brain which was still so alert, so overwhelmed by anxiety. It is, he says, a lifestyle, not just a job you can walk away from. And he felt he had done well, created friendships and built trust with the locals and he wanted to carry on. And if he went back maybe he would finally understand why they were there and the guilt he was feeling might be assuaged.

Deemed fit by the doctors he went back to the army base in Germany and the girlfriend he had left behind. But all he could think about, all his brain would do, was replay the whole seven-month tour in Afghanistan over and over in his head. And then he discovered his girlfriend, who had promised to wait for him, devote herself to him, had cheated on him while he'd been away. Desperately hurt – his brain racing, constantly analysing, questioning, having flashbacks – he knew he couldn't stay in the army any more, couldn't stay in Germany just waiting for the next tour. He needed structure, something to take his mind off Afghanistan. So he joined the French Foreign Legion, passed the selection and then realized that he couldn't do it. Couldn't do anything. He was struggling, sinking, deteriorating.

Post Traumatic Stress Disorder – or PTSD – is a term that has become familiar to most of us. But I wonder how many of us really understand what it is. If I'm honest I thought it was one of those hyped-up – even fabricated – conditions much loved by the no-win, no-fee-type lawyers when dealing with whiplash cases. And that is part of the problem for sufferers like Sam, because it is a term used widely and generally for a condition which can be relatively mild and manageable, or it can be severe enough to take over life and destroy it.

Sam was released from the French Foreign Legion and returned to England. He moved into a council flat and was given treatment – antidepressants – by the National Health Service. But he couldn't hold down a job, became addicted to the antidepressants, and when they ceased to give him the peace he craved he turned to illegal drugs too. Anything, he said, to try to kill his mind. But it didn't work.

He lost his flat because he couldn't pay the rent. Homeless, desperate and plagued by sleeplessness, stress and anxiety, addicted to drugs, Sam was at the end of his tether. Six years after he left the army he attempted suicide by hanging himself. It didn't work. He didn't die. Some time later he tried again. This time he lost consciousness, but came round. The third time he placed a rope around his neck, hoping it would finally let his mind rest. He said, 'I was on my last legs, but there was a tiny bit of me, a voice which told me that I could sober up. I could do something. So maybe I wasn't ready to die.' He decided to walk instead.

Sam's been on the road now for seven months and he's in Scotland – on the west coast. I've managed to track him down. We text a couple of times, then talk. I ask if I can come up and meet him and he agrees. I book a flight to Inverness, hire a car, find somewhere to stay near where he thinks he will be in a week's time. A couple of days later I get another text from him. The weather is so bad that he has been advised to change his route. He's going to cut inland, walk to Inverness and go back to complete the northern coast of Scotland in the spring. I find a hotel on the outskirts of the city, on the shore of a loch, and book us both in. 'See you there' he texts back.

The hotel is a country house, down a long drive flanked by damp spiky grass and towering conifers. Red squirrels chase each other across the lawn and up the trunk of a tree. 'Mr Doyle's arrived,' I'm told as I check in, and just as I'm handed my key a rather elegant dog walks down the stairs, so clean her white coat is gleaming, stretched over muscles as taut and defined as those of a race horse. Behind her is a young man, slight, almost scrawny. He has a scraggy ginger beard, dishevelled hair and his clothes have the look of being infrequently handwashed in streams. His voice has a soft, Northern burr. 'You must be Kate?' And we hug.

We settle on sofas by the fire in the sitting room. Jess, the dog, sits next to Sam, long limbs tucked under her, scrutinizing me across the coffee table. Sam sips his pint, I pour tea into a mug and ask him, Why? What made him set off on this walk? 'I wanted to give up the pressures of trying to live a normal life and sustaining a job, neither of which I was mentally capable of doing. I wanted liberation from the drugs. I wanted to exorcise my demons. So I threw myself out there and pretty much set off walking blind. I thought walking would make me accept that I had problems and make *me* deal with them, rather than looking to someone else – or something else – to deal with them for me. And now I feel like I'm in control, I'm able to feel responsible for myself. There's no better drug than liberation.'

The first day, setting off with an enormous rucksack that weighed almost as much as he did, but no map, he was almost swept away by the tide and only managed to cover about four miles. 'But I thought, I've taken the plunge now. It's either carry on walking and see what comes of it or go back to your drugs, go back to your alcohol, go back to your craziness and go back to doing nothing, but you won't last long.' And in the forefront of his mind were other veterans, similarly affected by their combat experiences, who had taken their own lives.

He talks about a young man called Lee Bonsall, who hanged himself five years after being discharged from the army. He, like Sam, was never diagnosed by a military doctor as having PTSD and never given any support by the Ministry of Defence. At his inquest the coroner called for a review of mental health procedures for soldiers. 'I thought,

I'm not going to be another Lee, because I'd seen the devastation Lee caused when he committed suicide. He didn't stop his pain from PTSD. He just passed it on. To his family. His friends.' He pauses, sips his pint, looks down, hiding his eyes, which have filled with tears.

Sam spent his first night under a derelict building. He was tempted to phone his mate and ask him to come and pick him up. Was tempted plenty of times throughout the first month. But he didn't succumb. By the second month he was getting used to the walking, by the third he thought, 'Well, I'm here now. But between you and me, Kate, I didn't like the walking. I didn't like the punishment of it. But I prefer the physical pain of walking because it feels like progression. And I knew, if I stopped, all I'd have is the mental pain of depression. And I could finally sleep at night, just because I was so tired at the end of the day.'

And it was in that third month that he realized the people he was meeting along the way were interested in his story. Interested in hearing about the issue that plagues so many ex-servicemen and women and so often goes unnoticed and untreated. So the talking as well as the walking became his therapy. He was interviewed on radio and for local newspapers.

PTSD Resolution got in touch. This small charity was set up specifically to help veterans struggling to re-integrate into normal work and family life due to combat-related stress or trauma. They told Sam what he was doing was amazing and offered to support him. It was a seminal moment. Sam was no longer the 'walking dead'. 'I'm alive again, walking for a cause, walking for a purpose: to tell people about PTSD.' And he set himself a goal. To walk the entire coast of Britain, however long it takes.

Not long later he was joined by his now-constant companion,

Jess the dog. 'I met a man trying to rehome her because he had a new girlfriend and her dog didn't like Jess and bullied her. Jess was pretty damaged when I got her – traumatized by this other dog. So we support each other. When I'm having night terrors she wakes me up and when she struggles I wake her up. I tell her everything. It's cool – when you're on your own and you talk to yourself, everyone thinks you are crazy, but talking to a dog is fine!' And together Sam and Jess have faced some tough physical challenges as well as dealing with their mental ones.

Sam tells me about trying to navigate along the shores of Loch Striven, 'knee-deep in clay and mud. Crying. Lost. Thinking we would never get out. I was struggling around there for nine hours.' And a day on the Isle of Skye when he was walking into an 80mph headwind and heavy, driving, freezing rain. Nowhere to take shelter or put up a tent. Carrying Jess. Symptoms of trench foot. Thinking about calling 999 for help. And I'm intrigued by this. This man, who just a few short months ago wasn't interested in living, will now struggle so hard to survive. Sam looks directly at me, fired up now. 'There's a lot to live for. There really is. And as weird as it sounds the harsh times make me appreciate the good ones. When the sun comes out. Climbing a hill just to see the beauty. The beauty of that openness as far as the eye can see. And it's the people I've met. A whole variety, rich and poor, it doesn't matter – everyone has been so welcoming, so kind.'

Sam thinks he is going to be walking for another three years. Maybe more. When he started out, he says, 'I was just completely lost. Now I'm lost and found. I'm just waiting to be collected! Time is the biggest cure, I think. There's a lot of curing to be done yet. This is just the start. Some time I'll find a place I can be happy, I can settle. But for now, I'll just keep doing what I'm doing. Hopefully I'll find an answer one day to help everybody. Not just me. But until then I'm happy walking.'

WALKING IN A WINTER WONDERLAND

*

We had been staying in Munich for the weekend to visit friends. They picked us up at the airport and we spent the journey to their house trying to work out when we had last seen each other. It was a decade ago. Ten years! How does that happen? How does time gallop along so fast? Munich was cold: a dry, bitter, continental cold. A physical presence that gripped the elegant streets, squares and parks in its frozen embrace. But it was festive too. Christmas markets, the smell of *Glühwein* and fir trees and cinnamon.

On Sunday morning it started to snow. Big, fat flakes that transformed the frigid grey buildings and the icy gardens, frosting them with a layer of soft white powder, turning the city into a Christmas card. And it was snow that meant our flight the next morning was cancelled. But not the snow in Munich, which had melted in just a few hours. This was snow that had fallen in the UK and the country was at a standstill.

We managed to get on a flight twelve hours later. It was approaching one in the morning when we turned up the narrow lane that leads to the track to our house. Both lane and track lead steeply uphill and we had no idea whether our car would make it: it was hard to judge in the dark how thick the snow was. Ludo drove with slow, steady determination. There were a couple of heart-stopping moments when the tyres didn't grip and the car started to slide, but Ludo held his nerve. We inched our way to the top of the track and stopped outside the house with an audible sigh of relief.

The light, when we wake later that same morning, is eerie and there's the muffled hush of a landscape cloaked in snow. We haven't had a big fall of snow here for seven years and when I look out of the window over the garden and see that everything is white, I feel as excited as a child. It is almost the shortest day of the year. The sun is taking its time to rise, and when it does the light it casts is pale and washed out. But a little later, when we are up, dressed in layers of thermals, in thick coats and bobble hats, the sun is clear of the horizon and shining with a bit more conviction. Everything is glinting and twinkling beneath a blue sky streaked with gauzy cirrus cloud. 'Oh, it's beautiful!' I exclaim, skipping and scampering out into the garden, making the dogs skip and scamper too.

The water pipes in the fields are all frozen. We carry buckets from the house for the livestock, break the ice and scrape snow out of troughs, feed everything. Then we walk. Climb the stile from our field into our neighbour's, crunch up the slope across ripples of snow that have been ruffled and sculpted by the wind. The sun throws blue-grey shadows: long, distorted images of us. The trees are living ice sculptures, every branch and twig encased in frost. Our warm breath condenses in the cold air. We blow steam, like dragons.

I have a silly belief that if the weather is beautiful on my birthday it bodes well for the year ahead. And today I am 49. Not a birthday of any significance; not one to shout about. But thanks to this glorious start to the day I don't feel burdened by my increasing years or gloomy that my forties are now basically over and I am officially middle-aged. Instead I feel light-hearted, optimistic, if a little bit stiff.

✳

More significant is my dad's birthday a few days later. He is 80 and we celebrate with some of his oldest friends and a lunch of his favourite things – shepherd's pie and bread-and-butter pudding. A year or so ago he was diagnosed with a chronic condition but drugs, regular check-ups and mum's dogged insistence that he eats properly and takes the occasional rest allows them both to lead pretty much their normal lives. Which, when I hear what they have been up to, makes me feel both exhausted and idle in equal measure.

They are astonishing, my parents. Both have had their share of serious illness over the years, but they've refused to let the mental and physical effects linger or dictate life afterwards. Neither of them uses a walking stick. Mum rarely uses her glasses. Neither of them would be seen dead wearing anything with an elasticated waist and I can't imagine either of them, ever, in any circumstances, spending a day – even an hour – watching daytime TV. 'Just because we are old, doesn't mean we have to behave that way,' is Mum's mantra. Which is why, when we talk on the phone the day after Dad's party and she says he's in bed and has been asleep for much of the day I know something must be wrong.

He's admitted to hospital the next day. I go and see him. He looks diminished. Pale and fragile beneath the unyielding hospital sheets. He has a kidney infection and a chest infection. He is plagued by a persistent cough and an upset stomach. He has no appetite, no energy, needs help to get out of bed. But the thing that floors me, that makes me weep in the car before I can drive away, is the expression in his eyes. He's scared.

As a family we have a pretty pragmatic approach to death. We talk about it. Have discussions that some would find positively distasteful about whether we'd like to be buried in a sack or a rhinestone-encrusted coffin. Whether we want to be burnt or left to quietly disintegrate under a hedge. Whether we want choirboys or rock music, a wake of tea and sandwiches or fireworks and gin. And if we had a gravestone, what we'd have on it – 'Discontinued' being a favourite.

We also all believe that one of the most fundamental human rights is that of being able to choose when to die and of not being kept alive against our will. When Dad was given his diagnosis a couple of years ago he wrote a letter and sent a copy to both me and my brother. He had not just laid out his wishes with regards to the end of his life and how he'd like the ending to be marked, he had also compiled a comprehensive list of the people we would need to call and notify – solicitors, bank managers, the executors of his will – along with names, phone numbers, account details and so on.

It was an act of supreme thoughtfulness and consideration, one that bowled me over with admiration and gratitude. I have heard so many stories of families being left in a state of complete disarray after someone dies, their legacy one of chaos, an incomprehensible jumble of paperwork and unpaid bills. Dad has helped many friends over the years facing this situation and is determined that we, his family, won't have to go through the same thing. So, as I say, we are pragmatic about death and its inevitability, but that doesn't make it any less frightening or heartbreaking when it appears to be close.

I stay with Mum that night. Cook her dinner, because despite the fact she is constantly telling Dad – and all of us – how important it is to eat properly, she hasn't been taking her own advice. She speaks to Dad in the morning and he tells her he is feeling OK, has managed a bit of breakfast. So I head home and we promise to keep in touch.

'Are you there?' It's a text, late the following morning. I phone immediately. 'Mum?' 'Oh, darling...' Her voice is brittle, strained with the effort of trying to sound normal. She's just come back from the hospital. The consultant is worried. Dad has had a fall trying to get out of bed. They are taking him for scans, concerned that something may be going on in his brain that is affecting his balance. 'He can't walk. They had to put him in a wheelchair. I felt so helpless watching him being wheeled down the corridor...' and her voice breaks. Never, until this moment, has she cried – not in front of me anyway. She keeps her emotions in check with an iron will, an unshakeable determination that by not giving in, or giving up, everything will be fine.

Now it's down to me to try to persuade her that it will be OK, that he will be OK. But I'm crying too. 'I'll come over now,' I say. 'No, darling, don't,' Mum says, rallying, 'the consultant's going to call when he has news. And I've got so much to do...' Underlying what she is saying is something else, something I recognize and feel too. She wants to be by herself.

Sometimes sadness can't be shared. It doesn't require articulation. It just needs to be given space, indulged with a little bit of acknowledgement and time. I put the phone down, put on my coat and my wellies, gather the dogs and walk out into the damp half-light of a chilly December day. My slow, steady pace over familiar paths quietens my mind, stills my fearful thoughts. Tears flow, unchecked, a warm stream over my cold cheeks and with them comes respite, release.

The ping as a text comes through. 'No brain tumour, not stroke, nothing nasty. I think he just needs to eat more than mashed potato. Feel like a new woman. Going for supper with the neighbours.' I go and visit Dad the next day, take him some headphones so he can listen to audio books. He is looking so much better, has colour in his cheeks and his appetite is returning. 'I might even be allowed home for a few hours on Christmas Day,' he tells me. The fear has gone out of his eyes and as I drive home in the wintery half light of the afternoon, I too feel relieved of a quiet burden of dread.

23RD DECEMBER

A BRIEF ENCOUNTER BECOMES A CHRISTMAS TRADITION

✳

We gather in a gaggle on a stretch of muddy turf just over the cattle grid behind the church. There is a general air of heartiness as boots are laced, waterproofs donned, hats pulled on. There are handshakes and hugs, jocular remarks about the weather. Which is not great. We are engulfed in low, grey cloud, making the nearby houses, the church and its steeple appear hazy and out of focus. The hill that rises just above where we've parked is entirely invisible. But unbowed, we set forth into the drizzle, spirits high.

Ludo and I have done this walk pretty much every Christmas since we moved to Wales. I am not a fan of Christmas – well, the Christmas peddled in films and TV ads at least. As I don't believe in god it has no religious significance for me and, as someone who loathes both shopping and parties, the secular approach to Christmas doesn't appeal much either. Nor do I like the food. Hooray for Scrooge and Bah Humbug to everyone else! But a few years ago, while on this very walk we are setting off on now, something happened that turned my well-honed, curmudgeonly view of this time of year on its head.

The walk takes us out of the village and down a track that leads to a sandy path. We walk down it, leap over a little brook at the bottom and then climb up, through the heavy loose sand of the dunes to join the cliff path. This is the Gower Peninsula, in South Wales, just west of Swansea. Right up there among my favourite places in the world. None of the friends we are walking with today have done this route before and already, in spite of the weather, they are captivated by its rugged, wintery beauty, the tang of salt in the air, the expansive vista of sea and sky.

Five years ago it was a very different sort of December day. It was cold. Cold enough for frost on the marram grass, but clear and bright, the sky unbroken blue, arching over our heads, meeting an unruffled sea that barely rippled against the sand. We descended, as we do now, a path that drops in uneven, well-worn steps to the beach. And what a beach! A broad, majestic swathe of dark gold sand that runs, uninterrupted, for well over two miles.

And like today we had the dogs with us and they raced ahead – playing chase, barking, ecstatic – and we followed, ecstatic too, but quietly so, drinking in the scenery, a little disbelieving that there was no one else here to experience this most perfect of mornings. But there was. In the distance we could just make out the hazy shapes of another little group walking towards us from the opposite end of the beach. As the gap between us narrowed, we saw that the group consisted of two men and, whizzing around them at tremendous speed – madly, gloriously – was someone in an electric wheelchair. We heard a cry – 'Dad! Don't go too close to the sea!' – as the wheelchair careened towards the water, only to pirouette at the last moment, heading back in great sweeping, swirling loops across the sand.

Our two little groups met in the middle of the beach. We exchanged Happy Christmases, remarked on the beauty of the day. But the man in the wheelchair, bundled up in scarves and blankets, didn't stop. When we parted and continued walking our separate ways, I looked back to see the wheelchair, already distant, continuing its dance in the winter sunshine.

When I recall this scene, as I often do, I wonder what it was that made such an impression on me. I think it was because that moment – that briefest of encounters – encapsulated something wonderful: a sense of liberation, optimism, recklessness and sheer, unadulterated joy. Something that if it could be wrapped up in shiny paper would make a Christmas present worth giving.

I now know the identity of the man in the wheelchair. Ludo and I met him again on the beach the following Christmas with his carer, Darrell, who later wrote to me to tell me a little about him. He is Professor Nigel Stott, who earned a CBE for services to primary care and general practice medicine. Darrell, who has looked after him for many years, recounted a warm summer's day on the same beach when he, together with the professor's wife Mary, took Nigel into the sea, deep enough so he could lie on his back and float, his head cupped in Darrell's hands. He had been almost entirely robbed of his speech by the stroke he had suffered but, in reply to Darrell's 'Are you OK, Prof?', after a short hesitation, Professor Stott said, 'Life is wonderful.'

'There you have the man,' Darrell wrote, 'summed up in three simple words.'

Meeting with Nigel and Mary and Darrell on the beach at Christmas has become integral to this walk. We see them now up ahead, walking from the opposite end of the beach, emerging from the swirling mist. Waving. The stroke Nigel suffered means that as well as not being able to talk, he can't walk either. But he can pedal and his bike – a side-by-side tandem – allows him to still be part of the family walks on the beach they all love. He and Darrell make up the advance party, pedalling towards us, braking with a flourish and a flurry of sand. We gather around the bike, introductions are made, connections discovered, people in common, shared memories. The walkers move off, but I'm not with them. 'Right, Nigel,' I say, as I climb onto the saddle beside him, 'be careful with me!' And we are off across the sand, putting up the gulls, dancing in the mist, our tyre tracks weaving through the footprints.

31ST DECEMBER

A GIFT

✳

A letter arrives. It is in an A5 envelope and has a London postmark. The address is handwritten in writing I don't recognize. I open it. There's a note and, with it, a packet with a clear plastic front and a white paper back. And tucked carefully inside it is a leaf. A sycamore. It has been dried. It is crisp, but still robust, and olive green. On it is a message printed in white ink.

Before I left the flat of the artist Paul West, just as I was packing up my things to leave, he said, 'I've been doing this project. It's on-going at the moment. It's called Silent Voices. I suppose it encapsulates my relationship with trees and the landscape.' And I stopped packing up, found myself sitting down again. He recalled a walk with his mum when he was a child. While they were walking she told her son the story of King Midas and why he had the ears of an ass. How he had been cursed by the god Apollo for judging his musical ability to be inferior to that of the god Pan.

Desperately ashamed of his outsize ears, King Midas hid them under crowns, or helmets, or huge scarves, so that none of his subjects would know. The only one who did was his barber, and he was sworn to secrecy on pain of death. The secret became such a heavy burden for the barber he went down to the river, dug a hole and whispered into it, 'King Midas has ass's ears.' And that is why, explained Paul's mother, whenever you hear the wind whistling through the reeds on the bank of the river it is actually revealing the barber's secret. 'King Midas has ass's ears...'

Ancient Greeks also believed that the words of Zeus were carried by the wind through the leaves of oak trees. And it was these myths that got Paul thinking, imagining that the leaves that fall every autumn carry messages that we have forgotten how to see or interpret. 'I started working on an idea of etching leaves, giving each one a different phrase that means a lot to me. And while I was thinking about this idea I collected about 300 leaves, dried them out and screen-printed a message on every one of them. And then whenever I went for a walk I would scatter a few. I never looked to see where they fell, or whether they were face up or down. Nobody knew I was doing it. But I wondered whether anyone would find one, whether it would trigger some sort of connection or memory.' 'And did they?' I asked. He handed me a piece of paper, a printout of an email.

'Dear Paul. I found a leaf in London Fields with 'WHEN YOU'RE FRAIL I LOVE YOU MOST' printed on it. I can't tell you how profound it was to find it so serendipitously, as I took a shortcut through a pile of leaves in October or November. My mother had just died, and it felt like a message from someone keeping an eye on me. It just jumped out at me as I walked along. I'm amazed I saw it.

I happened to see a picture on Instagram the other day and now having seen your website, I know who made it. I have the leaf on my mantelpiece next to a photo of my parents. Kind regards, Julia.'

I looked up. 'And she never would have found it if she hadn't been walking,' I said. 'No,' said Paul, with a smile.

I tip the leaf he's sent me out of its protective packet and it rests in my hand. I read the message. 'THIS IS YOUR STORY.'

And this is my story. But now it is ours. A shared story of Mother Nature and Human Nature. Of observations, discoveries and encounters. Of despair and bravery. Anxiety and relief. Helplessness and fortitude. Of creativity. Serenity. Happiness. Of connection. It is the story of walking. The small joy of putting one foot in front of the other.

AUTHOR'S ACKNOWLEDGEMENTS

✳

Huge thanks to my agent Rosemary Scoular for never giving up on the idea for this book. Stephanie Jackson and the team at Octopus gave it a home and their support, enthusiasm and nurturing made the whole process of writing it a joy.

I am grateful, as ever, to the Morlands and the Abels for providing solace in various forms in moments of panic and to the Ursell family for the perfect bolthole, sledging and 'tunch'. Thanks, too, to all my interviewees for their time.

Paul West was interviewed for the book and ended up doing all the beautiful artwork for it. Thank you, Paul (and Poppy!). You can find his work here: www.p-west.co.uk

If you would like to support Ursula Martin's cause to raise awareness of ovarian cancer, you can donate here:

www.targetovariancancer.org.uk

Sam Doyle and Jess are still walking around the coast of Britain. If you see them, do buy him a pint. You can find out more about PTSD Resolution and donate here: www.ptsdresolution.org

ACKNOWLEDGEMENTS

*

Grateful acknowledgement is made to the copyright holders of the excerpts used on the following pages: page 69, excerpt from *The Principles of Uncertainty* by Maira Kalman, used by permission of the author; page 105, excerpts from *A Day in the Life of the Brain* by Susan Greenfield (Penguin Books, 2017), copyright © Susan Greenfield, 2016; pages 118, 166 and 255, excerpts from *Wanderlust: A History of Walking*, by Rebecca Solnit, copyright © 2000 Rebecca Solnit. Used by permission of Granta Books and by permission of Viking Books, an imprint of Penguin Publishing Group, a division of Penguin Random House LLC. All rights reserved; pages 134 and 149, excerpts from *A Philosophy of Walking* by Frédéric Gros, used by permission of Verso Books; pages 131–32, excerpt from 'Laugharne' by Dylan Thomas, © The Trustees for the Copyrights of Dylan Thomas, reprinted with permission; pages 228, 229 and 230, excerpts from 'Walking and Friendship' by Deirdre Heddon, published in *Performance Research*, 17 (2), reprinted by permission of Taylor & Francis Ltd, www.tandfonline.com

ABOUT THE AUTHOR

*

Kate Humble is a writer, smallholder, campaigner and one of the UK's best-known TV presenters. She started her television career as a researcher, later presenting programmes such as 'Animal Park', 'Springwatch' and 'Autumnwatch', 'Lambing Live', 'Living with Nomads', 'Extreme Wives' and 'Back to the Land'. This year, Kate has appeared in several new BBC series, launched her Humble natural beauty range in supermarkets nationwide and embarked upon a national speaking tour.

Connect with Kate
www.katehumble.com
🐦 @katehumble
📷 kmhumble

THINKING
ON
MY FEET